THANK GOD AHEAD OF TIME

THANK GOD AHEAD OF TIME

The Life and Spirituality of Solanus Casey

Michael H. Crosby, O.F.M.Cap

Franciscan Press

Thank God Ahead of Time: *The Life and Spirituality of Solanus Casey*
by Michael H. Crosby, O.F.M. Cap.
Copyright ©1985 and 1989 Franciscn Herald Press.

Copyright © 1997, 2000 Franciscan Press, Quincy University, 1800 College Avenue, Quincy, IL 62301

Printed in the United States of America
Third Printing: January 2000
3   4   5   6   7   8   9   10

Cover Portrait:
Timothy Bodendistel of Grosse Pointe Park, Michigan

Cover Design:
William Dichtl and Blane O'Neill, O.F.M.

Library of Congress Cataloging in Publication Data
    Crosby, Michael, 1940–
    Thank God ahead of time.
    1. Casey, Solanus, 1870-1957. 2. Capuchins-United States—Biography. I. Title.
    BX4705.C33573C76 1985   271'.35'024 [B]   84-18737
    ISBN 0-8199-0879-7

Nihil Obstat:
Reverend Harry S. Benjamin
Censor Deputatus

Imprimatur:
Edmund C. Szoka
Archbishop of Detroit

June 22, 1984.

The Nihil Obstat and Imprimatur are offical declarations that a book or pamphlet is free of doctrinal or moral error. No implication is contained therein that those who have granted the Nihil Obstat and Imprimatur agree with the contents, opinions or statements expressed.

"Why not foster confidence in God's divine Providence by humbly and in all childlike humility venturing to remind him in the person of our divine brother Jesus that we are his children. We should remind him that we are, and at least want to be reckoned as among his "little ones." Therefore we should thank him frequently for, not only the blessings of the past and present, but THANK HIM AHEAD OF TIME for whatever he foresees is pleasing to him that we suffer. We should do this not only in general but in each particular case. We should leave everything absolutely in his divine disposal, including with all its circumstances, when, where, and how he may be pleased to dispose the events of our death."

Words of Fr. Solanus Casey

CONTENTS

INTRODUCTION

On August 31, 1956 I met someone whom many hope will be declared a saint. I was attending the ceremony at St. Bonaventure's Friary in Detroit where my brother Dan received the Capuchin Franciscan habit. Later in the day, as we were visiting, he invited me to meet a fellow-Capuchin, Solanus Casey. "Come and meet Solanus Casey," Dan said, "because he's going to be a saint someday."

Less than forty years later an event occurred in the Vatican which indicated Dan's prediction actually might be proven true; the first major step in the process of Solanus Casey's canonization was realized. On July 11, 1995, in the presence of Pope John Paul II, a decree was promulgated which stated:

> There is proven evidence that the theological virtues of faith, hope, and charity toward God and neighbor and also the cardinal virtues of prudence, justice, temperance and fortitude as well as other virtues have been exercised to a heroic degree by the Servant of God, Francis Solanus Casey, a professed priest of the Order of Friars Minor Capuchin.[1]

---

[1] Congregatio de Causis Sanctorum, "Decretum super Virtutibus: Beatificationis et Canonizationis Servi Dei Francisci Solani Casey, secerdotis professi Ordinis Fratrum Minorum Capuccinorum (1870-1957), *Acta Apostolicae Sedis Commentarium Officiale* 88 (1996), 118.

With this solemn declaration in the presence of the Pope, Solanus Casey not only was recognized as having lived a life of heroic virtue; from now on he could be called "Venerable."

Three weeks before, on June 20, the Congregation for the Causes of Saints had held its final discussion on the life and virtues of Solanus Casey. Led by Cardinal William Wakefield Baum (originally from the United States), the Congregation declared unanimously that the Wisconsin-born farm boy baptized "Bernard" and nicknamed "Barney" who became a Capuchin Franciscan called "Francis Solanus" had "cultivated the theological virtues and other virtues in a heroic degree."[2] His life proved worthy of imitation by the people of God. With the June 20 and July 11 declarations in 1995, the first major step in Solanus' becoming the first U.S.-born male to be declared "blessed" and a "saint" was reached. The declaration proved to be significant enough that even the *New York Times* discussed it in a story titled: "One Man's Life of Virtue Earns the Papal Spotlight."[3]

Little did I know when I shook Solanus Casey's frail hand in 1956 that it would be the work I did which would be accepted by the Congregation of Saints as the basis for its declaration that his life had been lived in a heroic way. How did this happen?

In late 1982 I was asked to write the "official" biography of Solanus Casey. I began my research by reading all his writings and the testimonies of people who knew him. Next I personally interviewed many people who lived with him, ministered with him, or met with him for help and inspiration, including his compatriots and critics. In doing so, I became convinced that, even if it would only be for myself, Solanus Casey had a message for our increasingly cynical and secular age: the story of one person's indefatigable faith in the existence and abiding presence of God surrounding us which invites us to cooperate with God in continuing the divine plan of creation.

The first result of my efforts came with the first edition of this book.

[2] *Ibid.*
[3] Gustav Niebuhr, "One Man's Life of Virtue Earns the Papal Spotlight," *The New York Times*, August 5, 1995.

A second result, building from this book, came when the Vatican requested that an "external collaborator" be appointed from the Province of St. Joseph to write two of the three volumes of the *Positio*. These would be used by the Congregation of Saints to determine the heroicity of Solanus' virtue. Thus, in 1987, when Brother Leo Wollenweber, the Vice Postulator for the Cause, asked me to be the "Collaborator" to the Relator for the Cause of Beatification of the Servant of God, Solanus Casey, I found it impossible to say "no."

The appointed "Relator" for the Cause of Solanus Casey was Father Peter Gumpel, SJ. He had the ultimate responsibility for the writings which would be presented to the Congregation. Now officially retired, he still is involved in some of the cases he was selected to shepherd through the Congregation. I had the distinct privilege of collaborating with him throughout the time of my work.

Never have I met a Vatican official with so much insight and integrity. Each visit I had with him in Rome only convinced me the more of the conclusion reached about him by Kenneth L. Woodward, religion editor of *Newsweek*. Woodward had gone to Rome to write an expose about the way the Catholic Church determines who and whether someone will be declared a saint. At first skeptical, his total access to Peter Gumpel (whom he called one of the Vatican's great "saint-makers" because of the key position and influence he held in the process), made Woodward a respectful interpreter of the process, the politics, and the promotion of candidates who might be declared "saint." The results of his work are found in his very popular: *Making Saints: How the Catholic Church Determines Who Becomes a Saint, Who Doesn't, and Why*. [4]

I submitted an outline for the two volumes for which I would be responsible to Father Gumpel. With his approval, I began my work. After reviewing the original sources used for this book, I read and re-read the 800 pages of interviews that represented the collected insights

---

[4] Kenneth L. Woodward, *Making Saints: How the Catholic Church Determines Who Becomes a Saint, Who Doesn't, and Why* (New York: Simon and Schuster, 1990).

of more than 50 people. These witnesses answered questions from a tri-
bunal of judges in Detroit using a 29-page questionnaire prepared by
the Congregation. The questions related to the life and holiness of
Solanus from his earliest days until and after his death. Their responses
were collated to become one of the three volumes known as the *Positio*.

Over and over I read the testimonies of these people—Capuchin
Franciscans, diocesan priests, lay people, religious, secular Franciscans,
and even Elmer Stoffel, the Capuchin who played his own self-appoint-
ed role of "devil's advocate" during Solanus' life. In all of them I found
sincere admiration and conviction that, in this simple friar, God had
done great things and that his name should be recognized as holy by the
official church.

When I finished my work, the volume covering the history within
which Solanus lived (1870-1957) and his biography was 327 pages.
The third of the *Positio's* triad, while the smallest of the three, would be
the most critical and detailed. This discussed "The Virtues." It attempted to demonstrate how Solanus practiced 15 virtues, including the theological and cardinal virtues, the spiritual and corporal works of mercy,
the three evangelical counsels and humility. Although this third volume
of the *Positio* is only 145 pages, it contains over 1,300 footnotes. Most
of these come from the other two volumes of the *Positio*, Solanus' collected writings, this book, and other sources. A good many of the footnotes have over 10 separate citations to support the statements made
about his practice of the virtues.

After being approved and supported by Father Gumpel, the three volumes were submitted to a "Designated Committee of Theological
Consultants." After extensive study, each of these nine theologians prepared a report and recommendated whether or not the materials presented had demonstrated heroic virtue on the part of Solanus Casey. On
April 7, 1995 the Designated Committee reached the unanimous decision "that the *Positio* contains reasons and elements sufficient to reach
the necessary moral certitude" that Solanus did, indeed, live a life of
heroic virtue. They concluded that "the Servant of God, Francis
Solanus Casey, was an authentic master through his words and example. His entire pastoral activity took place within the context of his

apostolic zeal, the integrity of his Christian life, and his exquisite fatherly love toward all who came to him."[5]

After this, the facts concerning the Designated Committee's findings were brought to the attention of Pope John Paul II. Accepting their judgment, the Pope ordered that a decree be written about the heroic virtues of Solanus. This decree, prepared by the Congregation for the Causes of Saints, was made public in an audience with the Pope on July 11, 1995. With the promulgation of the decree Solanus Casey had reached the first step in being declared a saint.

Less than 50 years before, in 1948, while he was in "semi-retirement" in Huntington, Indiana, Solanus had pondered about the role of saints in our spiritual journey. In his mind saints were exemplars offered by God to help us attain "familiarity with God" even here on earth. He wrote:

> Self-understood there can be no thought of our knowing God in our present state directly and as he is known in heaven. Our privilege here is to start such knowledge as can be perfected only in the great, blessed Beyond. Nevertheless, if we stop to think as we ought to do, there must be ways and means close at hand whereby, according to the lives of the saints, we may if we try, to ascend to great sanctity and to an astonishing familiarity with God even here as pilgrims to the Beatific Vision.[6]

My research and writings on Solanus Casey have offered me concrete "ways and means close at hand," whereby, as I read the life of this man I once met and who now has been declared "Venerable," I am being invited to a deeper, even "astonishing" familiarity with God. For this I always will be most grateful.

---

[5] Sandro Corradini, Promoter General of the Faith, in *"Super Dubium"* Report and Votes of the *Congressus Peculiaris* on the Virtues, April 7, 1995, *Congregatio de Causis Sanctorum*, P.N. 1400 (*Roma: Tipografia Guerra s.r.l.*, 1995), 114.

[6] Solanus Casey, "Think Over," in *Collected Writings* II, 253.

Little did I know in 1956, when my brother Dan invited me to "come and meet" someone who was "going to be a saint someday," that I'd be one part of the effort to make this happen. Whether or not he is declared "Blessed" and then "Saint Solanus Casey" really is not that important as I pilgrim my way to the Beatific Vision. The fact is that the man I came to know has touched my life deeply; I have been moved by his words and example. He has been for me the kind of "saint" he wrote about when he wrote about other saints for his own inspiration in 1948.

In writing the original version of this book, I was indebted to the people I interviewed in various places in Wisconsin, Detroit, and New York. While I thanked these, and others, in that earlier edition, I want to offer special tribute to the ongoing dedication to the Cause of three Capuchin Franciscan brothers of mine in the Province of St. Joseph: Richard Merling, Ignatius Milne, and, above all, Leo Wollenweber. To these and to the members of the Father Solanus Guild who have worked so diligently to share his message with the world I dedicate the revised edition of this book.

CHAPTER ONE
The Early Years
November 25, 1870—December 24, 1896

It was 1930. Solanus Casey, then sixty, reminisced about his parents and his life as "little Barney Casey." Writing to his sister Margaret, he recalled:

> Surely we were fortunate children that the good God gave us such sturdy, honest, virtuous parents. How can we ever be grateful enough? Thanks be to God! May their dear souls rest in the peace of the beloved! I often think of the wonderful designs of Divine Providence as revealed in the plans and strivings of these and similar "children of St. Patrick." They were often pioneers indeed. Our own dear parents were directed from city life in Boston and Philadelphia away to "The River Bank" (to) Prescott. It must have been little more than a village. [1]

How Solanus' parents, Bernard James Casey, from County Monaghan, Ireland, and Ellen Elizabeth Murphy, from Camlough in County Armagh (now Northern Ireland) were "directed" to Prescott, Wisconsin, makes good enough reading material for a book in itself.

When she was about seven, Ellen Murphy emigrated to Boston with her widowed mother, Brigid, an older sister, Mary Ann, and her three brothers. [2] Five years later, seventeen-year-old Bernard Casey came to Boston. There he learned shoemaking. Three years after this, in 1860, Ellen and Barney met at a typical New England Fourth of July picnic.

Even though Ellen was only sixteen, she was independent enough that Brigid Murphy felt free to move with other relatives to Hastings, Minnesota. Left alone in Boston, Ellen developed a deeper relationship with Barney Casey. When Ellen wrote her mother that Barney Casey had proposed, any independence she might have had was terminated. Ellen was told to leave Boston immediately and come to Minnesota.

The excuse for Ellen's move was to be that her sister, Mary Ann (who had married at sixteen a few years before with no apparent objections), had just given birth to twin boys.

However, when Ellen arrived, Brigid Murphy made quite clear the true reason for her decision: "You're still a girl," Brigid said. "You should enjoy the years of your girlhood; then you can take on family responsibilities."

Brigid arranged that Ellen would live with Mrs. Ignatius Donnelly, whom Mrs. Murphy had befriended throughout the course of their choir work at Guardian Angels Church. It was the "Irish Church"; a block away was St. Boniface, the "German Church."

As soon as she joined the Donnelly family circle, Ellen found herself thrust into a new world. Ignatius Donnelly was a well-known writer and lecturer. The themes he spoke and wrote about covered a wide gamut— from the benefits of Minnesota development, to the need for political reform, even to the origins of Shakespearean literature. Later when he became the youngest member of the House of Representatives and a U.S. Senator from Minnesota he began to have an impact on national politics.

After Ellen spent three years with the Donnellys, her mother finally permitted Ellen to marry Barney. When the Donnellys went to Boston, Ellen accompanied them. On October 6, 1863, Ellen Elizabeth Murphy and Bernard James Casey were married. They had just enough time for a half-day honeymoon. The Civil War had begun in 1861, and Barney was too busy making shoes for the Union soldiers. When the war ended in April 1865, the young couple moved to Germantown, Pennsylvania. Soon after they went to New Castle, Pennsylvania. In both places they and Barney's brother Terrence opened shoe stores.

These efforts at free enterprise soon faltered. Soon the bad times in the postwar months and the Casey brothers' reluctance to refuse credit to parents of shoeless children combined to hurt the business. If it were just theirs alone, their inconvenience might have been endured. However the first two babies of Ellen and Bernard made the hard times felt more keenly.

Meanwhile in Minnesota, Ellen's brothers, Owen and Patrick, were quickly becoming prosperous farmers. They urged their sister and brother-in-law to file a claim on some good land they found just below the town of Prescott, on the Wisconsin side of the Mississippi. Despite its distance from Pennsylvania, Wisconsin would be close to many relatives. Besides, business was bad. After many discussions between the Casey brothers and Ellen in New Castle, the decisions were made. Terrence would go to Boston (where he entered and subsequently graduated from law school). The young Casey family would take the train for western Wisconsin.

When the Caseys arrived in the Fall of 1865, Ellen's brothers helped Barney clear some of the 80-acre claim and build a three room log house overlooking the Mississippi. Bernard Casey was born in this house on November 25, 1870. Within a month (on December 18, 1870) he was taken to the little Mission Church of St. Joseph at Prescott and given the name Bernard Francis Casey. He was the sixth of what would become sixteen children.

Years later, in a rambling discourse, Barney Casey, Jr. would recall nostalgically the beauties as well as the difficulties of those early years on the Mississippi:

> Here it was, smiling down on the "Father of Waters," that five of us were privileged to breathe our first morning air and "sing our first baby music." No doubt little Bernard must have been proficient in that music; because it was during his term of babyhood that Papa went blind with ague. For two weeks he had to be led by the hand, and his little namesake got a rupture from which he never completely recovered. Like in all other trials, however, the good

God had his designs herein also, and we can say with fullest conviction and in all gratitude today: "The Lord knows best." May he be in all his plans eternally blessed!

How we must have thrived there in real unworldliness and innocence! Dangers of course were not wanting, to keep dear Father and Mother "on edge" and often, no doubt, in anxiety. Wild beasts and rattlesnakes seem to have been the most common cause of such anxiety, though two of our little cousins were drowned together just below our little retreat near that River. Otherwise it was so generous, so noble, so majestic.[3]

At Prescott, Barney and Ellen Elizabeth Casey created an environment of faith which developed a deep religious conviction in Barney. One of his earliest memories was the family's regular night prayers during which everyone would pray "for a happy death and a favorable judgment."[4]

In light of the shoe business failure in Pennsylvania, the move to farming in Wisconsin proved to be fortuitous. By 1873, Barney Casey, Sr., was prosperous enough to move a few miles away to Big River, Wisconsin. The new farm was part of an area called "The Trimbelle" in honor of the nearby river. It proved to be even more successful. According to Solanus:

The public road, such as it was, ran just past our little log cabin—a one story mansion about 12 × 30 feet. You may smile at this title to honor it with, especially when you learn that it had a single partition only below. This was for "the bedroom" with Father and Mother on the one side and the little girls, Ellie and Mary Ann and little Mattie on the other. In the loft above, the little boys slept. In the morning, they sometimes played till they quarreled as little boys are wont to do.

An ordinary man could walk straight downstairs, but there was one young J. B. Fahey—six feet two, who was careful not to bump his head on the crossjoints and, therefore, had to stoop a little. The only door led in from the sunny end, while a single window on each side let in light.

Winters were often severe and snowbanks sometimes mounted as high as the top of the gable roof. But poor, dear Father took care before the cold weather set in to bank well wherever he might. As a result, we were fairly comfortable no matter how the wind howled or the mercury sank.[5]

Barney Casey had enough to feed his milk cows during the long Wisconsin winter. He even sold excess feed to the surrounding neighbors. His vegetable and fruit garden prospered too, enabling all his children to have a year-round diet of wholesome foods.

Barney Casey, Jr., loved his second home. In later years, as Solanus Casey, he often reminisced about his happy childhood there:

> Trimbelle too!!! How removed! How primitive! How picturesque! How rich in its variety and abundance of wild flowers and fruits and nuts and berries!!! To the South were valleys and rolling prairies down to Diamond Bluff five miles below on the Mississippi. There was a fair pasture field for cattle as well as deer and other wild animals.[6]

Although it was filled with beauty, like all pioneering situations, Trimbelle had its regular disasters as well:

> It was also a fair race track for our most dreaded enemy, the prairie fire, that nearly every year would darken the sky in its crackling rush toward us through the abundant wild grass, prairie-tea, hazel, and other brush. On such occasions "Lamb's Road," running east and west on the ridge about thirty rods to the south nearly always proved a great protection. If the gale were not too strong our dear neighbors would have time to come to our rescue, as they often did by lining up along that road and preventing the fire from crossing. It was just a private road to a twenty-acre field off to our southeast from the Miller farm on our southwest.[7]

As he searched his memory, Solanus believed "he had never seen a picture—in Bible history or elsewhere—so nearly like an earthly paradise as he remembered that scenery to be—with deer in twos, threes and more, stopping on the hillside or valleys to gaze at what he might be doing. No doubt," he said, "what heightened the appreciation of those days was our innocence (from sin). . . ."[8]

Barney's "innocence" and faith were cultivated through the regular practices that were part of nineteenth-century Catholic pioneers. Besides daily prayers in the morning, at meals, and at bedtime, whenever possible the family traveled six miles for Sunday Mass. Fasting since midnight, those going to the 10 A.M. Mass would start off at eight. Because there was only one horse and wagon, the members of the family had to take turns going to church. One Sunday half of the children would go with one parent and the next Sunday, the other half would go with the other parent. Those staying at home would have their own service; precisely at 10 A.M. the home-staying parent would gather the remaining children and read the prayers of the Mass for the day.

Barney had fond memories of these Sunday morning services at home. They made the little log house more than ever a real "mansion." "You'll be wondering, why it might be called a mansion," he wrote to his sister Margaret:

> Well, every decent mansion has a chapel of some dimensions. Ours was at times all chapel, and at times something of a church. As long as we lived in that little abode—a "hovel" possibly outside, but clean and neat as a palace within—we were wont to say morning and night prayers together; and on Sundays at 10:00 A.M., Father would read Mass Prayers.
>
> Of course when the weather permitted and the roads were any way decent, he would trudge away to church about six miles taking short cuts. Then Ellie or James or one of the others would lead the prayers (at home). Sometimes they seemed pretty long.[9]

For a little boy anything beyond ten minutes seems "pretty long." Barney was no different.

Despite their faith, the Casey family was not immune from tragedy— even on Sundays. "It was such a Sunday," Solanus recalled:

> that Papa and Jim had gone to church when we saw the black cloud of smoke rising from the far side of some of the hills off to the South. The wind was pretty strong too and poor dear Mother seemed quite anxious. She was giving instructions what to do and getting ready for what must have looked like a probable burnout.
>
> Ellie scratched a little "hoe-mark" out in front of the house and sprinkled holy water in it about half way down to the barn. By this time the fire was crackling through the grass and brush this side of Lamb's Road and the smoke rolled over our heads in thick, dark clouds. Then the barn took fire, some ten rods east of the house, and we all went down, carrying some bedclothes, to the lone tree that for a long time stood in the middle of the original, four-acre field. . . . As we huddled together under said lone tree (my own little face hidden in mother's dress from the smoke) I heard mother saying in accents of relief: "Thanks be to God! Some of the neighbors have come and let the pig out." It was a big white one and had broken out of the pen itself where it had been a contented prisoner right near the barn. We saw it running for safety.
>
> Papa and James got home shortly after noon and some of the neighbors came to sympathize with us. It seemed a fresh, clear day, but our barn was in ruins and the hills were black in every direction, except our fields and up to the northwest where the fire did not cross the high- way . . . except to burn our barn.[10]

While nature's rhythm could create havoc, more often than not, the days at "The Trimbelle" provided an atmosphere of tranquility and rest for the Caseys. Much of the time the older brothers helped their father in the fields and barn; Barney's job was to help his mother in the kitchen. Now and then, however, chores would take him into the fields. As he recalled it:

> Those hills formed a great part of our pasture lands where we boys, especially Maurice and I (till he left for Stillwater to study) used to watch the cattle and study our catechism. Sometimes we'd roll rocks down the hillside . . . or pick berries, or fish and swim till the cattle would stray away and get into mischief. Then we would have our own anxieties finding them. Sometimes we got our medicine for carelessness.[11]

At times, young Barney "got his medicine" for other kinds of mischief besides carelessness. Most times the medicine would be prescribed and executed by the stern and exacting Barney, Sr. When he was six years old, Barney, Jr., threw a fork at one of his sisters. "This is the first time you have ever done anything like this," his Father said. "So your punishment will only be three lashes. But if you do any such thing again, you'll receive six lashes. And if it should happen a third time, you'll get nine lashes." This "medicine" made Barney realize what he could expect if he let his natural stubbornness retrograde into fits of anger. Such admonitions helped him learn quickly that negative expressions of his feelings usually were not effective in getting what he wanted—love, attention, and a sense of security that comes from being wanted. Even though he was very emotional at this stage of his life, he realized he had to adjust his natural inclinations to new behavioral patterns before he would receive any affection and interest.

Besides mixing strictness with fairness, the Caseys shared their dreams of the future with their children. Often these dreams involved religion. When he was about seven, Solanus recalled one such incident that pertained to his brother Maurice:

> Even among near and dear ones, however (though the ideal seems to be common in the "Island of the Saints"),

comparatively few ever knew of the fact that our dear parents had mutually dreamed of the privilege of being parents to a priest in their family.

This ideal seemed to have buoyed their hopes from the earliest years wherein they recognized holy matrimony as a state of life in which to serve God and help him to save souls. Furthermore, when the writer was in his seventh year and there were three brothers among their five dear ones ahead of him, it just seemed self-understood as though planned before birth that Maurice was to be the Priest. Not only was this the case in our immediate family and relatives, but our neighboring children often spoke of it and seemed to revere him as so fortunately destined and chosen. So much was this true that someone even at that time and perhaps earlier, began to wonder if possibly there couldn't be two priests in a family—hardly hesitating that he would be the other himself.[12]

While Solanus himself was to become one of the "others" to be ordained, the path to the priesthood for Maurice proved to be very difficult. He entered the seminary around 1883. But after only three years "health failure of the senior brother in his early classics had sent him home from the seminary, heavy-hearted—a family disappointment."[13] Maurice's departure was precipitated by a nervous condition which affected him for the rest of his life.

During those years, health problems other than Maurice's depressions plagued the Casey Family. Black diphtheria hit in 1878 when Solanus was eight. It slowly strangled life out of twelve-year-old Mary Ann. "Who will take the place of Mary Ann?" Ellen Casey asked aloud as she held her three-year old Martha. Getting down from her Mother's arms, Martha walked to the corner and picked up the broom Mary Ann so often used. "I will, Mama. I will sweep the floor for you like Mary Ann." But the black diphtheria would not be so generous. Three days later Martha was dead as well. Although several of the boys, including Barney, also contracted the disease, all recovered. However, their recovery was not without its side effects. Barney's voice became weak and wispy. Many believed that his bout with black diphtheria accounted, in part, for the peculiarly high-pitched, yet soft-spoken voice Barney would have for the rest of his life.

While occasional illness, compounded by lack of modern medicine, brought much sadness and depression into the Casey household, the majority of the time found "The Trimbelle" filled with happiness and spontaneity. As pioneers, the Caseys transformed their frontier more than being controlled by it. They brought their Boston-Irish culture into their environment. Though both Ellen and Bernard, Sr., had left Ireland at a comparatively young age, they never forgot its folk songs and stories. For many an evening, these were shared around the table in the log cabin.

In later years Solanus continued his parents' tradition of sharing songs and stories with their children. Having no children of his own, he handed on to his nieces and nephews the traditional stories. In this, Solanus was a true *seanchaidhe* (shan-a-kee), the Irish word for story-teller. To one nephew he recalled (probably embellishing the story as it had been embellished to him):

A certain overgrown John Joseph M., a contemporary of your Great Grandfather, a namesake and probably a relative, skipped school at thirteen because he was ashamed to go to class with little boys. He joined the British navy and went to the Far East. Later he failed in an enterprise in London. He first joined the Hudson Bay Company and then joined an Indian tribe and became the famous "Chief Black Eagle of the North." He was very charitable to the poor Indians whom, from the beginning, he had learned to love. But he was called to something greater.

Deep in the wilderness he came across a sort of little clearing. There in the crotch of a big tree he met a weather-beaten statue of our Immaculate Mother. Calling his braves together shortly thereafter, he resigned. He disposed of his vast estates, went to Rome and after five years was ordained a priest. He returned to Ireland and after several years of mission in London, became the famous Fr. John of Cork.

> Who does not get a taste of the Cross one way or another and, if only with resignation: "The bigger the cross, the greater the crown."[14]

At a time when television and movies were not even imagined such stories and songs provided the Casey family with sufficient entertainment. Especially when snows land-locked the family, this kind of entertainment kept spirits from becoming morose. Often the children played games. Other times Barney, Sr., and Ellen gathered everyone around the dining room table for an evening of literature. Barney, Sr., would read the poems of Tom Moore besides those of Longfellow and Whittier. Stories like Cooper's *The Deerslayer* held the children fascinated for long periods of time.[15]

In later years, Solanus loved to thankfully recall the impact which these family activities at Trimbelle produced. In many ways these experiences instilled in him not only a deep love for literature but for writing as well.

Bernard and Ellen Casey were creating a caring environment which enabled young Casey to become well-integrated and balanced. For their roles in his spiritual formation, the future Solanus would be forever grateful.

In many ways Solanus was able to be who he was precisely because of the way his parents nourished him in his youth. According to William Johnston, writing in his *The Inner Eye of Love: Mysticism and Religion:*

> . . . relationship with parents (even when these parents are already dead) seems to be the key to success in other adult relationships. Nor can it be taken for granted that everyone honours his parents with an adult love. Quite often suppressed anger and resentment and fear and childish fixations linger on. And it is precisely here, in the deep, deep unconscious, that barriers fall down in the mystical journey. Love penetrates to the caverns of the unconscious, allowing the suppressed anger and fear and clinging to surface. Exposed to the light they melt away and a deep, adult ongoing love for one's parents becomes the basis for a universal

love. Indeed, there can be an experience of enlightenment in which all barriers which separate me from others collapse and I discover that I am one with the human race, that no one is excluded from my compassion and love, that no rancour exists in my heart. This experience of union with the human race can be found, I believe, in the mysticism of all the great religions.[16]

From his parents, Solanus seems to have learned a very positive approach to "union with the human race" as well. His family related ecumenically with other ethnic Catholics and the neighboring Protestants before the word "ecumenical" was ever known. Possibly because many of these Irish, German, and French-Canadian neighbors had experienced bigotry and left their countries because of this discrimination, the Caseys seemed to realize the futility of arguing over religion if it would mean unnecessary alienation.

"Spic and span"[17] Alihue, the neighboring town where many Methodists and Lutherans lived, was the location for many "revivals." Some Catholics of that generation belittled such manifestations of religion. Yet, despite the fact that Catholicism then was very staid, Solanus later remembered the people of Alihue merely as "mostly honest, good Christians."[18] The seeds of his later ecumenism were sown early by his parents' spirit of toleration and charity.

Five miles beyond Alihue (which was four miles farther than Trimbelle) was Burkhardt, Wisconsin, in St. Croix County. Needing a bigger house and wanting to capitalize on his farming success at Trimbelle, Bernard Casey moved the family to a 345-acre farm there after the harvest of 1882.

Bernard Casey's relative prosperity had made the new six-room, clapboard house, two barns, large ice house, and deep root house possible. The Willow River flowed nearby and Dry Dam Lake (which proved excellent for fishing and swimming) was on its border. One of the attractive features of the new farm was the fact that a railroad line ran through it. This made St. Paul, Minnesota (thirty miles to the west) less than an hour's ride away.

Bernard Casey was not satisfied with meeting the basic needs of his growing family, which now numbered twelve. Wanting to give them a little more, he became a distributor for religious goods. He also sold subscriptions for the *Irish Standard* and *Extension Magazine*. After buying books at the religious goods store in St. Paul, Bernard would return with them on the train. As the train neared the farm, he lugged the book-laden canvas bag to the train's rear platform. Then he'd heave the bag into a snowbank where the boys waited to pick up the new supply. When the train stopped at Burkhardt, Bernard would walk back from town. He encouraged the family to read the books before they were sold—as long as they remained unsoiled. In this way he could make sure that his family was keeping up with all the latest in religious thought.

The local parish was St. Patrick's in Hudson, nine miles away. Two weeks before Barney, Jr.'s First Communion, he went to Hudson to be drilled in Catholic church doctrine. It was 1883, and he was 13. Although the Casey children began studying their catechism when they were seven and reviewed it regularly, the two week course provided Barney a concentrated approach. Staying in the houses of city parishioners, the communicants would attend morning and afternoon instructions. Fr. Thomas A. Kelly, the pastor, had to be certain that the young people in the pews in front of him would be able to defend clearly the Church's chief teachings. When he was satisfied they had sufficient knowledge, they were allowed to receive Communion. As a rule, children received their First Communion when they were twelve. Due in part, to sickness and family chores which kept him at home, Barney's First Communion was delayed a year. Following the tradition in many Irish parishes at that time, he used the occasion of his First Communion to "Take the Pledge." The "Pledge" was a promise not to drink alcoholic beverages until one's twenty-first birthday.

When he was fifteen, Barney nearly completed his elementary grades at the District School. But the last two crops had failed and the winter of 1886 was bleak. Family necessity demanded that he take some time off to augment the dwindling family finances. Because of the critical times, the Caseys had added a petition to the usual fifteen minutes of family evening prayer, a petition that the harvest not fail totally. Besides joining in family prayer, Barney had decided he would recite the rosary each night at his bedside.

One night after a hard day's work with chores, he felt like skipping the rosary just to get more sleep. While he had the feelings, he sensed a drive deeper than his need for rest which wouldn't let him go to bed. His natural doggedness and need to follow through on commitments kept him from going to sleep. Instead, he knelt down, determined to recite at least one of the five decades of the rosary. He knelt upright, without support, following the example of his mother and sister, Ellen (a practice he would continue throughout his Capuchin years). To his surprise, he was able to stay awake until the whole rosary was completed.

That night he dreamed that he was suspended over a huge pit of flames and was almost falling into it. Looking around for something to hold onto, he saw a huge rosary hanging just above him. He grasped it firmly. Now, he was secure. Later on he recalled that this dream reinforced him in his special relationship with the Blessed Virgin. What began in his youth would be built and sustained many times in days to come.

But, work and rosaries had to go hand in hand, so Barney, Jr. left the financially troubled farm and went to Stillwater, twenty miles away seeking work. During the days he worked the log booms, unjamming the felled trees which choked the St. Croix River. Although the log boom boss may have had his doubts about the scrawny young lad applying for a job, he hired him to work on the catwalks built over the lake of "still water" which gave the city its name. Barney's job was to feed logs into the Stillwater mills. At night he stayed with his mother's brother, Fr. Maurice Murphy, who was the Catholic pastor in Stillwater.

With winter coming and the waters freezing, Barney returned home to finish school and to help on the farm. Although the wheat had failed, the other summer crops had been good. Barney's help from his Stillwater job and the money from the good crops made it possible for all the debts to be cancelled. In fact, the farm experienced the first surplus in a long time.

During the final year of grade school, when he was seventeen, Barney became interested in the principles and practice of debate. Debates were a natural outlet that appealed to Barney's rebel side. While he was quite objective about life at this time and sought all the facts of a problem, his natural tendency to argue about the facts gave him a good outlet. Debates were the way he could give vent to his desire to compete. He was open to challenge from all comers. Argumentation was the nonviolent way he could engage in combat. Thus he could actually go out of his way to provoke a debate.[19]

During those days, debates would not be just an academic exercise; they were a public affair, open to people throughout the district. Attending debates was one of the ways people in a community recreated. One such debate in Burghardt treated a popular subject in those days which preceded prohibition: "Resolved: that the intemperate consumption of alcohol has been a greater evil than war." Barney was joined on the team by his older brother, John, and his father, who by now had become township treasurer and a school trustee. Although the debate began with decorum and dignity, it ended up in heated words.

One person who seems to have attended the debate was fifteen-year-old Rebecca Tobin. To young Barney Casey, she was the kind of person he could envision dating. Although he was only sixteen, they began to spend time together at school as well as afterwards.

In 1887 Barney completed his elementary grades. Today, that would seem an extraordinarily long time for a seventeen year old just to finish eight grades. However, situations such as the need for more money, family moves, sicknesses, chores, and other needs kept Barney out of school for long periods. But with graduation he was able to set off on his own and help the family even more.

One of his first jobs was working in a brick kiln around Stillwater, Minnesota. One day the workers stopped after some hours to take lunch. Barney did not know this in advance. He had no lunch with him. Some of the German-speaking workers noticed this and offered him some of their lunch, which consisted of bread and limburger cheese. After he had eaten the lunch, the workers asked him whether he had ever eaten this kind of cheese before. He replied: "No, I never ate it before, but I often stepped in it."[20]

During this time Ellen Casey gave Barney a Brown Scapular of our Lady of Mt. Carmel. As Solanus later recalled, it proved to be a most providential gift:

> Outside next to the building there was a large deep pit filled with water. I saw a man fall in, and I dove into the water, with all my clothes on and grabbed hold of him. He struggled with me and was pulling me down among the weeds so that I couldn't free myself.
>
> Suddenly I grabbed at the scapular I was wearing and with it I was somehow pulled up. Then another man who saw us, dove into the water and pulled the man away from me. However, the drowning man struggled so hard that the would-be-rescuer had to let him go, and so he drowned. I think I could have saved him. I know the Scapular of our Lady saved me.[21]

After his work at the kiln in Stillwater Barney worked at the local penitentiary as a part-time guard. He roomed with his Uncle Pat and Aunt Mary Murphy. While at the prison he established friendly relationships with many of the prisoners inside. They appreciated him for his sensitivity and openness. Notorious among those were the Younger brothers, Jim and Cole, who had been part of Jesse James' gang. Barney befriended Cole Younger and spent a good amount of time talking with him. Cole gave him a clothes trunk which Solanus kept for many years. Befriending the prisoners was easy for Barney; he was a people person. Yet he soon realized that he had to be on guard (literally and figuratively) so that the prisoners did not take advantage of his sympathetic nature. He found it very hard to say "no" to requests from the prisoners.

Although he liked his job at the prison, the newly opened electric streetcar in Stillwater promised him a greater opportunity for upward mobility. He applied for a job as motorman and soon was driving the new trolley cars.

During this time Barney and Rebecca kept up their relationship through correspondence and periodic visits. She was just finishing her studies in the elementary school and was almost seventeen. The relationship got serious. Although he was in love, Barney was also loyal to his Church's teachings on sexuality; he knew he should keep his drives under control. After a period of dating, Barney proposed marriage. However, even though she respected young Barney Casey, Jr., Mrs. Tobin would hear none of the marriage proposal. She refused approval and sent Rebecca to St. Paul to a boarding school. Barney would never see her again.

Rebecca might be out of the picture. Even so like any other red-blooded farmer from the area, Barney lost no time in taking an interest in other young people in Stillwater. One young person to whom he was especially attracted was Nellie O'Brien (who later became his brother John's wife). Yet he was somewhat cautious. Even though he was very people oriented and liked to be around them, he was very selective in those whom he chose as his close friends. Whether it was the experience with Rebecca or whatever, at this time of his life he preferred not to let people get too close to him physically. His personal body zone was rather wide and he did not want others to get too close to him. He wanted a wider space between himself and others; yet despite this distancing, he was not standoffish. He was considered very likeable and loyal.

One reason for this tendency to have only a few loyal friends may have been that he was not as self-confident as others perceived him to be. He was not an egotistical person. While he did not see himself in the positive light others did, he was not down on himself either. Possibly another reason for his distancing attitude was because he knew he was highly emotional and may have felt that he had to keep control by not letting too many people get very close to him.

Despite these defensive tendencies, he was an excellent mixer, especially on first contact. Because he was so people-oriented, his concern for them was obvious to all. People just naturally felt his concern for them and their problems. That trait created a bond of trust.

Barney fully enjoyed the convivial life that would be a regular occurrence with his friends and family. As a youth he had learned to play the violin; now he knew the latest dance tunes. Although his music was only passable (and never would get better), it was free and open hearted. These were other reasons why Barney Casey was a welcome guest at any party.

After a couple of years working for a new street car company in Appleton, Wisconsin, 230 miles away from home, he moved to Superior in the spring of 1890 to work as a motorman there. This was the fifth job in three years. While it may indicate a basic restlessness at that time in Barney, it was a move that would have a very positive effect on the fortunes of the Casey family.

Drought and chinch bugs caused successive crop failures in 1887 and 1888. Another failure in 1889 created a devastating blow to the once prosperous Bernard Casey, Sr. Not quite forty-nine, he was in no condition to continue relying on the uncertainties of weather to give him financial security. He needed a stronger economic base.

At that time Superior was one of the largest cities in Wisconsin. Barney wrote home that things were booming. Jobs were readily available. He urged the family to move there. Not long after, the three oldest brothers came, including Maurice who by now had been home from the seminary for several years. Once in Superior the brothers rented a house. Nell, their sister, left her school teaching job to help keep house for them.

Soon the five were trying to convince the rest of the family to move to Superior where a new farm could be tried. By 1891 the senior Casey was able to sell the Burkhardt farm, and load the house furniture, farm implements, fodder, cows, and horses into two box cars at the railroad siding. They unloaded at Superior where the brothers had rented a farm of forty acres. To the forty acres, one hundred and sixty more were soon added, providing good supplies of oats and hay for the livestock, plus vegetables and fruit for the family.

While the move brought the family enough security to build a new ten-room house in Superior, Barney, Jr., felt neither at ease nor at peace. He began to sense more keenly that he might have a vocation to the priesthood. This thought had been on his mind for years. Yet he had avoided any follow-through. Now that the family was secure again, the original excuse about needing to help the family was no longer relevant. Barney was running out of rationales for delay. On a late afternoon in the fall of 1891, as he worked at his conductor's job on the trolley cars, something happened which jarred him into action. It was a cold, dreary evening. As his trolly rounded a corner in Superior's "rough section," the motorman stopped it with a jolt. A crowd surrounded something lying on the track.

Barney and two crewmen ran up to the scene. There a drunken sailor was standing over a young woman. She was lying bloody on the railroad tracks. As he stood with a knife in his hand, the sailor continued to curse the woman. In a few moments two policemen arrived and disarmed him at gunpoint.

Getting back on the trolley after the policemen took the sailor away, Barney began to think about life more deeply than he had for a long time. He began to realize he could not just view this brutal stabbing and the sailor's hysterical cursing as an isolated incident; he began to sense that this experience somehow symbolized all the violence and anger of the world. As he prayed for the woman and her assailant, Barney realized he had to pray for all the violence and anger throughout the world. At the same time he felt he could not just pray to bring about change; he too had to heal the pain and problems of the world. At this point he knew he had to decide what he would do for the rest of his life. Something told him that the rest of his life would not be spent on trolley cars.

Two days later he went to his pastor at Sacred Heart rectory where he told Fr. Sturm that he wanted to change his life around and serve God in the priesthood.

The psychological process that led to this new conviction seems to have something in common with that which frequently precedes a major commitment of service for many mystics to-be. One's conversion is usually preceded by a period of reflection; the step to conversion itself is precipitated by some kind of shock. Like David's being told, "That man is you" (2 Sam 12:7) or Peter's being told, "Get behind me, Satan!" (Mk 8:33); only the deep pain connected to such a shock seems strong enough to reorder a new direction. For Solanus, his previous reflections on his emptiness and alienation, followed by the shocking experience of the violence around him, brought him to the point of conversion. By the time he got to the rectory for his meeting with Fr. Sturm, he had already begun to take the first serious steps toward the life of union with Christ. He had entered what spiritual writers call the purgative way, or the way of initial conversion.

Father Sturm recommended St. Francis de Sales Seminary in Milwaukee. This was the "German Seminary" which Maurice had attended and left, returning home with a nervous condition and a sense of futility and failure that would plague him for the rest of his life. For some reason, however, the German language used there and the fact of Maurice's failure did not seem to affect Barney's decision. He would go, even though it meant he would be attending the four years of high school with men many years younger than his own twenty-one years.

For his first year, Barney's academic grades were excellent as were his Application and Conduct. With the passing of semesters, though, his grades steadily declined. During the 1894–95 school year he was able to raise his marks sufficiently so he could enter Fifth Class, the equivalent of the first year of college (in the fall of 1895). For the second semester he got low-to-mid 70s in Latin, algebra, geometry and history, high 70s to low 80s in German, and the equivalent of today's "B" in vocal music, U.S. History, and natural philosophy. He was now 12th of 15 and steadily dropping a notch in his class each semester.[22] Although he was not failing, the seminary told him that he did not have the needed requisites to go on for the priesthood. Because he was poor in German and even poorer in Latin, and because both languages were used for all the seminary courses, the seminary officials did not believe Barney had the acumen to maintain the level of academic excellence they wanted to insure in their seminarians.

What happened? Barney was extremely analytical. He grasped subjects and issues quickly, being quite logical and methodical as well. While he had the ability to understand information quickly, he had a tendency to skim the surface for that needed information. Whatever information that might be readily available was used. Otherwise he did not probe much further. Not changing this tendency, coupled with the German-Latin structure which did not change combined to create more and more academic problems for the young Irishman. The seminary leaders decided he could not become a priest.

However, just because he might not be able to survive a seminary, the superiors did not believe that other kinds of church vocations were beyond his reach. They knew that his interest and concern for things religious were very strong. Theology was paramount in his life and the philosophy he did articulate was well-balanced. He was firm in his beliefs, yet very open to new ideas, concepts, and differences in others. His theological philosophy was not so closed and restricted that it prevented him from learning from others and broadening his horizons. Furthermore, his mentors realized that he had been a positive influence on the younger seminarians. The Barney Casey they knew projected the image of care for everyone. Although he was predisposed to intense likes and dislikes for people, Barney realized he had to direct these feelings.

They saw a young man refraining from showing the strong emotions which he felt inside, a young man able to control his feelings. He had developed self-control, diplomacy, and other restraining traits which were not the result of repression, but of integration. He was actually able to channel his strong feelings and emotions into deep sensitivity which made him very popular with the seminarians who felt he really did "feel" for them. Thus they had observed the way the younger seminarians respected Barney and how he was able to exercise positive leadership among them. They also admired Barney's ingenuity in the way he helped pay for some of his education by cutting hair.[23] While they did not approve of the way he doggedly refused to wear a catcher's mask when the students played ball—a sign of a rebellious spirit (which he carried throughout life) as well as a sign of impudence—they told him he had the makings of a religious vocation.

At their suggestion, Barney visited another "St. Francis Seminary" in Milwaukee. This one was conducted by the Capuchins, a group of bearded and sandaled men who followed the Rule of St. Francis of Assisi. Traveling the five miles from the lake shore campus of the diocesan seminary to the heart of Milwaukee, he was not impressed with what he found at the new St. Francis Seminary. Perhaps it was the Capuchins' austere appearance and strict observance of the Rule which repelled him, or perhaps it was the setting of the place—in the busy section of Milwaukee, not far from the downtown area. Maybe it was because the Capuchins were also German-speaking (at least in their studies).

Whatever the explanation, Barney had a negative reaction to Capuchins. He returned home for his summer vacation of 1896 very uncertain and quite unsettled. He had come to Milwaukee quite sure of his calling; now he did not know what God had in mind for him. The quinsy sore throat, which had gotten worse during his seminary days, now was becoming chronic, possibly aggravated by the deep anxiety and depression he was experiencing.

Barney began again to visit his former spiritual director, Fr. Eustace Vollmer, the assistant at Sacred Heart. Unlike Fr. Sturm, Eustace was a Franciscan, from the Observant branch of the followers of St. Francis. The Capuchins were another branch and the Conventuals were the third branch of the Franciscan triad. Fr. Eustace not only listened to what Barney Casey said, he reflected on Barney as a speaking person.

On the one hand he observed a young man who was very generous and open. While he was quite independent, he was available to most everyone in need—a good sign for a vocation. He had no abnormal repressions. He was responsible; he was as accommodating in dealing with everyday people on the street as he was to people in authority. Barney also had a certain degree of uncertainty coupled with and compounded by his tendency to play down his ego. There were no biases in his life, though he could become quite set in his ways once his mind was made up.

But this was Barney's problem: his mind was not made up. Barney was very confused, frustrated and concerned about his future. While he had negative feelings about the Capuchins, he felt somehow called to them. Furthermore, if he went to them, he was questioning whether he would be able to succeed. After all, hadn't he failed in school and shifted in many jobs? How did he know if religious life would go well? Thus he was afraid his long-term goal of dedication to the Lord might not be fulfilled. He was not as confident of himself as others perceived him to be because he covered those feelings with pride and dignity. However, Eustace was able to cut through these to address Barney's uncertainty about the Capuchins.

"You above all, Barney, should value the Capuchin beard!" Eustace joked. "Those beards protect the throat and chest. With that troublesome quinsy of yours, a heavy beard is precisely what you need!" Even though he was not impressed with Eustace's jokes or arguments, Barney decided to send a letter of application to the Provincial of the Capuchins, Father Bonaventure Frey, whose headquarters were in Detroit. But he also hedged his bets. He sent a letter to the Franciscans asking how he could be admitted to the Sacred Heart Province.

Barney expressed himself well on paper and could make himself understood quite clearly. This letter to the Capuchins as well as subsequent letters between Bonaventure and Barney made it apparent that it would not be long before everything was set for him to enter the Capuchin-Franciscans. Barney had written about his bill of $525 still owed at St. Francis for school and asked, "What should I do about that before I go to join you—supposing I could not pay cash?" Bonaventure replied, "In the Seminary of Milwaukee you will easily settle your accounts. If your father and brothers will offer the Rev. Procurator half of the amount of your debt, I have no doubt it will be accepted. I know neither the Most Reverend Archbishop nor the Reverend Rector will object to it."

Earlier in the letter, Bonaventure had written, "I will make no objection now to your application of joining our novitiate, as the Rev. Rector of the Salesianum thinks you have a vocation for monastic life. You may therefore come to Detroit, as soon as circumstances will allow you, or the sooner the better for yourself.''[24]

Ordinarily one would think that someone like Barney Casey would be extremely happy getting such a positive response. But at this time in his life it was natural for him to react first and think later. He tended to jump to conclusions and was more likely to form opinions because he did not wait until all the facts were in before he made up his mind. Thus he read the letter without enthusiasm; the initial negative feelings about Capuchins were too strong. By his own admission, Barney was prejudiced against the Capuchins; entering them was one of the farthest things from his desires that he could imagine.[25]

Still undecided, and thinking of the other branch of Franciscans to which Fr. Eustace belonged, Barney held off. To help reach a conclusion, he decided he would make a special novena to the Blessed Virgin. She helped him so many times in the past; possibly her approaching feast of the Immaculate Conception would be the occasion for insight.

During the novena, he came to the conclusion that, even if he was undecided about joining a religious order, he wanted to live celibately. Thus on December 8, 1896, he made a private vow of chastity, dedicating himself to God. Upon reciting his vow, he ''at once''[26] became intensely aware of the presence of the Blessed Virgin. He heard the phrase, ''Go to Detroit.''

Later friars would recall Solanus saying this experience (as well as an earlier experience of the Blessed Virgin at the time of his First Communion) was an actual vision.[27] Whether they were or not, their impact, especially the power of the experience during the novena when Barney heard the phrase ''Go to Detroit,'' remained forever in his memory.

Since he had been interested in both the Observant and Capuchin branches of the Franciscans, and since the novitiate for the Capuchins was in Detroit, Barney realized that the message coming to him was a clear sign that he should join the Capuchins.

While he might not be excited about the decision, at least he was relieved. Somehow the same God who had directed two Swiss diocesan priests to found the Order in the United States would help this former diocesan seminarian in the province they established. They made their first foundation at Mt. Calvary, Wisconsin, the same year Barney Casey, Sr., had arrived in this country. Perhaps something good could happen by the Capuchins' and the Caseys' coming together in the Calvary Province.[28]

Having earlier received the clearance from his local bishop along with the bishop's feelings that "no doubt you will become a good religious," Barney was ready to go to Detroit by December 20.

His family, realizing that once he entered the Order he probably would never be home for the holidays again, urged him to stay until after Christmas. But Barney's mind was made up. With his strong will power, he was determined and even quite enthused to begin. He would "go to Detroit" as soon as he could.

He packed his bags and left Superior for St. Paul on the 11 P.M. train. The snow his brothers predicted slowed the train to a crawl in many places. All night the train battled the drifts. When the crowded cars were not stifling and hot, they were bitterly cold. The air was dry and stale. When the train finally reached Milwaukee, there was a layover. Barney traveled the two miles from the depot to the Capuchin seminary at St. Francis. He spent the first part of the evening with the community in a "friendly recreation."

The next day he boarded the train for Chicago where he got another train Detroit-bound, which was pulled by two locomotives. Averaging twelve miles an hour through the increasing snow, the train arrived at Detroit station at dusk.

On Christmas eve, he arrived at St. Bonaventure's that he would later call "the privileged novitiate."[29]

CHAPTER TWO
Novitiate and Early Formation
December 25, 1896—August 3, 1904

Lugging his belongings—probably in the trunk given him by Cole Younger, the gangster—Barney found the right streetcar and arrived in Downtown Detroit. He made the transfer to the Capuchins' "monastery" of St. Bonaventure two miles east. The Capuchins had been expecting him. He was warmly greeted by the porter, the guardian, and his future novice-master, Gabriel Messmer. Although they offered him a meal, Barney refused; he was too exhausted. He only wanted to sleep.

Walking through the first floor cloister and up the winding stairs, Barney couldn't help but notice the starkness of the architecture which reflected the Capuchins' poverty and austerity. Opening the wood latch to his "cell," he saw a nine by twelve room with a single curtainless window. The window overlooked the large grounds behind the friary; it would have been a beautiful view in summertime. For someone as exhausted as he, it only looked desolate. Opposite the narrow iron bed was a one-drawered wooden desk with a straight-back chair. The two clothes hooks on the wall would hold all his clothes, if not then, at least once he became a Capuchin.

With the Capuchins gone and the door closed, Barney looked around. What had he gotten himself into? Recalling the December 8 experience, he asked in confusion, "Why did our Blessed Lady send me here?" Suddenly all the former negative feelings and prejudices against the Capuchins seemed to envelop him; his fatigue only added to the sweeping depression that came over him. Taking off his coat, he lay on the bed with a blanket thrown around him. Only a deep sleep quieted his fears.

The next sounds to reach Barney's ears came from the corridor, down the hall from his room. Straining to hear the sounds more clearly, he gradually determined that someone was periodically ringing hand chimes, mixed with strains of men singing STILLE NACHT. As sounds came closer to his room, he began to smell the scent of incense.

Barney Casey had arrived at St. Bonaventure's to experience one of the most tender and touching rituals of the Capuchins, the awakening of the brothers for Christmas Midnight Mass with songs, bells, and incense. Opening his door, he was greeted by a small group of singing friars who stood at his door. Some other friars came from their rooms to join the group as it moved from door to door. Putting on his shoes, Barney joined the bearded men in their procession. Somehow the gloom that had descended on him just an hour before was forgotten. Maybe, just maybe, the Capuchins were not so strict and inhuman after all.

Midnight Mass, and the Mass of Christmas Day, plus the feasting and recreating among the friars would help anyone forget their personal doubts, fears and anxieties at least for awhile. The whole Christmas season, in fact, found so many new and exciting experiences that Barney's doubts seemed to recede into the past.

However, with Epiphany they were resurrected again.

In those days, Epiphany began one of the many fasts of the Capuchins. An example of a Capuchin fast is "the Fast of Benediction" lasting forty days or into Lent, which ever came first. For Barney these days of fast renewed his prior doubts and fears. With investiture into the Capuchin novitiate slated for January 14, 1897, his negativity and foreboding seemed to increase. The questions, doubts, and confusion about his future as a religious were creating more and more anxiety. By the 13th, Barney's doubts had reached a peak. In the small book of the Rule of Francis and the Constitutions of the Capuchins, he would note that this "day of anxiety" was "dark indeed."[1]

Barney's fears seem to have remained with him until the very ceremony of taking off his suitcoat to be invested with the chestnut brown habit of St. Francis. Once robed and clad in his sandals, however, the new novice at last experienced peace. He was just now named Frater[2] Francis Solanus, after St. Francis Solano, a violin-playing Spanish bard, a Franciscan who worked in the South American missions during the seventeenth century. This peace would put an end to his fears.

Solanus' entry into the novitiate straddled two other groups of novices. For the first six months he was classmate of Fraters Leo Steinberg and Salesius Schneweis. Like his associates in Wisconsin and Minnesota, Steinberg and Schneweis too found in him a loyal and caring friend. In July, after his first six months, he was joined by seven new novices.[3]

The novitiate day would begin for the household with the sound of the "clappers." These were two pieces of wood eight inches long by four inches wide by two inches thick. They were to be clapped together to the tune of "Sur-gi-te, Fra-tres" (Get up, Brothers). With few exceptions, each morning would follow the same schedule:

4:45	Rising	
5:15	Lauds (Morning Praise) followed by Litany of the Saints	
	5:40	Meditation in common in choir
	6:00	Angelus followed by Mass
	6:25	Thanksgiving meditation after Mass
	6:40	Personal time in silence
	7:00	Breakfast

At breakfast the Capuchins drank their coffee from bowls. If such a ritual caused negative feelings in Solanus, they were certainly short-lived. He began to do the same. Later he not only put coffee in his bowl, but his juice, corn flakes, and whatever else seemed to fit, making a kind of porridge which he would eat with great gusto.

The more Frater Solanus got into the routine of classes and "clericalia" (household chores), the less inviting Superior, Stillwater and Appleton seemed to be. The first entry in his little book of reflections notes: "I labor for eternity; not $100 per day or $1,000 a month."[4]

Barney Casey, layman, was settling into being Frater Solanus, Capuchin.

Since he was by nature conscientious and even a bit scrupulous at that time, the regular schedule appealed to his need/desire to fit into a regular routine. He did not have strong tendencies to instigate projects but, within structures he could become very determined and even enthused to develop follow-through. Those planning to be priests in the Order (cleric novices) had three classes a day. They learned how to pray the Divine Office (as the Prayer of the Church was then called) and how to chant parts of the Office as well. Once or twice a week they would rise to chant Matins at midnight. In between time, the novices helped in the household chores or studied in their rooms.

Noon and evening meals, except Thursdays and Sundays, were always eaten in silence. During those times, various books and articles would be read out loud. Sometimes the selections would be the Rule and Constitutions, other times, a papal encyclical; most often it would be some light book of piety. Free time came on Thursday afternoons and, of course, on Sundays when there would be only one lecture. Thursday and Sunday evenings were for "recreation."

In the classroom, the eager Solanus was discovering more and more about himself. He was learning more about his drives and ambitions and how these could be directed toward spiritual growth. He tended to act first and think later; he could act impetuously. Thus he realized the need for effective controls to his highly emotional nature. While these characteristics reflected his inate nature, few if any of his classmates experienced him acting out these tendencies. He realized they had to be controlled.

During novitiate, Solanus became increasingly aware that his initial enthusiasm and efforts might be colored as much by a desire for a good reputation and to be respected as for the honor of God. Having this realization he copied a quote in his notebook:

> As for desiring to do things which may deserve glory,
> though it is what magnanimity desires, yet the magnanimous man desires it not for the glory that arises therefrom

but only that he may deserve the glory without possessing it. On the contrary he has raised himself so high above the opinion of the world, that finding nothing estimable but virtue and looking with the same eye on the praise and scorn of man, he does nothing for love of the one or through fear of the others; his flight is higher. It is for love of God and virtue that he is moved to perform great actions; all other motives have no influence on him. Virtue is so excellent a thing that men cannot either reward or recompense it sufficiently. God alone can do this.[5]

God alone was what Solanus was beginning to desire; his heart was becoming purified. Yet, to reach this goal of the spiritual life, there were certain goals he had to pursue. He remembered what he had heard from St. Bonaventure: that perfection consists principally in love and its perfection and that this perfection must exclude those inordinate attractions (like avarice, pride, and lust) which are the enemy of charity. Such tendencies are the opposite of that root and principle of perfection which Francis called ''most high poverty.''[6]

One could not reach the goal of the love of God, the aim of ''most high poverty,'' without certain practices or steps. In particular, Solanus decided, that he would begin to practice in the novitiate and try to develop controls which would make them part of his permanent approach to spirituality:

MEANS FOR ACQUIRING THE LOVE OF GOD[7]

1. ''Detachment of oneself from earthly affections; singleness of purpose!
2. Meditation on the Passion of Jesus Christ
3. Uniformity of will within the Divine Will
4. Mental Prayer, meditation and contemplation
5. Prayer: ''Ask and it shall be given to you'' (Mt 7:7)

In many ways, the first means to acquire the love of God, which Solanus noted, is the heart of spirituality; detachment and singleness of purpose are both linked to the purification both of the senses and the spirit itself. If he was going to experience God and God's love, Solanus realized, he had to develop a pure heart, free of those obstacles which might get in the way. Furthermore, he could not just be detached, or give up certain ideas, phobias, memories, material things or other people. He had to combine the negative element of detachment with the positive step of singlemindedness in his approach.

Singlemindedness was not just a spiritual goal for Solanus; it was part of his personality. He knew that once he set his mind to do something, it was going to get done. This stick-to-it-iveness was tinged with a strain of perfectionism that resulted from a combination of his strict up-bringing and a scrupulous conscience. Gradually, by purifying these natural inclinations, and by becoming more abandoned to God, he would be able to learn to be free both from excessive rigidity and anxious scrupulosity.[8] His singlemindedness would become a strong basis for his spirituality. "By every good work, how small soever it be, which is directed to all with love and with an upright and single intention, we earn a greater likeness and eternal life in God," Jan van Ruysbroeck the Belgian mystic wrote:

> A single intention draws together the scattered powers into the unity of the spirit, and joins the spirit to God. A single intention is (the) end, and beginning, and adornment of all virtues. A single intention offers to God praise and honour and all virtues: and it pierces and passes through itself, and all the heavens, and all things, and finds God within the simple ground of its own being. That intention is single which aims only at God and in all things only at their connection with God. The single intention casts out hypocrisy and duplicity, and a man must possess it and practice it in all his works above all other things; for it is this which keeps man in the presence of God, clear in understanding, diligent in virtue, and free from outward fear, both now and in the Day of Doom. Singleness of intention is the single eye of which Christ speaks, giving light to the whole body—that is, to the man's works and his whole life—and

cleansing it of sin. Singleness of intention is the inward, enlightened and loving tendency of the spirit; it is the foundation of all spirituality, it includes in itself faith, hope, and charity, for it trusts in God and is faithful to Him. It casts nature underfoot, it establishes peace, it drives out spiritual discontent, and it preserves fullness of life in all the virtues. And it gives peace and hope and boldness toward God, both now and in the Day of Doom.

Thus we shall dwell in the unity of the spirit, in grace and in likeness, and shall always go out to meet God by means of the virtues, and offer to him with a simple intention our whole life and all our work, and ever more and more, we shall increase our likeness, and pass through ourselves and go out to meet God without means, and rest in him in the abyss of simplicity: there we possess that heritage which has been prepared for us from all eternity. All spiritual life and all works of virtue consist in Divine likeness and in singleness of intention."[9]

While detachment and singleness of purpose were the first of Solanus' five "Means for Acquiring the Love of God," it is significant that the last "means" he noted for his spirituality was a specific kind of prayer: "Ask and it shall be given you." This promise of Jesus to his followers, combined with Solanus' single-minded conviction and union of his will with God would translate into a powerful testimony of ideals-in-action in his later years through the healing ministry.

In developing relationships with his fellow novices (who were not allowed by the Constitutions to associate with the Capuchins who had professed vows), Solanus was discovering the need for community skills. While he was a "people person" among his peers, in his perfectionism and idealism, he also began to notice that, at times, he was judging his confreres harshly. The more he reflected on these tendencies, the more he realized he should be judging himself and become more sensitive to what may have caused the novice to act in a questionable way he observed. He came across a passage which seemed to be "speaking" to him about the issue of judging, so he jotted it down in his notebook:

> If a fault of anyone disturbs you, know that it is more a weakness for him than for you, and that he suffers more from it. Perhaps, however, it is but "a mote in thy brother's eye" which, on account of "the beam in thy own" appears so great. At all events, have the charity to pray the Lord to deliver your brother and if the latter be the case, it will prove a double blessing.[10]

In his classes Solanus learned to pray formally. He was given the tools which would serve him well not only for prayer in common, but, in particular, for his personal prayer. Aided by the silence of the monastery (which was total unless for the Thursday and Sunday dinners and suppers or the occasional dispensation for special occasions and regular recreation periods), Solanus discovered the value of recollection and the means he could use to maintain a sense of the presence of God. There were two in particular which he thought would be helpful. Again, he jotted these down in his notebook: "I. Raise your heart to Him by frequent ejaculations (little mantra-type prayers) and II. Make a good intention at the beginning of each work and frequently during its execution."[11] Frequent meditations on the passion of Jesus, helped by the Stations of the Cross, became prayer forms that could also help him reach his aim: acquiring the love of God.

As the days evolved, Frater Solanus was being considered by the professed Capuchins as a good prospect for profession. He passed his first two "scrutinies" with nine votes in favor. On the last scrutiny, November 17, he and Frater Maurus received eight positive votes and one negative vote. Frater Damasus Wickland received two negative votes. While it is not recorded why he received the negative vote from one of the professed Capuchins at St. Bonaventure's, it could have been because there was some concern about his ability to know Latin and German well enough to become a priest. Based on his classes with Fr. Gabriel, the novice master, it was becoming clear that the fears of the superiors at St. Francis Seminary in Milwaukee were not ungrounded.

The Capuchin superiors approached Solanus about their own concerns. They feared he did not have the necessary grasp of his subjects to qualify him to become a Capuchin priest. With first vows coming soon, they also wanted to discover the motivation for Solanus' entry into the Order; was it to be a Capuchin or a priest? In those days, many people came to the Capuchins to become priests, since Capuchin priests were the only priests they knew. Solanus had been told that he could not become a diocesan priest; he had come to the novitiate to become a Capuchin. If one day he might become a priest in the process, fine. However that would be up to God.

Even so, the Capuchin superiors asked Solanus to state his intentions clearly on this point. To allay their fear about his future abilities at the seminary, Solanus made the following "Attestation" on July 20, 1898. It was the day before he would make his first vows:

> I, Fr. Solanus Casey declare that I joined the Order of the Capuchins in the Province of St. Joseph with the sure intention to follow thus my religious vocation. Although I would wish and should be thankful, being admitted to the ordination of a priest, considering the lack of my talents, I leave it to my superiors to judge on my faculties and to dispose of me as they think best.
>
> I therefore will lay no claim whatsoever if they should think me not worthy or not able for the priesthood and I always will humbly submit to their appointments.[12]

Whether it took much struggle and purification of motives to write such an "Attestation" will never be known because Solanus never was known to express any bitterness about the way superiors ultimately determined his "worthiness." Whatever the unknown feelings, the words themselves indicate that the year in novitiate had found that Solanus Casey was already manifesting those signs that reflect that higher stage of spirituality called the illuminative way, or the way of positive growth in the life of detachment.

Now he was ready publicly to vow his life to the Lord "in the presence of all the people" (Ps 116:14). An inner vow to be totally dedicated to the Lord had already been offered December 8, 1896. That private vow had gradually been strengthened during the novitiate through Solanus' single-minded effort to be faithful to what he had promised. The "Attestation" added to his detachment. Their public expression came on July 21, 1898. On that day he knelt before Fr. Bonaventure, the Provincial who had accepted him into the novitiate twenty months before and declared: "I, Frater Solanus . . . vow and promise to . . . live in obedience, without property, and in chastity."[13]

Immediately after making his vows, Solanus and his classmates took the train to Milwaukee. They would continue their studies at the Capuchin's St. Francis Seminary.

Although the Capuchins presently loan the building which housed the Seminary at St. Francis for use by poverty programs, when Solanus arrived at Fourth and Harmon (Brown) Streets, the complex looked basically the same as it does now. The friary seminary extended like a "U" on its side, from the left of the large Romanesque church. This created a cloister garden which was ideal for relaxing, as long as you did not talk or laugh in such a way that you would disturb those in their rooms on the second floor. The friary chapel extended behind the Church proper. On the second floor, in the upper left corner of the building was a classroom.

Because there were neither enough Capuchin faculty members or students, the classes were rotated on a four-year basis. The Director of the program was Father Anthony Rottensteiner. While some might have laughed at his unique surname, nobody made fun of his approach to education, especially the young Capuchin clerics. He was all seriousness and demanded the same of the seminarians.

Anthony had founded the educational program for the seminarians of the province. He also was the province minister from 1888–91, the first provincial who was not one of its two founders, Francis and Bonaventure. Their terms had covered a twenty-four year period, including those years before the Calvary Province became an official province.

Anthony was elected for just one term of three years. To be elected for only one three-year term was rare in the province then as well as now. It was usually a sign from the electing delegates that they were displeased by the way leadership had been exercised. At the Chapter of 1891, Minister of the Order, Bernard of Andermat, made it clear that he wanted leaders to be more sensitive and more humane in their approach. Since Anthony was known for his severity, this may be a major reason why he was not re-elected.[14]

Returning to teaching at St. Francis, Anthony tried to make sure the clerics had other outlets to balance their studies. Consequently, Solanus was given charge of the friary chapel and the altar boys for the parish church of St. Francis.

In taking care of his assignments, Solanus was conscientious to the point of perfectionism. According to a classmate, Father Boniface Goldhausen:

> As far as his work is concerned, he was always on time. I do not remember that he ever came late for religious exercises or for the work to be done. It was always perfect. . . . He was very exact and painstaking. At times I would go down to the choir when he was busy there. I would observe him. I was highly edified. On feast days he would put perhaps three candles and three bouquets out. Then he would put candles on each side and he would go way back and look at it. If it wasn't exactly perfect he would go back and move one candle until they were just where he wanted them. It was the same things with the bouquets. If everyone would take so much care for the Lord it would be wonderful. It took him at least a half hour to trim that simple choir altar. But at the same time he seemed so recollected. When he was finished, he made his adoration. One would notice that he was deeply absorbed spiritually. That's one thing I cannot forget.[15]

Fr. Boniface remembered such details about Solanus after almost seventy years. This in itself indicated that some things about Solanus already at that time were causing him to be remembered.

While such a detail might be recalled, little is revealed about Solanus' dealings with the other seminarians, except that he fit in as well as anyone else and that he liked to play checkers. While others regarded Solanus as quite normal, he never regarded himself as good as others said. He was aware of failings others didn't see. In his notebook, he wrote to himself, "Patience, therefore, *with* your faults."[16] Solanus not only had to be patient with himself; sometimes his patience ran thin with others. The controls over his strong emotions, especially anger, could flare up. Now and then he responded indignantly to his associates. Then, after thinking it over, he would ask forgiveness, feeling much better as a result. But the tendency to judge wouldn't go away easily. Even when he didn't verbalize his feelings, he knew he had his share of judgments about others, so he cautioned himself: "Beware of silent criticism."[17]

In those days the style of spiritual formation tended to reinforce the inner-orientation reflected in his self-admonitions. Despite this, Solanus was also beginning to be aware that holiness could not be limited to the confines of the cloister. He had noted that the "Traits of Saintly Characters" consisted of three things: "(1) Eagerness for the glory of God; (2) Touchiness about the interests of Jesus; and (3) Anxiety for the salvation of souls."[18] Since some of those souls which "interested" Jesus very much were the poor, Solanus began to realize the poor had to become his interest too. "Our lot," as Capuchins he would write, "has been cast among the simple lives of the poor."[19]

One of the first quotations Solanus had noted in his little book came from Pope Clement XIV while he was still a Cardinal:

> Be not contented with giving, but also lend to him that is in need, according to the precept of the Scriptures. I do not know a more contemptible object than money if it be not employed to assist our neighbor. Can the insipid pleasure of heaping up crowns be compared with the satisfaction of conferring happiness and the felicity of attaining heaven?[20]

In his communications with others, he also urged them to do what they could for the poor. He reminded his sister Ella to "admonish" their brother Owen "not to neglect the most salutary (deed)—almsgiving for the poor and orphans."[21]

While the superiors saw to it that an environment would be created to facilitate the vowed living of Capuchin-Franciscan spirituality, the bulk of the time and effort of the young clerics was spent in classes and study. With Anthony Rottensteiner's stress on excellence, Solanus began to find some difficulty in his final semesters of philosophy. He was just below average in his class of six. As his records show he found philosophy itself especially difficult. Text books were in Latin and discussions were in German. These had been two of his most difficult subjects in the first year of philosophy at the "other" St. Francis. He almost failed in Latin. More and more Solanus was finding the nuances of the language and interpretation of theories in them becoming increasingly difficult.

When he began his first semester of formal theology, in the fall of 1899, the superiors voiced serious concern whether Solanus would be able to make it within their academic regime. Instead of changing the system which demanded German and Latin, their approach demanded that the change be made in individuals. Consequently the structure took its toll on its victims. Instead of blaming the system, the superiors placed the blame on victims like Solanus; he simply was not smart enough.

Although the general impression was that the educational problem rested in Solanus' deficiencies, the leaders in the system did not deal with him severely at all. Despite his severity otherwise, Anthony Rottensteiner sensed something good about Frater Solanus. He did whatever he could to coax answers out of him and others having difficulty, especially when he believed their hesitation and stumbling were not for want of understanding, but because of the nuances of the German and Latin languages.

A report card[22] of his first theology shows that Solanus' first year was his most difficult. Based on a system wherein 1 = good and very good, 2 = average, 3 = passing, and 4 = failure, Solanus was definitely below average.

	DOGMA	MORALS	CANON LAW	SACRED SCRIPTURE	LITURGY
Dec. 1900	3	2–3	2–3	3	2
July 1901	3	2–3	2–3	3	2

Reviewing his grades in 1901, the superiors were very concerned. Solemn vows would be made July 21, and Solanus was appearing less and less able to complete his courses successfully. If he took solemn vows, Solanus had to realize that it did not necessarily mean he would be ordained, or, that if he was ordained, he would be able to fully function as a priest.

Solanus understood his situation quite well. But to make it clear, the superiors wanted his understanding to be put in writing. Thus, on July 5, 1901, Solanus signed a German statement that declared his intentions:

> I, Fr. Solanus Casey, having entered the Order with a pure intention and of my own free choice, wish to remain in the Order, and I therefore humbly ask for admission to solemn profession. However, since I do not know whether as a result of my meager talents and defective studies, I am fit to assume the many-sided duties and serious respon-sibilities of the priesthood, I hereby declare (1) that I do not want to become a priest if my legitimate superiors consider me unqualified; (2) that I still wish to be able to receive one or other of the orders, but will be satisfied if they exclude me entirely from the higher orders. I have offered myself to God without reservation; for that reason I leave it without anxiety to the superiors to decide about me as they may judge best before God.[23]

To subscribe to such a statement reflects a deep humility. Solanus would abide in these traits of humility and self-deprecation throughout his life.

Meanwhile life continued with a few things happening now and then to break the academic routine. From Solanus' notes we read of the rise of Count Leo Tolstoi and his strong influence over people of that time. At the triennial meeting of the Capuchin leaders ("the chapter") that summer it was decided to split the northern section of St. Francis Parish into a new parish. The new Capuchin parish was named after Elizabeth of Hungary, the Franciscan Queen, noted for her concern for the poor. Because the new building needed much work, especially free labor, Solanus and the other seminarians were recruited regularly.

The notebook also speaks of periodic visits from the members of Solanus' family. After seventeen years away from the seminary, Solanus noted that Maurice had informed his family that he was thinking of returning to study. On July 20, 1903, another brief entry was jotted: "Death of His Holiness Leo XIII." A few weeks later he added: "Pope Pius X elected August 5th, the 7th ballot. Crowned August 9th in presence of 70,000."[24]

Meanwhile, as he continued his studies at St. Francis, Solanus became preoccupied with a physical problem. He had developed sore eyes and was beginning to become quite concerned about what would happen both to them and to himself. The more he thought of his pain and the way he was reacting in such fear of it, the more humiliated he felt. Not able to find peace in his approach, he decided to change his attitude. He would try to be more positive and thankful. It worked; in his notebook he briefly penned: "Thanksgiving for same June 12; consolation on 13th, 1902."[25]

Another consolation of a more practical nature was the fact that, with the 1901–1902 school year, Solanus' grades began to improve. Possibly thinking that Solanus might continue to improve, the superiors allowed him to receive tonsure, the first step into the clerical state.

During his second year of theology, Solanus worked at his grades as hard as he could. His efforts began to show even more improvement, although the improvement was admittedly slight. The first semester of his third year brought him the best marks he had received thus far in Theology. Things were definitely improving. Despite his improvement there were still questions being raised about whether he possessed the resources to function fully as a priest in the Order.

Solanus was trying hard to integrate these problems with his spiritual life. More and more, he realized that his vocation as a Capuchin demanded that such difficulties be accepted not only just in a spirit of detachment, but in a spirit of thanksgiving as well—even when it meant doing violence to his original dream. He wrote:

> "Penance is the primary end of the Friar Minor. Therefore a vocation to the same implies *penance* first of all, and whatever is of pain or death must be received at least with resignation and, better yet, with gratitude . . . If the *Creator* desires or requires penance, what better can the creature do?"[26]

In concluding, possibly as a sign of his effort to show gratitude, in the face of his own fading dreams, Solanus added and underlined the words that would rise to the tip of his lips for most of the rest of his life: "*Deo Gratias!*"[27] Somehow, if his will was united to God's and that God's will was somehow communicated through his superiors' decisions, he had to give thanks even though it might be terribly hard.

Solanus celebrated the seventh anniversary of his vocation to "Go to Detroit," by receiving the subdiaconate. While this signaled his inauguration into major orders, it still was not clear if he would be ordained priest. The final decision seems to have been deeply affected by something which occurred two months later. In February 1904, Solanus' first semester grades indicated that something serious had happened with his studies. He received no marks at all for Sacred Scripture and Liturgy. Despite this, he was still promoted to the next steps toward the priesthood. But would he be able to function as a full-fledged priest? Solanus wrote his sister that he would "probably be ordained deacon and priest before August. May the Holy Ghost direct my superiors in their decisions in this regard and may his Holy Will in all things be done."[28] This time, under his signature, Solanus wrote "*Resignation+*"; this was one of the few occasions he signed his name this way. Given his future which was being decided by his superiors, perhaps it was asking too much of him to show gratitude for the penance he was about to receive; resignation was all he could muster!

In the next few months, the faculty was becoming very concerned about what was happening with Solanus. While his grades in Dogma, Morals, and Canon Law together were the best average he had ever achieved, he did not seem to be adequately handling Sacred Scripture and Liturgy.

	DOGMA	MORALS	CANON LAW	SACRED SCRIPTURE	LITURGY
Dec. 1900	3	2–3	2–3	3	2
July 1901	3	2–3	2–3	3	2
Feb. 1902	3	2–3	2	2–3	2
June 1902	2–3	2	2–3	3	2
Jan. 1903	2–3	2	2	2–3	2
July 1903	2	2	2	3	2
Feb. 1904	2	2	2	—	—
June 1904	2	2	2	—	—

There is no written record of the meetings at which the subject of Solanus Casey's receiving priesthood were discussed. But, if his academic record was being discussed, it was not in isolation. Of six in his class, there were three clerics with mostly all "good and very good" and "average" marks. There were three others who received almost all "average" and "passing" marks. Solanus came just behind Frater John O'Donovan and quite a bit ahead of Frater Damasus Wickland.

Not one of these three had ever gotten a "good and very good" or even a combination of these with "average." Furthermore, none of them seem to have completed their Scripture and Liturgy courses to satisfaction. What could be done with them?

It is known for certain, however, that the decision was made to ordain Fraters Solanus and Damasus, but to withhold the faculties of hearing confessions and preaching dogmatic sermons for the two. There is a dispute whether the superiors decided to withhold the right to hear confessions and to preach dogmatic sermons to Frater John O'Donovan; some say the superiors did withhold "faculties" but that John fought the decision and won the day. Others do not believe he had any faculties withheld.

Solanus in particular did not have the grasp of German sufficient to be an effective minister in the confessional, they reasoned. This decision was not based on an anti-Irish bias, for John O'Donovan "knew German better than the Germans." However, because the Irish Solanus was a part of the German Province, he had to suffer the consequences of its structures if he would minister in it. When it came to discuss Solanus' case and his future ministry, the superiors remembered the words which Anthony Rottensteiner had said at the time they considered Solanus for diaconate. "We shall ordain Frater Solanus," the Director of Studies had said, "and as a priest, he will be to the people something like the Curé of Ars"[29] (referring to the candidate for canonization, John Vianney, whose faculties for hearing confessions and preaching dogmatic sermons had originally been withheld, although they were later instated).

Frater Solanus and his five classmates were ordained in the parish church of St. Francis on Sunday, July 24, 1904. The ordaining bishop was Archbishop Sebastian Messmer, the brother of Solanus' former novice master. Two days later, in Rome, the head of the Capuchin

Franciscan Order, Bernard of Andermat, signed the letter giving Solanus his "Preacher's Patents" for the Order. The letter stated that he was to be:

> a messenger of the divine word and for the merit of obedience we enjoin upon you the office of preaching, so that, after having first obtained the Faculty from the superiors and the Ordinaries to whom the matter pertains, you preach the Word of God everywhere in a worthy and fruitful manner, with well-considered and simple language, and, as directed by our Holy Father Francis, proclaim what is vice and virtue, punishment and glory.[30]

Though he received the papers from Rome giving him the power to preach the Word "the superiors and the Ordinaries to whom the matter pertained" would not give him permission to use it, or to hear confessions. Solanus would remain a "Simplex Priest" for the rest of his life. It was simply figured that he was not smart enough to function fully as a priest.

But is this the case? Recent evidence shows that Solanus Casey had an I.Q. around 135.[31] Why, then, did he not make the grade? Certainly part of the problem was the system that demanded solid Latin and German; Solanus was proficient in neither. However, besides the system's imperfections, Solanus' own personality created an obstacle too. While he was very analytical and logical and loved to have the facts, he did not like to probe issues deeply. He tended to skim the surface. If he did not grasp something immediately he tended to give up.

Interpreting this reaction to studies as a lack of intelligence or ability, the superiors did not challenge Solanus' mind by giving him methods on how to go beyond the surface facts to logical insight and understanding. Instead the interpretation about him coming from the diocesan seminary professors at St. Francis de Sales was reinforced, and a self-fulfilling prophecy about Solanus Casey began to evolve. He lived the consequences of this mixed-up situation for the rest of his priestly life.

At that time the Province had legislation that "First Masses" had to be said in that Capuchin parish which was nearest to the newly-ordained's home. Since Appleton was the closest to Superior (200 miles away), Solanus' "First Mass" would be celebrated at St. Joseph's Parish there. In many ways, given the situation, it was not totally removed from Solanus' past experience. After all he had worked there as a motorman years before. On the Sunday after his ordination, a very formal liturgy was celebrated. The procession even featured a "bride" for Solanus—four year old Irma Roemer.

Despite the fact that he knew he would never do some of the things priests considered most important, Solanus could only look upon that day with thanks. God not only had been so good to him; he discovered that God was touching his brother Maurice as well. "On that occasion I met dear Mother for the first time since joining the Order eight years before. She and Father came down from Superior and Maurice, who was with the Railroad Mail Service, came from Chicago," he wrote:

> Poor, dear Maurice served on the Altar. I was told afterwards that for very joy Papa wept all during the Services at the thought that God had finally blessed his family with a priest.
>
> Maurice, who was destined to follow to the same sublime privilege, brought a tear to my own eye that day, when the two of us were strolling in the Monastery garden. He half-soliloquized, as though revisioning his twenty-year vocation: "By George, Barney, I think I'll have to try it over again. I'm getting tired of this blamed rail-roading![32]

Shortly after ordination, Solanus received word that his first assignment would be Sacred Heart Parish in Yonkers. His "Obedience," the official letter of his appointment, said that he should be there by August 4, 1904, four days after his "First Mass" in Appleton.

CHAPTER THREE
Yonkers, New York
August 4, 1904—July 14, 1918

Solanus Casey had never been so far East in his life. From the start it agreed with him. Situated on the top of one of its many hills, Sacred Heart Parish and Monastery in Yonkers was known throughout the area for the generosity and kindness of its "Capuchins on Shonnard Place." Solanus considered this industrial location north of New York City as "the city of fine schools, villas, and terraces."[1] While it might not be Trimbelle, it too was "picturesque and beautiful."[2]

A main reason for Yonkers' beauty lay at the foot of its many hills, the historical Hudson River. The room selected for Solanus offered him a view of the Hudson. From it he could reflect on nature as a part of God's grandeur. It contributed to his own sense of thanksgiving. When he wrote to his sister, Margaret, he noted how the view generated in him even greater thoughts about gratitude to God from whom he had received so many benefits in his life thus far:

> Surely the natural scene now before me when I turn my head to look at it is as picturesque as any scene of long ago. The mouth of the Hudson shines like a silver lake away in the horizon in the clouds. I was going to say, "with hills and valleys and human achievement between." But what is nature in light of the supernatural? Ah, a substratum!
>
> And what are natural blessings compared with the hope of immortality? I believe that I'd go crazy, yearning for something higher if I had nothing to enjoy or to hope for but

the natural, even had I all the natural gifts and blessings enjoyed by man. But thanks be to God for the True Faith! Thanks be to God for the simple, honest, faithful parents that God gave us! Thanks be to God for vocation and for strength to follow the call, at least imperfectly! Thanks be to God for the blessed hope that he gives us here in our exile of once being eternally united with his chosen ones in the peace of our true home, in the love of his Sacred Heart![3]

"The ideal monastery of the Sacred Heart in picturesque Yonkers"[4] had for its superior and pastor the man who had built it thirty years before as provincial, Bonaventure Frey. Since Solanus was in the unique position of being a priest, but not allowed to preach formal sermons or hear confessions, giving this new priest something to do proved quite a challenge to Bonaventure's imagination. At a loss to come up with anything else, he assigned Solanus the care of the sacristy and the overseeing of altar boys.

The job was hardly full time. It might also be considered something of a "put-down." But Solanus had resigned himself to the fact that he would always be limited to such ministries as a Capuchin. Even more his resignation had begun to turn to gratitude. By now, Solanus was not able to consider his assignment in any terms but positive. Whatever we do in faith and thanksgiving can be part of God's plan, he reasoned. Referring to his work in the sacristy, he wrote:

. . . something came to mind of our ineffable privilege in doing the little things we are able to do for the general welfare—most especially in a religious community. Each one is in his own place without thought or distinction as to what the work may be. To whatever office or service one may turn, it is not easy to say just which is more privileged, possibly excepting that of a sacristan.[5]

While Solanus considered his assignment as sacristan to be a distinct privilege, it was not the case with some others. They felt that a priest taking care of the sacristy and sanctuary was a real humiliation. One who tried to understand was Solanus' brother, Edward. Not fully understanding why the Capuchin superiors had not only limited his brother's priesthood, but now had given him assignments usually assigned to a lay brother. Edward, who would later become a priest as well, wrote him a poem. Entitled, "The Brother Sacristan," he tried to link the theme of fidelity to duty with the concern about details which he knew earmarked Solanus' approach to work:

> The God of Mercy, meek and humble, holds
> His reign of peace in tabernacled cell:
> While spotless order quietly enfolds
> The Place where man's Redeemer comes to dwell.
>
> With reverent love a modest figure kneels
> To pay the voiceless homage of his heart.
> Then silently from place to place he steals
> The worship of his fingers to impart.
>
> Each object there receives his tender touch—
> The snowy linen, flowers, burnished bell—
> While conscience whispers sweetly: "It is much
> For His dear sake to do each duty well. . . ."
>
> 'Dear Lord!' he whispers. 'Dearest! Crucified!
> Teach my poor heart in penance to repair
> In some degree, the luxury, the pride,
> The cold neglect that leaves You lonely there.'
>
> He lingers still, and fain would there abide,
> When evening shadows fill the chapel dim;
> At last he goes, but leaves his heart beside
> The faithful little lamp he loves to trim.

Solanus treasured this poem. It seemed to capture his feelings about his first assignment.

In his capacity as sacristan, Solanus worked with the Altar Society. He also was in charge of the altar boys who served the many public and "private" Masses of the friars.

Solanus discovered that it was not always easy to get or to keep well-behaved boys. Those he did get were not always conscientious. At times he let them know, in no uncertain terms, of his frustration at their pranks or their lack of devotion. On one occasion such corrections did little to change the situation. He began a novena to pray for a happy resolution of his problem. By the time he finished the novena of the Immaculate Conception, he noted, "immediately good boys asked to be servers!"[6] The day was December 8, the anniversary of his decision to join the Capuchins.

The altar boys did not like to serve Solanus' Mass. It took too long, given his sense of reverence, his scrupulous concern for exact wording, and his poor Latin. But they did love it when Solanus took them on outings. Unlike some other Capuchins, Solanus impressed them by playing baseball in his habit. What impressed them even more was the fact that he would never wear a catcher's mask—a continuation of his practice with the Casey brothers' team in Superior and at St. Francis in Milwaukee.

James Lawless was one of the many boys who were servers under Solanus. He recalled:

> I have fond memories of the good times we had under his supervision, such as the yearly outings for the altar boys. I remember on these occasions that we had to attend Mass and pray for a safe journey to and from our destination. These visits were to Rockaway Beach, to St. Patrick's Cathedral, and other places.
>
> Before heading home, Father always treated us to an ice cream soda. After that we would stop at the nearest church and say a few prayers for a safe return home.
>
> . . . Father Solanus was the personification of patience when it came to teaching us our Latin for serving Mass. He was a patient, dedicated, and devoted servant of God.[7]

While to their faces, Solanus might be the "personification of patience," oftentimes the servers' insensitivity and lethargy troubled him.

One time their inattentiveness had reached such a point and his corrections had fallen on deaf ears to such a degree that Solanus again decided
to take his troubles to prayer. He made another novena, this one in
honor of Our Lady of Perpetual Help, in the hopes that his anxieties and
fears about his servers would be resolved. Before he knew it, "or
thought how it came, every one showed new zeal."[8]

The entry above was one of four notations Solanus made between
1901–10 under the heading: "Favors of Our Lady and Blessings."
Another entry calls himself to task for being too easy on the boys and
for being a bad example by not making visits to churches which they
passed: "When writing about altar boys' outings, having them repair
their carelessness last Saturday and their ingratitude when, with them,
you passed so many churches without making a visit to Jesus, before,
during, or after the first outing."[9]

In 1906, Fr. Aloysius Blonigen succeeded Bonaventure as pastor and
superior at Sacred Heart. One of the first things he did was to give
Solanus another job. He was to become the doorkeeper, or porter, of the
friary.

As porter, Solanus quickly learned about the people's problems in
ways he never was taught in the classroom in Milwaukee. During the
early days of his new assignment in Yonkers, people came to the friary
to "talk to a priest." Solanus told them that he was a priest, but when
they asked him to hear their confessions they became confused when he
said he could not. They had observed him celebrating Mass at the side
altars, why couldn't he hear confessions? "I'm not able to," is all
Solanus would usually reply. As word began to spread about Solanus'
compassion, sensitivity, and gentleness with the many people who started to come to see him, the parishioners developed their own rationale
for his inability to hear confessions. They began to reason, one woman
recalls, that, "Father Solanus loved God so much that he could not hear
confessions because he might not be able to take it if he discovered how
many people were hurting God!"

When people came to see him, telling him about their problems,
Loretta Brogan (later Sr. Dolora, C.S.A.) remembers, "He never acted

as though he was what he wasn't. He accepted people wherever they were. If you were sick, he hurt with you. He was very compassionate. He could say a few words to you and you would be perfectly at ease."[10] Others recall that, of all the priests at Sacred Heart, there was something about Solanus that made him the one who was most approachable. He was the one who put you at ease and who would do anything for you.

Those who attended the preparatory seminary that was on the grounds of the Monastery at Sacred Heart recall the humanness of Solanus. "One time we were called to Midnight Mass by Solanus. Here he was," Walter O'Brien (later a Capuchin) recalls, "the censer on one finger, the bell on another, and he was playing *Stille Nacht* on his violin!"[11]

Above all, the people remember Solanus as approachable. People would come to the office where he was portering. They came with problems and concerns, asking for prayers or guidance. Generally Solanus would listen to the problem, then close his eyes for a few moments or look away in space in a reflective mood. Then he would give his response. His answers invariably brought new insights to deal with the problems. In some beautiful and significant way, the people began to sense, Father Solanus was in special touch with God.

When people with troubles could not come to Solanus in the front office, they often asked him to come to their homes. These included not only the Germans and Irish who felt a natural kinship with Solanus, because of language and background; the newly immigrated Italians also were secure with him because of the way he showed concern for their needs.

As an eight or nine year old girl, Carmella Petrosino acted as Solanus' interpreter for the Italian community. "If anything went wrong in the neighborhood, the people would say, 'Go, get the Holy Priest,'" she recalls:

> We lived in the neighborhood where there were all Italians who had just landed from Italy. Our parents couldn't speak English. We lived three blocks below the Monastery. In

between there were lots of woods. My father went to St. Anthony, the Italian church, but my mother went to Sacred Heart. I was in the third or fourth grade there.

I went from house to house, acting as Fr. Solanus interpreter.

My first experience happened with Mrs. Maria De Santo in our neighborhood. She had come from Italy with her three or four children, and was about to deliver another. In those days instead of doctors, they had midwives, so my Mother went over to help. In the process of delivering the baby, the woman got very, very sick. As the days went on infection set in. The doctor came, very concerned about her failing health. My Mother said, 'I don't think Maria is going to get over this; she's going to die.'

So right away I suggested that I go and get "the Holy Priest." To the Italians, they wouldn't say, "Fr. Solanus;" they would just say, "The Holy Priest." So I went to Fr. Solanus and told him that one of the ladies who just had a baby was going to die. So we started down the hill into the valley where we lived.

As soon as Father came in, he asked for holy water. But they had no holy water. Fr. Solanus said, 'Oh, poor, poor, poor.'' I ran over to our house and got some. When I came back he prayed over her, blessed her and from then on the woman got over her infection and lived a long time afterwards.''[12]

During their walks to the neighbors' houses, up and down the hills of Yonkers, Solanus and Carmella would have good talks. "And, Carmella, what are you going to do when you grow up?" he asked her one day.

"I'd like to be a Sister of St. Agnes," she replied, thinking of the Sisters from Wisconsin who staffed the school.

"You will be a Sister of St. Agnes," is all that he said. Carmella became Sr. Agrippina Petrosino, C.S.A.

Such an incident indicates that as early as his first assignment Solanus was beginning to develop keen insight into people's needs and how they fit into God's plans. His Yonkers days were sowing the seed of his future ministry of healing and prophecy. In seminal form these gifts, even then, were beginning to be nourished and used.

Recalling another incident where she acted as interpreter, Sr. Agrippina recalled:

> I don't know where this woman came from, but she came to our house. The woman had been having headaches for many years and felt she couldn't take it any more. She said to my mother: "Mrs. Petrosino, I heard that they have a Holy Priest up at Sacred Heart. And that if he prays over you, you get over your illnesses." (We didn't say "miracles" in those days, just that "you'll get better."). Then she said, "Could your daughter go up and get him?"
>
> So I ran up the hill and Father came right away. He had a little book with him. The woman said, "Father, would you put your hand on my head." So he did that, as he read from the book.
>
> I just imagine the woman got better because she never came back.[13]

In the two accounts told by Sr. Agrippina, Solanus used holy water one time and various prayers at another time. Invariably, Solanus always used some "instrument" in the form of a sacramental of the Church or some corporal or spiritual work. Thus, when any favorable response came to those in need, Solanus was merely reinforced in his faith in the efficacy of the Church's rituals or such means of mercy practiced by the petitioners. While the people would credit Solanus, he would credit the means used.

One work of mercy which Solanus stressed that others practice was membership in the Seraphic Mass Association, the brainchild of a Swiss lay woman who was very concerned about helping the foreign missions. Trying to find a way to help them financially, she convinced the Capuchin superiors that if she could get people to make contributions to the missions, the Capuchins ought to promise those people a remembrance in their Masses and other prayers. In fact, she argued, why not start an Association? The people contributing to the missions would become members of the Association. Benefits would go both to the Capuchin missionaries, in the form of donations, and to the people donating, in the form of Capuchin Masses and prayers. The superiors accepted the idea and the SMA was launched.

Each Capuchin front office had SMA memberships available. Thus, when people started coming to see Solanus in the front office at Sacred Heart asking for favors, he would often talk with them awhile, pray for their healing or intention, and then ask them, as a sign of their thanks for the blessings of God already at work in their lives, to support the missions through membership in the SMA.

Depending on the persons, Solanus would vary the action which he requested them to perform as their sign of faith when they asked for a favor. Solanus was open to people of all backgrounds. Italians, Irish and German Catholics sought him out and gladly performed the various actions he requested. But Solanus didn't limit himself or his care to Catholics alone. He realized while he might have a natural tendency to be clannish especially with the Irish or the Catholics, that he needed to be open to all people. Thus to make sure he wouldn't remain controlled by a ghetto mentality, Solanus sought out Protestants to be with them. At times he would visit them for simple reasons of friendship. At other times it was because many of them were really wealthy; they could provide jobs for people coming to Solanus looking for work.

> Non-Catholic neighbors over on Hudson Terrace especially where the more wealthy and the "millionaires" lived were wont to employ Catholic girls and young men.
> . . . Later on, when continuing such visitations I found that many of these dear good people would feel slighted if we failed to see them too. It just seemed sufficient to ensure employment if a Capuchin father sent anyone over where there was work to do.[14]

Solanus Casey was not the only "holy priest," sought out by the people at Sacred Heart. During his first years in Yonkers, Solanus was stationed with Fr. Stephen Eckert, whose cause for canonization was introduced in 1948. From a note he wrote much later, it is evident that he was quite edified by Stephen's spirituality. In his earlier days, it seems Solanus had a tendency to become envious of other people's material or spiritual success possibly because of his strong competitive nature. But by now he had become quite free of that tendency. Far from being afraid or jealous of Stephen's popularity, he was actually edified by it. Stephen's popularity was in no way a threat to his own. He revealed:

> Shortly after our ordination to the holy priesthood—Father Damasus, John, Fabian, Pius, and Maurus—I was sent to the Sacred Heart Monastery in picturesque Yonkers, New York. Father Stephen (who was about my age and had been ordained several years ahead of me) had preceded me thither at least a year or two. Even then, though second to the Very Reverend Pastor, Fr. Bonaventure Frey, he seemed to be the popular Father. His bell in the Monastery was continually ringing.
>
> From the very first he seemed to me a really earnest, zealous priest. He was always not only willing, but solicitous to help whom and where he might, without exception, high or low, rich or poor, learned or ignorant, Catholic or "Atheist."
>
> He was surely not overtalented. . . . Yet Father Stephen was friendly too and was seemingly missed by the clergy as well as by the laity whenever anything important was on; even though he never seemed to care about making personal friends. In fact, unless he could see an advantage toward doing something to benefit (others), he was decidedly reticient and preferred to be alone. He was wont to retire to Jesus in the Tabernacle as often as convenient without being noticed, even in time of recreation. [15]

If Stephen Eckert was discovered praying in the church at odd times by Solanus, it was because Solanus himself was praying there as well! In fact, people remembered seeing Solanus praying in a corner of the chapel as early as four o'clock in the morning.

Besides prayer in the quiet dark by himself and the formal Office prayer with the community, Solanus made it a daily practice to pray "The Little Office of the Blessed Virgin." When he missed it, he would correct himself as being ungrateful and insensitive. After all hadn't the Blessed Virgin Mary been solicitous of him throughout his life? Hadn't she been at the heart of some of the many unique religious encounters he had experienced?

To maintain "a happy relationship" with Mary, Solanus tried to cultivate a deeper understanding of her own spirituality. Much of his effort to do so revolved around a book he read soon after coming to Sacred Heart. "Shortly after my ordination to the holy priesthood," he wrote,

> I heard of a "Life of the Blessed Virgin." I was skeptical. "Who could think of presuming to write the life of the Blessed Virgin these days?" So I figured, erroneously taking it for generally understood that it had never been written. However, I was determined to see if it possibly might be more than a compilation of favors, etc., like the "Glories of Mary" which my Father used to peddle in the wintertime and give away.
>
> We found an abridged copy of *The Mystical City of God.* WHAT A REVELATION! What a treasure!
>
> From that first perusal of the simple but masterly introduction by the humble secretary, the actual writer . . . (Mary of Agreda, the Spanish mystic), my conviction has grown that the same *Mystical City of God . . .* is not only a genuine "Life" of the same Blessed Mother Mary, but, having studied it for more than forty years and on my knees having prayed the whole four volumes, I am

convinced that the work has been rightly referred to as the most opportune and authentic autobiography of the Blessed Virgin herself, the Queen of all Creation and chosen by the Divine Creator himself to be his own Spouse and our Mother. Glory be to God![16]

Solanus knew *The Mystical City of God* inside and out. He noted the key passages which he found helpful in understanding Mary's role in salvation, how these might apply to the Church, and their relevance for issues he was concerned about.

Another devotion which Solanus began to cultivate while at Sacred Heart was to Therese Martin, the "Little Flower" of Lisieux, France. He read her biography at least fifteen times during his life. In writing to his sister, Margaret, he mentioned his admiration of Therese, and how she might help Margaret with her daughter, named Therese:

> Therese ought to imitate the little Servant of God, Therese of Lisieux, the "Little Flower of Jesus."
>
> Dear Margaret, if ever there was a good for a family like yours, her autobiography is one. She died only fifteen years ago. Her cause for beatification is now in Rome and I am asking her for entire reconciliation between J.T. and T.J., as well as other favors. . . . You ought not fail in procuring this book. She makes sanctity so really attractive and so beautifully simple. I think the book costs $2.00 at P. J. Kennedy and Son's, Barclay, N.Y. Do not fail to bless your family with its presence."[17]

While Solanus developed a spirituality that was influenced by devotions to the saints and private revelation, his spirituality was not only inner directed, it also had the unique ability of being able to translate his faith concretely in the way he related to others, especially those in need.

The parishioners noted that when he was portering, Solanus would feed the "tramps," as the wandering homeless were often called in those days. People recalled seeing him sweeping the sidewalk in front of the friary. When strangers arrived needing help, he'd get them a big bowl of coffee, as well as whatever else might be available. The parishioners told each other that Solanus even would give the poor his own food. The friars knew he would take food from the friary and bring it to poor families in the parish and in the neighborhood. In a special way they knew he tried to help families with many children.

Solanus not only extended hospitality to the poor and strangers; he loved to show little kindnesses to the school children as well. He liked to play baseball with the boys. Cletus McCarthy, later a Capuchin, recalls that he would join in playing *fungo* and bat fly-balls to the boys. Or he would hit the ball on the ground "to see if they were good shortstops." [18] Physical activity was a natural outlet for his pent-up enthusiasm and competitiveness. Those who were boys in school at that time remember the robed and bearded friar throwing the ball to the pitcher, telling them tales of his bygone days on the Casey brothers baseball team.

Others who were school children have recalled still different memories of Solanus Casey. One such child was Loretta Brogan. She recalls:

> It was 1912 and I was seven years old. We were having a Field Day in school. We were free from classes and celebrated with outdoor activities. I had gone to the eight o'clock Mass. Yonkers is called "The Terraced City" and I lived in a valley below another hill and valley.
>
> Fr. Solanus saw me going by the Monastery and said to me, "Loretta, where are you going?"
>
> "I'm going home to get my breakfast."
>
> He put his arm around me and said, "No, you're not going to walk down all those hills. You come with me."
>
> He took me inside to the Office to an inner office. He brought me a plate with the biggest piece of bread on it I had ever seen in my life and a bowl of cornflakes and a great big cup of coffee. I had never seen such a cup of coffee in my life either.
>
> I was a very picky eater and never sat still long enough to

eat much of anything. And I was so embarrassed to be in the priests' house. I was afraid what my Father would say if he knew I was eating the priests' bread. I don't remember how much I ate, but when I was done, he took me over to school and saw to it that I was in good hands.

That's the way he was; he just had to help you. Everybody respected him."[19]

Gradually, besides his work as sacristan, as supervisor of altar boys and as porter, Solanus took on other jobs. One of these was "The Children of Mary," a sodality for young ladies. At the end of the meetings he would make sure that a big tray of cookies would be available for the young girls. Another group he monitored was the Sacred Heart League. Although he had not been allowed to give extended, formal sermons, Solanus used the occasion of League meetings or devotions in church, to give what the Capuchins called "ferverinos."

In the early days in Yonkers, these ferverinos did not come spontaneously to Solanus. He wrote them out with great difficulty. Yet, because he had a flair for writing, he rather enjoyed the tedious process of perfecting his thoughts on paper. One of his notebooks covers fifteen pages of such reflections which he wrote to share with the people. His thoughts and reflections were a departure from the typical "fire and brimstone" approach used by many preachers in those days. Instead of hell and damnation, the themes Solanus often stressed were unity, the love of God, the roles of the Sacred Heart and the Blessed Virgin, the nature of the Church, and the need to cooperate with God's graces. While he drew from his theological background, the spirituality Solanus preached reflected his own life, struggles, and experiences.

Typical of the generally realistic and positive approach he brought to his sermons is one he delivered on marriage. Using the text from the Wedding Feast at Cana, Solanus' reflections for his era need not be altered greatly to apply equally well to our time:

> The Holy Gospel of today brings us at once to the really beautiful and sublime subject of "Christian Marriage." It is

a subject that the Church has always proclaimed holy. It is a type of the love of Christ for his Church. It is fundamentally necessary for every kind of true progress and human prosperity.

Not that everyone must marry who wishes to have peace in this world and gain heaven in the next. That would be contrary to the counsels of Jesus Christ and his Church. But marriage should be held as it ought to be, and is, as something sacred, to be prepared for with purity and holiness of heart and embraced in a Christian manner. Those who embrace it should do so determined to bear the burdens of the holy state they enter. They should *remember* that their duties and privileges are one and the same and must be taken as such if peace is to reign in the individual soul, in the family, and in human society.[20]

Moving from a solid theological basis for marriage, Solanus then addressed the pastoral problem of growing alienation and divorces among married people:

How is it that there are so many unhappy unions in the holy state of matrimony? How is it that, where peace should abide and conjugal love reign (to the edification of the earth and the delight of heaven) that there is so much discontent, so much suspicion, so much hatred and quarreling? How is it that the divorces in our country alone are running away into the hundreds of thousands? *One single* divorce is a lot of scandal in a community. Why is it?

Is it not because of the levity with which so many of our young people prepare for and enter marriage? They worship at the shrine of amusement and pleasure while preparing, dreaming of nothing else. They cast away the thought of duty and obligation which indeed is so grave and so manifold. They trust to material advantages and to natural attractions in creatures, forgetting the Creator of all beauty and joy and holy pleasure. How can they but be disappointed? But alas, the worst of it is not for themselves but for poor children who grow up practically without father or mother and in cases of mixed marriages without definite religion.

But the marriages are not all so discouraging. Thank God there are still many who do prepare for this holy state and embrace it as God-fearing people ought to do. Many marriages in the Church, where the parties begin their new state at the steps of God's altar, receive the blessing of the Church and of God upon them and receive Jesus in their hearts. Such marriages are an edification to the parties themselves, a delight to friends, a joy to angels and surely at such weddings the Mother of Jesus is undoubtedly there also. For when Jesus is in our hearts, Mary will not be far away."[21]

While Solanus was very conscious of the problems facing married people and others who came to see him or whom he visited, he was also aware that they were influenced by forces beyond them in society. Even more so he discovered that people's alienation and problems often were created and reinforced by conditions and relationships in society.

During the time he was at Sacred Heart, the tensions between nations in Europe reached the breaking point with the outbreak of World War I. In another reflection, on the thirteenth chapter of Matthew's Gospel (wherein Jesus talked about the weeds sown among the wheat), Solanus found the weeds in the "sources of scandal" that the Pope at that time had said were causing nations to war against each other. Among these were:

The general craze among all classes for pleasure and amusement—very often sinful in itself—craze for the dance hall, the moving picture, the gambling hall, the ballroom. The Gospel's cockle can also be found in the sources of scandal which our Holy Father Pope Benedict XV complains of in his Encyclical to the Warring Nations:
1) Lack of mutual love among nations;
2) Disregard for authority;
3) Unjust quarrels among different classes; and

4) Material prosperity becoming the absorbing object of human endeavor as though there were nothing higher and better to be gained.[22]

Again, in making the link about the influence of society on the behavior of the people to whom he was preaching, Solanus added:

> As Leo XIII commented, "Our lot has been cast in an age that is bitterly opposed to justice and truth." And besides all these external dangers, there is a war going on within our own hearts as determined and as uncompromising as the world conflict now raging in the fields of Europe—a war between right and wrong—between the virtues of the soul and passions of our corrupted nature. As St. Paul expresses it, the spirit wars against the flesh and the flesh wars against the spirit. What are we to do? "And the servants said to him, 'Do you want us to go and gather it up?' And he said, 'No, lest you might root up the wheat as you are gathering up the cockle. . . .' " But what are we to do?[23]

For the rest of the sermon, Solanus listed various ideas to help the people live peacefully in the midst of both their own wars and those of society: patience, awareness of our obstacles to God's grace as well as our "unspeakable privileges" from God, prayer, and avoidance of those situations in society that can undermine fidelity.

In concluding his thoughts to those people attending the 10:15 Mass he urged: "Let us not sleep, therefore, in God's service, but be *grateful* and vigilant that when the time of harvest comes on the day of judgment, we may be gathered into the heaven of eternal glory. Amen."[24]

Solanus realized that while many of the problems of society rested in individual sin, there were social problems in society itself that had to be addressed and challenged. He realized that as a priest he had an obligation to make sure the people were aware of their need to get involved in public issues to promote the Gospel and the social teachings of the Church. The last entry in his Second Notebook highlighted a quotation from Pope Leo XIII about the need for such social involvement:

Let those of the clergy who are occupied with the instruc-
tion of the multitudes, treat planning of this topic of the
duties of citizens; so that all may understand and feel the
necessity of conscientiousness in political life, and of self-
restraint and integrity. For that cannot be lawful in public,
which is unlawful in private affairs.[25]

One of the issues that deeply troubled Solanus at this time dealt with a
problem his friends at Graymoor, New York, were facing from people
he perceived as acting unjustly.

Solanus had become a friend of the well-known Anglican convert,
Paul Francis Wattson. Wattson had brought his Anglican community of
religious men into the Roman Catholic Church as the Atonement Friars.
Solanus was present at Paul Francis' ordination and preached for his
friend's "First Mass" on July 3, 1910, at Graymoor, New York, the
home of the Atonement Friars. Paul Francis was their superior. Paul
Francis' "Clare" was Sr. Lurana. Like Francis of Assisi who supported
Clare of Assisi in her effort to begin an Order for women as he had done
for men, Paul Wattson affirmed Sr. Lurana in bringing the dream of
unity to the world through her Atonement Sisters. She was the superior
of the women's branch of the Anglican Order of sisters which also
entered the Catholic Church at that time.

Upon entry into the Roman Catholic Church, the sisters discovered
that a benefactor who had deeded their convent to them now wanted to
take it back, alleging it had been given to them because they were
Anglican Sisters. Because they became Roman Catholic Sisters the
benefactor demanded it to be returned. The whole matter created quite a
legal scandal at that time. Even though the sisters resisted the man's
effort, Solanus was edified at the "Franciscan" way they represented
themselves. He wrote to Sr. Lurana:

> . . . I take this occasion also, Dear Sister, to assure you
> that I thanked Almighty God—and do thank him—for hav-
> ing inspired someone with such truly Franciscan sentiments
> as were manifest in your gentle protest to the plaintiff attor-
> nies of that Graymoor Church property case.

I am fully confident that there are too many upright lovers of justice, even among our separated brothers and sisters, who read *The Lamp* (the Graymoor Magazine) and paused at that letter ever to hold their peace while an act of such injustice were perpetrated as would be perpetrated should your community be ejected from Graymoor. In my opinion there is no sane man who has a spark of Christianity who will hesitate (when he knows the facts and the present circumstances at and around Graymoor) to second these sentiments, and acknowledge your sentiments as really Christian. Continue, Dear Sister, in your determination never to quarrel, as our Holy Rule enjoins us and be sure you will have more powerful patrons on your side than intrigue with irreligion and silver and gold can ever procure."[26]

After a lengthy legal battle, the sisters lost their appeal in 1917. They were evicted from the property. True to his personality which could be adamant on matters of justice, Solanus was tenacious in his belief that the sisters had morality and justice on their side. He felt that their eviction represented "the killing letter of the law." It enabled unscrupulous men to score against them. He believed that "the majority of our separated brethren will condemn it as done in their name and will regret it."[27]

While the sisters might be experiencing this persecution for the sake of justice Solanus did not become self-righteous. He did not urge retaliation. Instead, he wrote Sr. Lurana about the kind of disposition he thought should guide a Christian's response in such a situation. "Needless to say, we all hoped that things would never come to such a farce against common justice and charity," he wrote:

However, the victories of the world are short-lived: "Man proposes but God disposes." We may be sure that Almighty God has not permitted things to take such a course without some good design of his own—to turn evil into good.

At all events the words of our Divine Master, "Blessed are you when they revile you and persecute you. . . ," should be a consolation to you and an encouragement. The sisters will hardly be able to do anything better than pray earnestly for their persecutors, according to the same divine authority: "Do good to those who hate you, and pray for those who persecute and calumniate you."[28]

In concluding his supportive letter, Solanus enclosed a "little donation . . . to help you in your present need." It came from the superior of Sacred Heart, a very human response to some friends and co-workers facing a very difficult situation.

Life for Solanus wasn't all front office work, visiting the sick, helping the poor or those in trouble. There were plenty of times for celebrations as well. While he liked to be alone and spend time by himself in prayer, these celebrations brought out the human, playful side of Solanus which delighted the people.

One of Solanus' favorite celebrations was Sacred Heart's Labor Day Parish Reunion. Starting with a "High Mass," the parishioners would celebrate together for the rest of the day in an all-parish festival. Parishioners and nonparishioners alike would mill around the playground, mixing with each other, playing games of chance, and drinking good German beer.

Solanus' gregarious personality was at its best in such celebrations. His natural desire to be around people, to become close to them, to share his enthusiasm and optimism for life and God seemed especially evident. These attitudes in Solanus were reinforced by the peoples' realization that Solanus simply loved them. Not only was he their "holy priest," he was a priest who had a great sense of humor, who loved to joke and enjoy people—as long as no person or group would be hurt in the process. In addition the people sensed in their friend not only generosity, but loyalty. They experienced him as extremely loyal, especially in the way he honored the confidence they placed in him.

Such mutual admiration only increased Solanus' enthusiasm and zeal to be among the people as friend and minister. Besides being able to deepen friendships, even the games at the parish celebration seemed to bring out the enthusiastic side of Solanus, including his desire for risk and good competition. Possibly this is why Solanus liked to play the wheels of fortune at the festivals. Even years later, when he was stationed in Brooklyn, he returned to Sacred Heart on Labor Day for the Parish Reunion, eating hot dogs with onions, renewing acquaintances, and enjoying taking part in the festivities.[29]

Another highlight of Solanus' years at Sacred Heart was the celebration of his parents' Fiftieth Wedding Anniversary. In the autumn of 1913 the entire family of four daughters and the ten sons, including three priests, joined together to celebrate their "dear parents" fifty-years of life together. Fr. Edward, ordained for two years, was celebrant. Maurice, who had been ordained for three years, was the deacon. Solanus was the subdeacon and preacher.

Years before the celebration, he recalled his parents' example for good as a way of encouraging sister Ella who was facing personal difficulties:

> . . . I only pray you to content yourself for the present and pray and hope—even as you know poor dear Mother did, at the River Bank and at Trimbelle. You must know that there were trials in those places and indeed patience and resignation exercised. Now, after so many years, Father speaks of great consolation. It is really enough to draw a tear of admiration and gratitude for God's merciful providence, if one only considers the past of our dear parents and now beholds their present circumstances and prospects. May their sky continue to brighten as their end approaches.[30]

When he reflected on the impact made by Barney and Ellen Casey on their fourteen children, Solanus could only be thankful. In his sermon for the celebration itself, Solanus developed this theme—gratefulness for the past years shared between husband and wife with each other and their children, gratitude for their present health, and prayerful thanks for their holy and happy future.

During the week of celebration, the family spent much of the time reminiscing. Years later Solanus recalled some of those reminiscings with his brother James:

> Probably you remember when, at the Golden Wedding in 1913, we were all musing over scenes and events on the River Bank and in Old Trimbelle. Someone remarked, "Wouldn't it be nice if we could go back there again!" Dear mother, gently sighing as if revisioning the trials of those days which outweighed their beauties and pleasures, half-whispered an exclamation: "Thanks be to God, I'm glad it's over."
> Many a time since I've thought, how beautiful was that little exclamation. It was really Christian![31]

Two years after the Golden Anniversary, Barney Casey, Sr. died a slow and painful death.

Three years after her husband's death, Ellen Casey joined her beloved Barney in a "beautiful death at the second ringing of the Angelus."[32]

This was the time of the middle-years for Solanus. He was in his mid-forties. And true to so many at this stage of life, he had experienced the loss of those closest to him. Far from embittering him, the loss made Solanus deepen his desire to draw closer, in union, with God. In his prayer, he was able to deepen his relationship with that God who dwelt within him. At the same time, he seemed to grow even more concerned about God's people—a sign that his contemplation was authentic. Whether it was a widow needing consolation, or a laborer needing healing, Solanus was discovering that he was being led to be a channel of God's comfort in proportion to his own trust in God. As more and more people came to him, he was discovering that his words were bringing people new strength and peace.

At this time in his life at Yonkers, much of Solanus' way of relating to the people in their needs was based on a mixture of his own intuition and the faith that flowed from his prayerful union with God. When people came talking about their problems and needs, he did not spend much time probing. Something in his personality made him unconcerned about details; he seemed to skim over surface issues. To some this reflected superficial thinking; others thought it implied that he might be too easy with the people; still others said it might be because of the great numbers of people coming to the office. For their part, the vast majority of people found in this approach a Capuchin whose care for them in their need manifested a deep love for God which brought them healing rather than further embarrassment. They knew his world revolved around loving God and listening to them as they were.

At this time too, realizing the positive things happening in his ministry with people, Solanus seemed to develop much more self-confidence and assurance in relating to others. At times he risked giving responses to people that may have bordered on bravado. The initial positive results in being a channel of God's healing word and touch to people in pain, invited Solanus to even deeper trust and confidence that God would respond to people who asked; they would receive. This inward faith in God's power at work reinforced Solanus' natural tendency not to probe people who came. If they had a problem, he would just pray for its solution. He would give thanks ahead of time that the problem would be solved.

Probably at no other time in his life was Solanus more enthusiastic and confident. The time at Sacred Heart found him gaining more control over his strong emotions. His earlier tendency to argumentativeness and debate was waning. He no longer had times of temper flare-ups. He was becoming more sensitive and empathetic. While these attitudes would stay with him they were almost boundless at this time. The result was a kind of bravado that was what the Scriptures call boldness or courage. While these virtues evidenced a maturing of his personality, they showed even greater maturing of his spirituality.

Solanus also was discovering that the scriptural promises about Jesus' healing sickness and diseases of every kind were as much for Yonkers as for Galilee. The resulting confidence which the people sensed in Solanus was really the fruit of his growing, prayerful confidence in God and God's promises. In fact, it was becoming clear that precisely because he had good self-confidence and ordered humility, Solanus was able to base himself in even deeper confidence in what God wanted to do in him and through him, for others.

While his self-confidence was building, like other men in their forties, Solanus would also experience strong sexual drives and increased sensuousness. In analyzing his feelings, he tried to maintain a proper control, balanced with deepening commitment to God and God's people. He coped with these difficult times by his celibacy, and also found himself isolating himself from others when necessary. He continued the practice of his younger days of selecting his associates carefully. In this way he would be less prone to temptations.

In July 1918, the Capuchins had their triennial "Chapter" or meeting at which new assignments were made. At this time, the superiors decided Solanus Casey had been at Sacred Heart long enough. He would be transferred to Our Lady of Sorrows in Manhattan on the lower East Side.

While sad to leave his "first assignment, first love," the years at Yonkers had built a solid foundation for Solanus' future ministry. Not only had he found his ministerial niche in the Province; he had found himself. His desire for responsibility had found its expression in a unique ministry that was helping others physically, relationally and spiritually. Whatever earlier doubts and confusion he may have had about the religious life and priesthood seemed resolved; there was little or no confusion as how he could minister as a Capuchin-Franciscan. He had developed a rhythm and timing that spoke of solid integration and openness to the future.

In this sense, the news of the transfer was bittersweet. While it would be difficult to leave friends and friars, Solanus' personality manifested someone who dreamed dreams for the future. In some way, he felt, God's plan for him could be furthered by this new assignment. Such strong determination and enthusiasm to be faithful to his God made the transfer that less difficult. Because his goals were now more future-oriented than immediate, he could not but sense that his future held good, not woe. With these attitudes in mind, Solanus prepared to go to lower East Side Manhattan knowing he was leaving a beautiful part of his life behind.

He dropped a note to his sister, Margaret, giving her his new address. In the note he shared his mixed feelings about the transfer:

> I am just about to leave Yonkers for a new field, down in the very heart of the metropolis. In a way I almost feel sad to leave the Sacred Heart Monastery and Parish where I've been laboring (if laboring is the right word) for close to fourteen years. We had a provincial Chapter in Detroit last week (July 11–14) and we just learned today (July 16) of the changes made. . . . Well now, "Good-bye" for the present from Yonkers. My new address will be 213 Stanton Street, New York City, New York.[33]

Solanus left Yonkers immediately. He began his new assignment the same day.

CHAPTER FOUR
Manhattan
July 15, 1918—July 31, 1924

When Solanus arrived at Our Lady of Sorrows, the parishioners still constituted the same ethnic group of German immigrants who helped create the parish in 1867. After Mount Calvary, in Wisconsin, "Sorrows" was the first Capuchin foundation of Francis Haas and Bonaventure Frey. It was the Eastern anchor of a grand scheme which took almost one hundred years to materialize: the creation of not one province, but two—with Mt. Calvary beginning the province in the "West" and Our Lady of Sorrows being the base for a future province in the East.

The parish had a unique start. About its foundation Bonaventure Frey wrote to his partner, Francis Haas:

> So your soul is again at rest; and you see that I did not lounge around New York during fourteen months for nothing. . . . Yesterday I was so lucky as to acquire a billiard saloon (121 Pitt St.), which will now be dedicated as a provisional church, as poor as Portiuncula (the place where Francis initiated the Order)—or even as the crib of Bethlehem. I pay one hundred dollars rent per month and have obtained it for half a year and now I will quickly organize my parish, which is very eager, and open up sources of revenue. If you have no objection and leave it to my choice, I will name this new cradle Portiuncula; it's really the cradle of our Order and will distinguish it from all other churches of New York. I hesitated between Portiuncula and Sor-

rowful Mother—since, however, the neighboring church is
a church of the Blessed Virgin, Portiuncula will be better. . . . S/Fr. Bonaventure, Pastor of Billiards.[1]

When Solanus arrived at Our Lady of Sorrows, he came full of high
hopes. While he was not searching for any new theological horizons and
was content with his religious beliefs, he was not closed to new ideas
either. He was again given the tasks of being director of the altar boys
and the Young Ladies' Sodality. He could share his deep religious
convictions with these groups.

It does not seem that he was given the job of porter; thus he had more
time on his hands. Far from frustrating him (as might have happened
before), he saw in this extra time the chance to deepen his understanding of the Scriptures. He wrote many of his favorite passages in a new
notebook. He wrote thirty-five pages (with some blanks) in his little
book, covering biblical themes of resignation, patience, gratitude, injustice, the Eucharist and the Blessed Virgin.

Solanus also used the time to learn more about his own weaknesses so
that he might work to be converted from their control. He realized that
he was quite sensitive to criticism from others, and he knew he liked to
be stroked or complimented on his abilities. He also realized that he
could rationalize some of his negative tendencies. Many of his weaknesses, he was discovering, dealt with subtle forms of pride. For instance, he knew people were making positive comments about his sermons. He also realized that he was being hypocritical in the way he
often responded to their affirmation, acting as though their words of
affection and congratulations did not affect him. In his little book, he
noted one incident, probably as a caution to himself not to be controlled
by the desire for adulation from others: "Affected to be little conscious
of the beauty or success of sermon yesterday."[2] Such insights show that
Solanus was realizing, he too had mixed motives. He would have to
accept the fact that he had a shadow side besides that which he tried to
portray and which had touched so many people for their good and
growth.

Another self-imposed caution which he noted at this time related to his feeling of being insensitive to the needs of the poor who approached him for help: "Refused 5¢ (one time and) 2¢ to unfortunate."[3] Two entries away from his notation about refusing help to the poor, he jotted a reminder of what Deuteronomy said about the way the poor are to be treated: "Therefore I command thee to open thy hand to thy needy and poor that live with thee in the land (Deut. 15:2)."[4] Such notations manifest someone struggling to be faithful to the long process of conversion—moving from ego-controls to the true freedom of a child of God.

Not much is remembered about Solanus' years at Our Lady of Sorrows, yet his concern for people was growing even deeper and wider. This was a sign of both positive sexual sublimation and deepening charity. The only available recollection of any lay person who knew him at that time is from Sr. Rose Cecilia Ascherl, an Amityville Dominican. She was in grade school while Solanus was at "Sorrows." Even as a child, she recalled, "Fr. Solanus made a deep impression on me. His gentleness with the children, his way of speaking and friendliness I always cherished."[5]

Other than this childhood recollection of a parishioner, the materials collected since Solanus' death in 1957 show nothing from others about his stay at Our Lady of Sorrows on Pitt and Stanton Streets. Yet, internally it appears that this time was one of the most significant for his spirituality. "OLS" would be Solanus' time for deepening. It would offer him desert time for further purification of motives and dreams.

At this time Solanus' personality shows that he was moving from more practical goals to visionary goals. Increasingly his deep generosity toward people was being mixed with an almost exaggerated enthusiasm and zeal. In Solanus' retreat notes for 1919, of all the references noted, the most refer to "Zeal for Souls." He copied Luke's words of Jesus and underlined the first words: "*I am come* to cast fire on the earth and what will I do, but that it be kindled" (Lk 12:49). He then continued to speak of a link between the union with God that is achieved in ecstatic prayer and the desire to bring others into a similar union with God. He quoted approvingly St. Catherine of Siena's words after she woke from an ecstasy wherein she had a vision of heaven: "Oh wonder! Oh wonder! How can I begin to describe the ineffable and the indescribable?" As a result of this religious experience, Solanus commented, Catherine "was ready to give her life a thousand times to save even one sinner for such glory."[6] Gradually, Solanus seemed to be saying, he too desired to grow in contemplation and in the knowledge of God experienced by the mystics and ecstatics.

Solanus' writing during this time reveals that he was moving from being unduly influenced by his "shadow" self to his true self—the point at which he could be touched more clearly by God. He was progressing in what many spiritual writers called the "three-fold" path toward God in conversion. One of Solanus' favorite writers, St. Bernard, described the progress of the soul as passage through three levels of truth. The first of these, the truth of self, begins the process which ends with the ecstatic knowledge of God.[7]

For Solanus, this first pathway and level of truth was the recognition and admission that he himself was a sinner. His sensitivity to these sinful tendencies at this time was very keen, a kind of humanity-as-truth. Often he would ask people to "pray for my conversion." In his eyes (unlike those who could find no fault in him), he was not the holy man but the sinner in need of growth and conversion. He may have been on the way to holiness, but that way demanded continual conversion and growth lest there be extinguished, St. Francis wrote, "the Spirit of holy prayer and devotion to which all other things of our earthly existence must contribute."[8]

The second pathway and level of truth was Solanus' knowledge and truth about others. In his early years he had acted on intuitions about people. Many of these intuitions were simply projections gained from his own self-knowledge. In turn, this self-knowledge led him to greater acceptance and love of others. "The soul that is perfectly aware of its misery," John S. Maddux notes, "realizes that all other men share in his condition. . . . As the awareness of personal misery reaches the deepest point, it is transformed into compassion: the individual realizes his communion with his larger self, the mass of humanity."[9]

The more Solanus became aware of his own "shadow-self," the more he realized that his own individual feelings could easily be projected in the way conflicts, not only within each person but between groups were worked out. Thus the tension between his shadow-self and real-self were expressed in the conflicts between races and nations, the rich and the poor. In turn, these wider conflicts returned to find a home in individuals like himself as well. He gradually came to realize that he also was like those individuals and groups toward whom we feel prejudice, intolerance and rejection. What we reject in these "others," he was discovering, was possibly what he rejected in himself.

The first two stages of truth—that about one's self and that about others—lead automatically to the third level. According to Maddux, this is the level of rapture, in which "the soul is illumined with the truth of God."[10] Not afraid to face the truth about himself and others, Solanus was open to experience the truth of God "with unveiled face" (cf 2 Cor 3:18). The more time he took to be still and know the Lord, the more the peace, joy and consolation of God seemed to invade his being. This experience invited Solanus to further union.

While Solanus never wrote explicitly about his experience of this union, his writings about Catherine of Siena and the fruits of the Spirit gradually becoming more manifest in his charity toward others bespeak the mystical reality already quite present in his depths. Paradoxically an external experience he had under the influence of drugs might just reveal what was happening internally in Solanus at this time.

From his own recollections, Solanus came close to Sister Death as a result of some kind of gangrenous infection. The experience of deep pain made him very aware of how difficult it is to be grateful to God— especially when people are in deep need. As he recalled, "I had been in agony for at least forty hours, though no one else seemed to know it, and while I tried to thank God for it all, my principal prayer—at least a thousand times repeated—was 'God help us.' "[11]

In his recovery at St. Francis Hospital on East 142nd Street, Solanus described the experience which brought him in touch with the possibility of death and his reaction to it in a detailed, although somewhat hard-to-follow letter to his sister:

. . . You will probably wonder what the cause for my being in the hospital. Well, I did not come here for pleasure, of course. Yet I thank God for the whole experience here since my arrival. No doubt a few details will be interesting, and I hope, profitable. I will give you some of them now and tell you their purpose afterward.

When I was examined by Dr. Edgerton (an excellent physician) Saturday night, my case was pronounced gangrenous. Because of its urgency, it would be a Sunday case. "Tell Dr. Kirchen to be here at 10:00 tomorrow," he said, and then said to the nurse (our cousin Joseph Parker), "We'll give him a whiff of gas and slit that open."

I had counted the hours all night. I wondered at times if I'd be possibly able to say Holy Mass at 6:00 as prearranged. I considered how I might hold out until 10:00. Thank God I said Holy Mass, but with great difficulty.

At about 11:00 "Parker" came in to tell me that an urgent case of appendicitis had come in just as they were about ready for me. He said, "Have a little patience." I had started a couple of cards to our Reverend Brothers (Maurice and Edward) by this time and I think my pain had become less acute. My most frequently repeated prayer was "God help us!" Sometimes I said, "Deo Gratias! . . ."

After some joking with the doctors . . . they took off their "long faces" although they kept on their white caps and gauze-covered mouths. Dr. Edgerton concluded: "Well, roll him in here now, head first." With my sixth breath of gas, and with effort, I called out: "All right!" (after the first couple of breaths, I almost doubted if the stuff was any good).

Life and light were going by fast when beautiful bells began to ring (from St. Joseph's Hospital for Consumptives across the street). A voice gently and piously reminded: "There's the Angelus." Oh, how sweet was that music to my soul and the announcement, how confidence-inspiring!

Then I realized that consciousness had come to the very end. The description of Mother's beautiful death three years ago at the second ringing of the Angelus flashed on my memory and my heart was only able to respond: "Behold, be it done to me according to your holy will."

I can realize now as never before how beautiful in the sight of heaven Mother's death must have been. With the above act of resignation, I came to "perfect *darkness* and *death*." A shorter instant, however, than that death lasted could not be imagined. With electric quickness the bubble broke. What peace! What solemnity!!! The very breath of my experience seemed to be principles of wisdom and truth, such as "To the pure, everything is pure." "Charity knows no evil . . . is not suspicious," etc.

At about 12:15 P.M., I heard Dr. Kirchen urge Dr. Edgerton: "Hurry up! Hurry up!" I seemed to see the latter cutting away the last fleshrags as I actually felt him do it without the slightest pain. I could only weep out with joyous wonder: "Deo Gratias! Deo Gratias! Thanks be to God! . . ."[12]

Solanus' experience of coming into "perfect *darkness* and *death*" which resulted in the experience of unity through identification with the very principles of wisdom and truth was influenced by the "gas." However, there is nothing in the same memory which he used to reflect on it later that is divorced from that experience. Thus, by being able to actually experience those principles and values in which he had believed prior to coming to this point of unity, and being able to consciously recall them afterward, argues to the strong possibility that Solanus was writing about an on-going form of a mystical experience.

While it is true that Solanus' reflections were induced by the anesthetic, since it called up Scriptural archetypes to his consciousness ("to the pure, everything is pure"), it is not wrong to believe that Solanus' unconscious had been at the point of purity of heart; the peace and solemnity which he experienced in this purity were merely surface emotions of mystical reality present before and present later.

Solanus left the hospital in a short time. His greatest happiness was not so much the fact that he was leaving, but that he had been able to offer Mass almost every day. That specific infection never returned, although he would begin to be bothered with chronic poor health in a short while.

On October 25, 1921, a trade was made between Our Lady of Sorrows downtown and Our Lady Queen of Angels in Harlem. The *Chronicle* for Queen of Angels starkly notes: "Fr. Cajetan transferred from here to Pitt Street at 'Mater Dolorosa.' His place was taken by Fr. Solanus from Pitt Street."[13] No rationale for the transfer is noted; but in those days the only rationale ever given was the vow of obedience. So much for the significance of Solanus Casey's transfer, as far as the friars were concerned. To them it was just one more on the list of new assignments. As long as he did his work like everyone else, everything would be fine.

Events would show at Our Lady Queen of Angels that Solanus did do his work. The most immediate significant thing about Solanus' new assignment at Third Avenue and 113th Street was that, for the first time, he was not appointed to the sacristy or to take care of the Young Ladies Sodality. Realizing the potential for good that was being accomplished through his door-ministry of hospitality, the superiors gave Solanus the main assignment of being porter or doorkeeper. He would work in the front office to meet the varied needs of the people who came for help.

When people came with their problems, Solanus continued the practice he had initiated at Sacred Heart of enrolling people in the Seraphic Mass Association. In his eyes, the SMA was a most powerful instrument which could benefit its benefactors and its donees, the Capuchin missions. He explained its benefits to someone whose child had been enrolled:

> A friend of your daughter, Jenny's, Miss Rose Faris, writes me that Jenny is very low with polio and asks for prayers, that, if it be God's holy will, she recover. I am enrolling Jenny in what we call the Seraphic Mass Association for prayers of hundreds of thousands of people.

The members of this Association are asked to pray for our foreign missions and their work and for one another—those members, of course, who can pray. Also those who can afford to do so are asked to help with an offering of some kind (for the missions) besides by prayer and Masses. I am confident that this will help your Jenny. This (will help) especially if you and yours do your part.[14]

Although Solanus wrote this letter later in his life, the dynamics he outlined describe the way he dealt with the people who came to him asking for prayers. After the people shared their problems, Solanus would make some comments about their physical, relational, and spiritual condition. In his gentle way, he would touch the area of a person's pain or concern with deep sensitivity and care. Many times he touched the very area that might not have been shared as a concern by the person who came for help. After commenting on the problem, Solanus usually talked about God's goodness, and the need to thank God ahead of time for working so powerfully in each person and in all of creation. Then he would invite people to manifest thanks, ahead of any possible outcome (that might or might not accord to the petitioner's original desire). He also asked people to do something concrete, such as enrolling in the SMA or performing some spiritual or corporal work of mercy. He stressed the need for some kind of action as a sign of "expectant faith"; thus his previous quote to the mother of "Jenny": "I am confident that this will help . . . especially if you and yours do your part." The "part" which more and more people did was to enroll the object of their concerns, or "the poor souls" in the SMA. Thus, as Solanus envisioned it, enrollees would benefit from all the Masses, prayers, and good works of all the worldwide Capuchins, plus their benefactors.

When people understood that they were helping the Capuchin foreign missions as well as receiving spiritual benefits for the people they enrolled, they did not think that the requested fifty cents for an annual enrollment was too extravagant. However, when some could not afford that amount, Solanus would enroll them without cost. By being named an official "Promoter" of the SMA for the Capuchin Order by the superior in Rome, Solanus was free to give a certain amount of free memberships to those he determined were in need.

As he promoted the SMA to the people coming to him, or urging them "to do their part," people began to notice that their prayers were being answered. Soon the word began to spread about the phenomena taking place at Queen of Angels through Fr. Solanus. Persons with personal problems were being resolved; marriages were achieving peace; people with sicknesses were saying they were healed. As the word spread, more and more people came. Before very long, Solanus was busy all day counseling people, praying with them and for them about their problems, getting them involved in doing some charitable work, and, always, blessing God for "all his designs."

Because so many persons started coming to Queen of Angels with reports of favors received in answer to their prayers, the Minister of the Province, Fr. Benno Aichinger, began to be quite interested. During his annual visit to the Parish and Friary in 1923 he talked with Solanus about his portering and what was happening in the front office. Solanus told him about the various favors being granted, never identifying them with himself or his faith; as they were always attributed to the SMA, to good works, prayer, or some form of gratitude. Touched by Solanus' simplicity and humility in narrating the many wonderful things being done, Father Benno told Solanus to start keeping a record.

That very day Solanus obtained a twelve-by-ten-inch letter-type book with heavy covers and lined pages. The first notation under "NOTES ABOUT SPECIAL CASES—November 1923" referred to Benno's request: "Nov. 8th, 1923. Today Visitation closed. Father Provincial wishes notes to be made of special favors reported as through the Seraphic Mass Association."[15]

The choice of words Solanus used for his notebook—favors reported *as through* the Seraphic Mass Association is significant. Solanus Casey had an almost unshakable faith in the efficacy of the Mass and membership in the SMA. He was convinced that any favor people might receive was for two reasons: God had heard their prayers and they had witnessed to their faith and confidence in God by doing some good work for their neighbor. The "secret" of the healing of the person or the happy resolution of the problem rested not in Solanus but in the person's membership in the SMA or whatever other good deed each was asked to perform, be it "going to confession" or helping the poor and needy. Since many of the favors were granted through such works of charity as enrollment in the SMA, Solanus refused to be identified with the positive results being reported. In his mind, it was as clear as that. It was the SMA, not he, that was related to the source of their help. He noted to a person who shared his problem with him, that results could come to anyone who enrolled in the SMA, at any Capuchin office. Other Capuchins, he said, "can enroll you in the Seraphic Mass Association as well as I can, and that is a big feature in the 'secret' of the many notable favors reported. . . . Thanks be to God." [16]

His first entry in the "NOTES ABOUT SPECIAL CASES" book opened with the phrase Solanus used to begin and end so many verbal written utterances: "Deo Gratias!" Then it continued in Solanus' unique method of abbreviations:

This P.M. Marg. Quinn—who enrolled her neighbor Mr. Maughan against drink and consequent anger (on) October 26, as also her sister, E. Remy of Philadelphia against severe inflammatory rheumatism, reports wonderful improvement in former and (reception of) letter this A.M. from (her) sister (writing): "Thank God and the good prayer society, I'm feeling fine." [17]

The first page has notes about people in many stages of life and death. It refers to someone praying for "the grace of a religious calling and strength and grace to accept it." It mentions hitchhikers who had been "terribly beaten-up." Someone (whose husband drinks) had "two partial strokes." A woman's "16-year-old had vanished a week before" and was "found next day in Jamaica." Another woman had "a nervous breakdown." Someone else whose brother had "been drinking for five years" and was "very careless about Church" had lost sight in one eye. The period for these entries on page one covered the days between the book's inception on November 8 and December 9.

Every now and then, about every third or fourth entry, the notation is written in such a way as to indicate that a positive resolution of the problem had taken place. Page after page sketch the "pathetic stories" (as Solanus would refer to so many of the cases)*:

- An eighteen year old boy was staying out Sunday mornings until 4:00. Although he was a practicing Catholic, he remained in bad company. That and his drinking were upsetting the family's peace. Nineteen days after this entry, another entry is made noting that he "went to the sacraments Christmas," escaped the "terrible and notorious misfortune of (the) former comrade" and was doing "ideally." His sister noted, "Nothing less than miraculous."
- A mother with two fine babies suffered pneumonia and was given three days and then three hours to live by her doctor. She "recovered completely."
- A woman with an address on Lexington Avenue had improvement in her serious heart failure attacks. The doctors were surprised that she lived.
- A man working on the subway enrolled his wife who fell eight years before and lost "her memory completely" so that he had to leave "a note on table for Sunday morning (saying) 'This is Sunday' to remind her to go to Holy Mass." He came back to report, "My wife's memory is evidently improving. Thanks be to God!"
- A woman enrolled herself and her husband who was "an inmate of asylum on Ward's Island." She came back to report that her husband was home and mentally well.

About half of the cases reported in the first pages give full names and addresses. The places of residence range from a few blocks from the church to Danbury, Connecticut, and to places in New Jersey. Solanus' reputation was growing. His increasing popularity was reinforced at his silver jubilee celebration January 14, 1922; the house Chronicle notes that it attracted "a great multitude of the population of New York."[18]

The first extended entry came on St. Valentine's Day, February 14,

1924. Under the heading *Use of glasses restored.* Solanus detailed the account of a 73-year-old woman from East 88th Street:

> Extremely anxious lest operation for double cataract be necessary. Promises to do all in her power for missions if use of glasses be restored without operation. This was November 1. She returned on January 20th, wearing her glasses but not yet satisfied. She renewed her promise that day. Today she returned jubilant and perfectly cured. In fulfillment of her promise, she joined herself (to the SMA) perpetually, and re-enrolled her parents and brother besides paying for a heathen child ($5.00).[19]

The various incidents reported by Solanus filled seven such notebooks by the time of his death. As far as Solanus' attitude went toward keeping the accounts, it was simply a matter of obedience. As far as the superiors were concerned, it was a matter of having a kind of insurance. They needed Solanus' comments about what actually was happening in face of the inevitable rumors which were beginning to create for Solanus the reputation of being a "miracle worker."

While some people at Queen of Angels sought out Solanus for his blessing, to share their problems with him, or that they "might be cured," still others were led to a deeper sense of God's presence by observing his religious faith. The Italian children in the school spontaneously referred to Solanus as "The Saint." "We just observed him," one former third-grader recalls, "especially when he was in the back of the church where the Calvary scene was located. We all looked in awe at him and were compelled not to talk or cause any disturbance as though (to do so would be) a sin."[20]

Others, like Fr. Justin Joos of the present New York–New England Province remembers how Solanus not only brought consolation to his family at the time of the death of his brother, but a prediction that he (Justin) would become a Capuchin. He recalls:

> He was a great friend of my mother and father. My Mother was Prefect of the German Third Order and my

Father was head of the Ushers in Harlem. This was in 1924. I was only eleven at the time, kind of a roustabout who never took things too seriously.

My brother was a Capuchin seminarian, Frater Romuald. He had been in a hospital in Appleton, Wisconsin. He was at Marathon, Wisconsin, in theology and was about to be ordained subdeacon. He got sick and they thought he had a thyroid, although he never had a goiter problem. They gave him medicine and then he developed tuberculosis. For awhile he had to recuperate at Calvary; then he went to Detroit for treatment and finally to Appleton.

My father went out to Appleton where Frater Romuald was in the hospital. They assured him that everything was going to be all right. Two weeks later, on February 24, my father got a phone call that he was dead.

My father wanted his body brought back here but it was not permitted, so my father was the only one able to go out to the funeral. After he came back, he was quite distressed about the sudden death and that he alone was at the funeral. He went to Fr. Solanus to share his concerns. He explained that he wanted to have a priest in the family. Fr. Solanus told him, "Don't worry, you will have a priest in the family."[21]

At that time the eleven year old John Joos had no intention of going to the seminary. Years later when John had become Frater Justin, Mr. Joos told his son about the incident which had brought him and his wife comfort in their bereavement. He had not told his son because he didn't want Solanus' statement to influence John's decision to go to the seminary.

Others remember Solanus as not tolerating the antics of servers who misbehaved during Mass. Something in Solanus was triggered when he would discover their "shenanigans." Although he would get frustrated and correct them "quite consistently,"[22] the corrections were never couched in anger; his charity and gentleness always overcame his momentary impatience. He realized "boys would be boys."

Where Solanus did show his emotion of anger very clearly related to situations wherein he perceived that the rights of other people were abused and maligned. Probably the harshest extant writing Solanus ever wrote, is a stinging "Letter to the Editor" of the *Catholic News* of New York. He scored the editorial writer for "a regrettable one-sidedness of information." Solanus believed this bias resulted from what he considered was the undue influence of the "atheistic" news agencies. His specific concern arose from an editorial in the Catholic paper about relations between Ireland and England. The paper's treatment of the anti-Irish tensions, Solanus wrote, "might be expected rather in a London Daily, or in any of our Metropolitan Yellow Jackets—everyone of them heart and soul in sympathy, not with a crucified nation (Ireland) or with Catholic principles, but with the Brazen Brutal British."[23]

In justifying the tone of his letter to the Editor, Solanus believed he was merely "aggressively" challenging the Catholic press to that kind of information which Popes Leo XIII and Pius X said was necessary to confront the secular press. These popes believed the latter was often "bitterly hostile to justice and truth."[24] Solanus' letter (which extends five full pages of single-spaced small type) recalled "centuries of Britain-broken treaties" and other incidents.

Solanus perceived himself as a "correspondent not doing this (writing) in any spirit of vindictiveness or out of malice to anyone." Rather he used many principles of debate which he had learned as a teen-ager. His energy, enthusiasm and determination to right wrongs were at their peak when he used his pen to hammer away at his point, marshaling example after example to support his position. He peppered the editor with one argument after another to show why the paper was not being even-handed toward Ireland. "Aye, Ireland unarmed except by her Faith in God! Unoffensive except for her surpassing determination to stand by the principles of righteous Freedom—principles for which from 1914 to 1919 humanity has bled white! Great God! Is it to be all for nothing?"[25]

Mustering all the supportive arguments he could garner, Solanus even attacked the allied nations for their postwar degradation of Central

Europe. Somehow he was able to connect that "hypocrisy" with Britain's dealings with Ireland and the need to implement what the popes said was necessary: an aggressive Catholic press defending the claims of truth and justice.

Let no nation, much less individuals deceive themselves: God will not be mocked forever! And the allied nations, and their civilization have been mocking the honest peoples of the earth, and surely not less the Eternal God of honest people. Who is to blame? Where is our ideal Catholic Press? Offensive and defensive? God help us! Aye, God help us, and forgive us!

That individual leaders have been and are guilty of that criminal silence and that mockery, is as positively clear as the fact that nations are made up of individuals. They seem now, however, to be going further into crime. Instead of blushing for shame, personal as well as national, that no one has arisen like Daniel of old to convict the hypocrites, some of them are beginning to come out on the side of shame itself, on the side of the bulldog and the lion [England], the side of the archravager of nations. They speculate with the coolness of gamecock gamblers on hair-splitting points of morality. Thus they wittingly or unwittingly divert attention from the real source of [the] troubles in Ireland—the presence of British soldiers and of British corruption. Is not this clearly a case of the Scriptural, "Straining at a gnat, and swallowing the camel?" Shame on the "blind guides!" Pardon me if your correspondent [Solanus] seems acrimonious, and may the Lord help us to see clearly! For bitterness like falsity and exaggeration are to no purpose in an honest cause.

But history, it seems here as well as elsewhere, must repeat itself. It was a bishop that condemned St. Joan of Arc for witchery and who, a little later (duressed as he was by the British who were supposed to be Catholic) exposed her to unmentionable cruelties and finally burned her at the stake as a heretic. If reports be true, there are one or two priests in America who would do the like for a number of Irish "Joans," even without British duress.[26]

Probably because of such allusions to the bishops of Baltimore and Boston (who had made negative comments about Eamon DeValera, the IRA freedom fighter who became head of the Irish Republic), as well as the passion and rhetoric of the letter itself (to say nothing of its length). *The Catholic News* rejected Solanus' letter. Not to be daunted, Solanus sent it to *The Irish World* which ran it *en toto*.

This would not be the only letter from Solanus Casey which *The Irish World* would print. The son of two Irish immigrants who had filled him with stories of "The Old Sod" and the British often used his flair for writing to promote the Irish Cause.

Someone reading the entire letter cannot help but question the anti-British sentiments of Solanus Casey. What cultural script was being played out? What happened in Solanus' past that could trigger such passionate and negative feelings? How can such an incident square with the fact that people think Solanus Casey, the Irishman, should be a candidate for sanctity?

First of all, candidates for canonization are not perfect (there is only one who is [cf. Mt 19:17]). Rather they are people who *tried* to "be perfect in the way your heavenly Father is perfect" (Mt 5:48). It does not mean they are without fault or have no failings, just that they have manifested a kind of heroism in the way they struggled to be faithful to the way of perfection. It does not mean that they are free of their "cultural script and biases"; after all, even Jesus used the pejorative phrase of the Jews which called the Canaanites "dogs" (Mt 15:26). When the Scriptures were written, women were not considered equal to men; from the legal perspective they were like children. From the law as well as the mind of the scriptural writers, they did "not count!" (cf. Mt 15:38).

However, as Jesus did with this particular Canaanite woman, Solanus went beyond group biases to minister to persons, not the member of this or that group. As an Irish descendant of immigrants, he would have found it impossible to be emotionally divorced from his roots. One is not raised in a family with parents who were forced to leave a country because of famine (which they knew was not only caused by weather but by economic policies of the occupying alien government) without feelings which would be communicated. When one has such feelings the tendency is to paint the opponent in diabolical terms and to have "selective attention" to faults on one's own side. Solanus showed the tendency quite clearly.[27]

From the strength of his arguments, Solanus fully believed in the innocence of the Irish vis-à-vis England. Consequently, he would have been the first to believe that he wasn't prejudiced. But he was. Prejudice is a social sin that is inherited from one's environment. It is not necessarily *willed*, but it is part of one's emotional response received from society. Because it is so deep-seated, it is not extricated from one's emotions overnight. If it took Jesus until the resurrection to extend his and his disciples' ministry beyond "the lost sheep of the tribe of Israel" (Mt 10:6), certainly Solanus Casey should be allowed to mellow in time (which he did). His struggle to overcome his received cultural biases is evidenced in the way he never limited the Gospel to any person coming to him, no matter what nation or racial group they may have represented (cf. Mt 28:19).

While Solanus believed his anger was justified in the case of the Irish "Troubles," he could be equally strong, though more gentle, in dealing with justice and injustice among the Capuchins themselves. During his days at Queen of Angels, a Brother was being pressured to leave the Order under some degree of duress. He confided in Solanus. Solanus took up his cause. The Brother seems to have had few friends in the Order; in fact, friars seemed to have shunned him. The definite impressions was that he was neither welcome nor wanted. Solanus was aware of how the community had dealt with the Brother. While he himself did not accept all the things the Brother had done, he tried to find some saving features and basis of hope. Believing the possibility of conversion was there, Solanus wrote to the Provincial, Benno Aichinger. He explained the nature of the advice he gave the Brother and noted that he believed the local superior may not have given the Brother a "fair deal":

> . . . I told him as much as that I had not been personally edified at what seemed to me was his want of fervor or devotion to Holy Communion while he was with us in Our Lady of the Angels. I thought he ought to turn earnestly to Headquarters—meaning the Tabernacle—and make some promise to do better in this, or some other regard, if things adjusted themselves favorably to his peace.
>
> Then he said something about making a retreat with the Jesuits. I told him that would, in my opinion, be the best thing he could do. I told him I would write you about him and he said he wished I would. I wanted to tell Father Guardian of my visit to him (which was made without the Guardian's knowledge) and of my proposition to write you all about the case, but I decided it as prudent to say nothing to him about it. Before I had a chance to do so, before deciding, he forbade me to correspond with "Br. P." and at culpa before dinner gave quite a little admonition, in a general way, bearing on this case, while we all knelt as (though we were) novices.
>
> Now Dear Father Provincial, I do not wish to blame anyone or to excuse anyone else. "Brother _____" seems to me willing to be directed. He seems quite conscious that he did not receive entirely "a fair deal" with the superior above. Well, may our dear Lord direct him and us all![28]

What happened with the particular Brother and the "bad blood" between him and the local superior is not known. However, from the tenor of the letter, Solanus believed the local superior was part of the problem as well. Perhaps Solanus was right; many times his intuitions were strikingly accurate. But perhaps it could have been another case when Solanus was taken in by another's hard luck.

Solanus' unbounded trust in the goodness of every human being could be exploited. He was not always consistent in applying his prophetic gifts for good in all situations. Whatever the situation, Solanus Casey could be counted on to speak his mind whenever he believed people were treated unjustly. As for the times he himself was misunderstood, however, he would merely shrug off "put downs" and other forms of belittlement. He never was known to justify himself or to try to make his detractors look negative or foolish.

At the July Chapter which preceded this letter, Fr. Benno was re-elected Provincial. At that time it was also decided that Solanus should come to the headquarters of the Province, St. Bonaventure in Detroit. Stickler to details that he was, Solanus noted that he received word of his transfer at 1:15 P.M., July 30, to be in Detroit by August 1.

He arrived, he notes again, exactly on August 1, 1924.

In Detroit, Solanus would often nostalgically look back on his days in Yonkers and Manhattan with much gratitude and happiness. He noted, "While I never long to go back to any old place from which Divine Providence has seen good to remove me, yet I must acknowledge that I have a natural inclination that way—like the Israelites in the desert naturally yearned (many of them) to go back to Egypt. No doubt, we are all naturally inclined that way."[29] Having had so many positive experiences in the New York area, the uprooting was made easier for Solanus in his perception that the move was simply part of God's plan for him.

CHAPTER FIVE
Detroit
August 1, 1924—July 22, 1945

When he arrived in Detroit, Solanus found that St. Bonaventure's was a novitiate, a friary, and the provincialate. None involved many people coming to the door from the outside. Consequently, the front office was quite quiet. The head porter, Br. Francis Spruck, had enough time on his hands that he had the added job of being habit-maker and tailor for the growing Province. At that time the Province had 176 solemnly professed friars in ten friaries ranging from Wisconsin and Michigan to New York.

Although he had been the main porter at Sacred Heart and Our Lady Queen of Angels, Solanus was assigned to porter at St. Bonaventure's as an assistant to Br. Francis. Francis was a very affable person; kind of a Friar Tuck-type. His wit and humor made him very popular not only with the friars but with the people who walked through St. Bonaventure's front door. The tailor shop was on the right side of the entrance hall and the porter's office was on the left. This arrangement made it easy to hear the doorbell no matter where he was.

Within a few weeks of Solanus' arrival more and more people started to come. It was not long before Francis realized that his assistant was creating a conflict with his neatly arranged ministry at the entrance of St. Bonaventure's. Furthermore, people were coming not to see Francis Spruck, but Solanus Casey.

For his part, Solanus continued filling his notebook with reference after reference about "people of every illness and disease" (cf. Mt

4:23; 9:35). At the sight of them, Solanus' heart, like that of Jesus, was being moved with pity. From the growing list of accounts, the power of Christ within St. Bonaventure's new porter seemed to be going forth to touch all who were afflicted (cf. Mt 8:16).

The majority of the 64 entries for the period of August 1–December 31, 1924, contain no follow-up notations indicating what, if anything, happened to people after they came to see Solanus. Yet there are enough significant things noted to explain why the front office at St. Bonaventure's was getting more and more crowded. Healings of every kind were beginning to take place as evidence in the entry about a woman who came during the first month:

> (August 30) Mrs. Clara Kowalski (23, of 3392 Palmer Ave.) on August 18, extremely anxious lest x-ray examination demands (an) operation for dead bone in (her) ear. Joins Mass Association. Today (says) nothing was found yet in photo x-ray.
> (Sept. 1) Danger disappearing, good color returning.
> (Nov. 1, 1925) Perfectly cured. Deo Gratias.[1]

As one month flowed into another during this first year at St. Bonaventure's, the notebook shows more and more problems. A good number were positively resolved. The kinds of people being enrolled and the nature of their difficulties cover a wide spectrum of humanity's physical, relational, and social ills:

- (Sept. 7) Protestant woman enrolled for the sake of peace by a Catholic neighbor. Mrs. H. Johnson and Emma Smith run the Scientific Beauty and Corsett Shop. They are very much at variance. Each is having a lawyer, to the scandal of (their) surroundings. Papers (have) already been served in Court.
    (Sept. 12) Amicable settlement effected. Deo Gratias.
- (Sept. 12) Lost Mental Faculties Restored. Wilfrid J. Vincent Noonan, 27. He (has been) in St. Joseph's Retreat,

Dearborn, since June 15. Once a very successful student, seemingly called to be a priest or religious, but to help poor parents decided on course of medicine. Broke down completely. Is enrolled today for two years by (his) broken-hearted mother.

(Oct. 24) Saw him today. Naturally not much hope; (his) poor Mother weeps bitterly. . . .

(Aug. 2, Portiuncula, 1925). Now back home since March and (spent) first night (as) intern doctor in hospital. Deo Gratias. Loss of mental faculties restored indeed. Now thanks be to God!

N.B. Said that W.J.N. got his "degree M.D." in October 1927 (and) in June, 1928 was made superintendent of (a) big hospital in Detroit, Delray Hospital.

- (Oct. 6) Sugar Diabetes Cured. Joseph Kajeski, 3320 Montgomery (35 years old) had been an invalid for two years with diabetes. He is a hopeless case. He was enrolled on Sept. 3. He went to work Oct. 6. Deo Gratias.[2]
- (Nov. 18) Gall-Kidney Stones Cured. Mrs. Margaret S. Homan (45) of 1063 E. Grand Boulevard. Enrolled Sept. 6 against terrible kidney stones. She was to have operation which took place on Sept. 9. Operation surprisingly successful as also the rapid recovery. Today returns to report as perfectly cured after seven years suffering.
- (Oct. 20) Suicide Positively Averted. James John Kulick, 37, of 4933 Vinwood, makes all preparations for death by suicide (final will in all details, even to the choice of coffin). Ready to go on boat to Cleveland. His two sisters received a leaflet and word of explanation about the SMA, at their father's funeral. They enroll their desperate brother that day, October 16. Today, sister Grace returns in tears of joy that every vestige of danger disappeared that night. Her brother is now in hope and is praying. Will go to work November 24. Today enrolls brother, Ed, against tuberculosis.

(April 18) Same Edward reported in perfect health. Deo Gratias!

- (Dec. 5) Father away from Church two years enrolled by anxious son. Theophilis Rohr, 65 years old (has been) away from practice of religion for two years. The children of his second wife (have been) taken out of Catholic School. Estranged and bitter against older children and against religion. Is enrolled for year by oldest son, who reports a week later: "Father is completely changed."
- (Dec. 29) Benedict F. Morvitt, 44, father of two is gone two weeks from family on Dec. 24. His brother is in anxiety. Enrolls him for one year. Before two days (pass) he comes home alright, weeping and happy. When asked what had happened, answered, "Please don't ask me any questions."
- (Dec. 29) Louis de Simeres, 39, 2421 Helen. (Got) typhoid poisoning; given up by doctor and already lamented by friends. Is enrolled second time in a week. Died in peace.

As more people came to see the new porter at St. Bonaventure's, the room was enlarged. Solanus' desk was placed at the right of the entrance, and additional chairs were placed along the wall. Solanus would talk to people at his desk. Francis' desk would be a few feet behind him. The chairs had to be set up, not only because of the growing numbers, but because Solanus was taking so long with each person who came. Whoever had a problem would receive Solanus' full attention for as long as they wanted.

Francis was surprised that nobody seemed to get impatient at these long waits. When persons were asked why they would wait so long, and with so much patience, they merely replied that they knew they also would receive Solanus' fullest attention when it came to their turn.

If the people were not getting impatient with what was happening at Solanus' desk in the front office, Br. Francis Spruck was not among them. According to Fr. Marion Roessler (who was a novice at St. Bonaventure's the year Solanus came):

> Brother Francis was really the chief porter of the Monastery. Brother Francis was a very efficient person and

Ellen Murphy Casey and Bernard
Casey, Sr., with Daughter Ellen,
sometime around 1878.

The Casey Family in Superior Wisconsin, August 14, 1892. Bernard Casey, Jr., 22, is seated
third from the left on the porch.

Close-up, Bernard Casey, Jr., August 14, 1892.

Minnesota State Prison at Stillwater in 1885. Bernard Casey, Jr., worked in the guardhouse about 1887.
(Minnesota Historical Society)

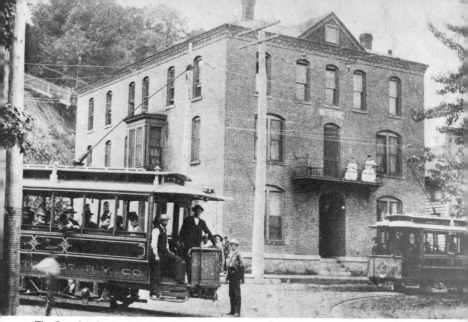

The first electric street car lines in the Northwest at Stillwater. Barney Casey, Jr., was a conductor around 1888. (Minnesota Historical Society)

St. Bonaventure Chapel and Monastery as it was in 1896 when Barney Casey came to the Novitiate. The Novitiate wing is in the back of the building, not pictured here. (*Detroit News*)

The Souvenir Holy Card of Solanus Casey's *First Mass*. Note the biblical quotes he chose for this occasion.

Sacred Heart Church and Monastery and the adjoining field at Yonkers as it was when Solanus Casey came in 1904 for his first assignment.

Solanus Casey, 40 years old, at Sacred Heart, 1910.

Solanus with his priest brothers at Maurice's Ordination to the priesthood, June 1911, in St. Paul, Minnesota. Maurice is on the right. Edward, on the left, was ordained in 1912. Note Solanus' Scripture quotation from Daniel.

"All ye works of the Lord bless the Lord ... All ye servants of the Lord bless the Lord; Praise and exalt Him above all forever!" Dan III

Praised Be Jesus Christ! 19/7/18.

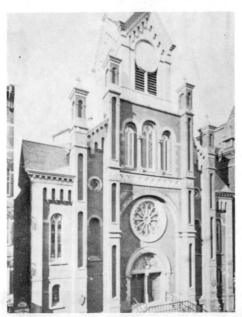

Our Lady of Sorrows Church, Pitt and Stanton Streets, Manhattan, as it was when Solanus Casey came for his second assignment, 1918.

Interior of Our Lady Queen of Angels, 113 and 3rd Ave., Harlem, as it was when Solanus Casey came for his third assignment, 1921.

couldn't stand Fr. Solanus' slow easy manner, letting people talk on, letting people wait for hours to see him. He felt
he had to keep people moving. He would scold Fr. Solanus
before an office full of people, calling him "Casey" when
he was piqued. Brother Francis would tell people that they
could bring their enrollments to his desk and he could take
care of them. Father Solanus would acquiesce and say that
Brother Francis could enroll them also. Of course people
would want to wait for Father Solanus and did so no matter
how long it took. But it was a humiliation before all these
people.[3]

At St. Bonaventure's, Solanus' "official" day started at 4:45 A.M.
Lauds or morning praise began at 5:15 followed by the Litany of the
Saints and meditation in common. At 6:00 Prime and Terce were
chanted, followed by the "Conventual" or community Mass at 6:15. If
he had not celebrated Mass privately beforehand, Solanus would do so
after conventual Mass. Then he would eat breakfast. At noon two more
"hours" of the Divine Office, Sext and None, were chanted for about
15 minutes, then followed by the main meal. Afterward, there would be a
short time spent in relaxation. Vespers and Matins were recited at 5:15
or 5:30 until 6:00 when supper was served. Before retiring prayers
were shared in common, including the Litany of the Blessed Virgin.

In between the daily "horarium" and often until late at night, Solanus would meet people in their needs, respond to telephone calls, and
answer letters. The demands and needs of the people were great.
"There were so many callers that I had to give personal attention to,"
he recalled, "that I worked for 18 hours a day. Sometimes I could not
attend to one quarter of my personal letters."[4]

Within the rituals of community life, along with personal ministry
and prayer, Solanus lived out his life. However, while the community
might rise at 4:45 (always to the sound of the "clappers"), Solanus
often had been up long before, praying in chapel. And when the friars
had all gone to bed, Solanus would just be saying good-bye and "God
bless you" to the last person in the office. Then he would take out a

mop and a pail and clean the office. After this he would go to chapel to pray some more. Finally he'd go to bed. "I have plenty to keep myself busy for at least eighteen hours a day," he wrote to his sister:

> I console myself occasionally with the thought that sooner or later the day will come when they will say of poor Father Solanus: "He's gone." Please God the struggle for existence will then be over. I just hope that by that time I'll be able to exclaim with St. Paul, when shortly before he died a martyr he said, "I have long desired to be dissolved and to be with Christ!" O well, it will not be long. What are fifty years of pain to the endless joys awaiting us above?[5]

The January after his arrival, Solanus struck up a relationship with Earl Eagen from Smiths Creek, about forty miles northeast of Detroit. He had come to Solanus after telling his son, "I don't have much longer to live. You take care of your mother and your brother and sisters; you are the oldest." As Solanus recalled the incident years later to Mr. Eagen's daughter, Dorothy:

> It was Saturday morning, January 10, 1925, that a neighbor-friend of theirs from Port Huron, brought your dear parents to St. Bonaventure Monastery in Detroit. Your poor father was hardly able to talk. He tried, however, to tell briefly how he felt and that the doctors said he had "ulcers of the stomach." Later on I learned that they had sent him home as a hopeless case of cancer. I told him quite a little about the Seraphic Mass Association and suggested that he do something for the missions.
> "Now I have your name, Mr. Eagen," I said. "And you can enroll perpetually if you wish. If you are anyway short, however, I would advise that you enroll for just a year now and promise perpetual enrollment as soon as convenient, if things go favorably."
> I took him to be seventy-five years old or upwards. Your poor mother looked old too. Sunday morning, eight days

later, your father drove his own car down to keep his promise. From their appearance alone I would hardly have known them; but the moment he spoke I thought, "This is the fellow from Port Huron!" He looked thirty years younger. He was only thirty-nine at the time.

"But, Father," he said, "The doctors in Port Huron want to take an x-ray. What do you think?"

I asked him, "How much is it going to cost you?"

"Twenty-five dollars."

"What do *you* think?" I asked your smiling Mother. They were both smiling all over.

"Father, he doesn't need it. Look at him," she exclaimed.

"Listen," I said. "You make a promise to the poor souls in purgatory that, if you are able to forget that appointment tomorrow, you'll enroll them for a part of it."

"Gee," he said. "I'll give them half of it. I'll go fifty-fifty!"

After that he drove down every week for several months. On February 29, I believe he had the whole family down. After enrolling some other member, as he nearly always did, he concluded about as follows: "Now, Father, I want to enroll the Poor Souls as I promised them I would do. Put them down for a good half of that twenty-five dollars. Enroll them for fourteen dollars."[6]

The letter above which was sent by Solanus twenty-two years after the event took place, was in response to Sr. Cecilia Eagen's request for an SMA enrollment. In her request, she did not mention her baptismal name Dorothy; yet Solanus vividly recalled what happened when he first visited the Eagen farm.

Solanus had asked to be introduced to the family. All but little Dorothy were introduced; she was too embarrassed to come downstairs because she didn't have any shoes. Sensing someone missing, Solanus asked if he had met all the children. At her mother's urging, eleven year old Dorothy was coaxed to come downstairs. In the way Solanus greeted her, the self-conscious Dorothy immediately became fully at ease. Solanus noted in his letter to Sr. Cecilia Eagen: "And just incidentally, it was on that occasion that I remember seeing little Dorothy as a possible candidate for a convent or a missionary."[7]

On March 12, 1925, a few months after the incident with Earl Eagen, Solanus entitled an entry: "*Big Company Enrolled*" in his *Notes about Special Cases*. Since a subsequent letter of Solanus described the situation, it serves to explain the kind of spirituality that was beginning to be manifest in Solanus. His letter is not only unique, it also indicates an uncanny awareness of a kind of corporate sense which Solanus sometimes articulated:

> I hardly think I ever told you about our enrolling companies and projects in the Seraphic Mass Association. The following, first of several similar to it since, I am sure will please you.
>
> The slump of the 1925–26 winter was a tough one on Detroiters. Every auto factory in the city shut down for at least a week at Christmas, without a word when they would start up again. Only a day or two before New Years' it was announced that Ford would start up again, on such and such a day after New Year's Day and would continue at three days a week till further notice. That was quite a "beam of hope" for perhaps millions. The other auto companies followed lingeringly, but most of them just worked one and two days each week. One of the slowest seemingly was Chevrolet. As we learned only a year or two later, it had already started negotiations toward bankruptcy.
>
> On the 12th of February, Thursday after 9:00 P.M. John McKenna, who had become enthusiastic about the SMA the first months after my arrival back from New York, August 1, 1924, came to the Office. He was evidently discouraged, notwithstanding his otherwise wonderful Faith.
>
> "Father," he began, "I don't know what to do. I can't support a wife and family with the hours I've been working. I haven't had a full day now in two weeks. Today I had only

two hours. They're always finding an alibi to send the men home." All at once, as though by inspiration, he said, "Father! Enroll the Company! (Chevrolet)"

"That's new," thought I. Twenty times quicker than I could tell it, however, so that it seemed absurd to hesitate, (something) flashed on my mind: "If a single Holy Mass must help any legitimate cause, why should not five hundred Masses daily in connection with the holy foreign Missions help?"

"All right, John," I answered.

"Yes, Father; I'll give them fifty cents" (for an annual membership in the SMA).

That same night the company received an astounding order. Two nights later McKenna waved triumphantly: "Father! We had overtime yesterday and today and we heard this afternoon that the company has an order for 45,000 machines, wanted in thirty days."

It was believed that order saved Detroit itself from bankruptcy.[8]

If the average priest was in Solanus' sandals talking to John McKenna, his inspiration about enrolling the Chevrolet Company in the SMA would have been countered with theological arguments why such an idea was untenable. Moralists would have raised all sorts of rationales to say why a corporation (despite its legal constitution) is not a person. But many of these theologians and moralists operate out of set, traditional theological and moral virtues. They would have argued that doing such a thing would not have been virtuous. However, by now, Solanus was operating not only from the virtues, but especially under the inspiration of the gifts of the Holy Spirit. He was beginning to judge situations from the influence of the seven gifts of the Holy Spirit—gifts which everyone has, but not everyone uses.

Traditionally mystics have gotten in trouble with people who consider the law from a framework of the virtues, or traditional categories of knowledge and understanding. Solanus, as well as people like Gandhi,

Martin Luther King, Jr., Clare of Assisi, or John XXIII use knowledge and understanding; however they are influenced from the perspective of the gifts of the Spirit. Such models possess that kind of wisdom which was manifested in Solanus when he responded to McKenna's idea: "That's new, thought I. Twenty times quicker than I could tell it, however, *so that it seemed absurd to hesitate . . .*," he agreed to the proposition.

Some friars and others who operate from a strictly legalistic approach to life were hard-pressed to find virtue in Solanus while he was alive precisely because of incidents such as this. Many of the things he did intuitively, or from the gift of wisdom, were highly unorthodox in his times. Today they have come to be accepted as normal. His approach to non-Catholics and to Jews, wherein he did not pressure them to become Catholic, was unique. The way he counselled people who were having marital problems or were divorced only recently has been accepted.

Another unorthodox practice of Solanus was the way he "heard confessions without giving absolution." It was as exceptional as it was humane and practical—from the perspective of the penitent, if not the traditional casuist. Solanus (who was not legally allowed to give sacramental absolution) had a unique arrangement with Fr. Herman Buss. According to Fr. Herman (who began working with Solanus in 1926):

> A person would come in (to Solanus) and talk and talk. Father Solanus got the story. Then he would say to the man or woman, "Now go over to the church and I'll call Father Herman and he'll go over to hear your confession." Father Solanus could not give absolution, but many, many persons told him of their lives. Father Solanus would say, "Now you told the whole story. Just give a resume to Father Herman. He will understand that you talked to me and he'll give you absolution." Then Father Herman heard their confessions.[9]

Invariably, Solanus' approach to people arose from a deep sense of compassion for them in their pain. Realizing many of them were in very embarrassing situations, especially when it came to such sensitive situations as revealing their sins, he somehow used their very sharing with him as a burden-lifter. He spoke with them very quietly and calmly. He had no pretensions of education or formality or aloofness. He operated the same way with everyone whether that person was Mayor Frank Murphy of Detroit or Br. André of Saint Joseph's Oratory in Montreal (in front of whom he knelt for a blessing after André had asked Solanus for a blessing).[10] He didn't relate to people to win their favor. Unemployed people, women, Jews, blacks, as well as his fellow Capuchins found him simply himself. His way of relating to them always flowed from a growing inner freedom that resulted from his deepening abandonment to Divine Providence. His inner freedom became nonthreatening to the most fearful persons. Many peolple recall that even crying babies seemed to relax when Solanus would get up from his desk and take them from their perplexed mother's arms.

When people approached Solanus for a favor, his method always seemed gentle. Yet he never allowed people to remain passive. He always invited them to further growth in God's life and grace. After talking with a person, he would build on some positive thing he discovered in what they said; then he would embellish that point with references to God's goodness and love for them. After this, he would invite them to develop their goodness in unique ways by deepening their relationships with God or by doing some good works for others.

To a man who was a professed atheist and whose son had drowned, Solanus invoked the example of the man's wife Kathleen. Solanus tried to help him remember her "example of never failing Christian virtues." It was "just six weeks after the son's death," that "his wife Kathleen also was taken, leaving him three children to mother for himself as best he might."[11] Yet Solanus was not afraid to invoke her faith to encourage her grieving husband.

He might ask non-Catholics to discover for themselves the differences between their own religion and Catholicism or why Catholics "try so much to imitate Jesus in his love and reverence for Mary, his own dearest Virgin Mother." All Christians, he believed, should be faithful to their own beliefs about religion and act on them:

If religion is the greatest science of all ages—"The science of our happy dependence on God and our neighbor," which no one seems to question—then there can be but one religion. In like manner if—"We are Christians only inasmuch as we believe in Jesus Christ and keep his words"—his doctrine—so there can be but one Christianity. Therefore, it is up to each one of us individually to examine into our own conscience whether we be Christians in reality or only in name. Too, it ought to be our happy privilege to perfect ourselves in the faith more and more, and to find out its infallible Guide on earth.[12]

To nonpracticing Catholics he might be a bit more direct than he was to Protestants and Jews. Often he asked them about the frequency with which they celebrated the various sacraments. Then he invited them to be more faithful. Solanus not only used this approach to individuals. He also urged groups of persons sometimes in unorthodox ways to be more energetic in their faith. One time, according to William Tremblay:

I drove Father Solanus to St. Joachim's Church, which is the old French Church of Detroit. As they were short of priests, the Capuchin Fathers used to go and say one Mass there sometimes. It happened one Sunday that I drove Father Solanus there for 10:30 High Mass. When it came to Communion time, he turned around and held the Host waiting. But there was nobody that came to the holy table for Communion. There weren't many people in the Church. Maybe one hundred people, but it used to happen that nobody went to Communion. He was so surprised and seemed to be hurt about it. He said to the people as he held up the Host, "Please come, the Lord wants to go to you, please." And everybody was so surprised that they all just looked at him. Then he turned around and put the Hosts back in the tabernacle. It was just another incident to show you his love for the Holy Eucharist and how he wanted the people to be helped. He knew that God could help them through Holy Communion. He was just surprised and hurt that nobody went to Communion and he just had to tell them.[13]

Once he got people to "do something" extra as a sign of their love for God, Solanus would then bless them with the sign of the cross, or with holy water, or with a relic of the True Cross, or some other sacramental. In all situations, however, he honored their integrity, their freedom and their conscience.

His pastoral approach somehow empowered people with a deeper sense of peace and hope. At times, to put people at ease, he would use his Irish wit to full advantage by beginning to look very serious only to end up telling a funny joke or story about the Irish. He would play on his last name, Casey, saying he had the shortest surname: only two letters—K. C. Even when people came to him in a very agitated state, he somehow was able to calm them and invite them to experience their better selves and to hope.

His calm approach to people who were upset is one that came in handy at night when people would call the monastery. Sometimes Solanus would be in chapel praying, or other times he would be in bed. If he heard the door bell or the telephone he would respond immediately. "One morning," William Tremblay recalls:

> A man came to the Monastery at 4:00 and as you know, Fr. Solanus was always the first one to go to the door. He always thought that the poor Brothers would be too tired, so he would always get up himself. Well, that morning he answered the door and a man was waiting there.
>
> He asked, "Where's that guy, Solanus?"
>
> Fr. Solanus said, "Well, he's here, what do you want with him?"
>
> He said, "I came here to kill him."
>
> "Well, that's something that should be discussed," said Fr. Solanus.
>
> The man had a few drinks, so Fr. Solanus invited him to the office and helped the man talk. The man told him that he was secretary of the East Side Communist Party. His mother belonged to the Monastery and she was a great friend of Fr. Solanus. His mother cried all the time because he had those meetings in his home and the things they discussed broke her heart, because he didn't go to church and he kept

meeting those Communist men and having them in his home.

So, Fr. Solanus let him talk until he sobered up a little bit and then after awhile, he began to talk to him. Before the man left, he wanted to go to confession. He got on his knees and begged Fr. Solanus for mercy and asked him to bless him and he wanted to go to confession. Fr. Solanus said, "No, I want to see if you'll make a man of yourself. I want you to come to confession during the day and some other priest will confess you."

And as far as I know the man went back to church with his Mother and he left the Communist Party. Fr. Solanus told me this story himself.[14]

Solanus was invariably able to bring out the goodness in almost all the people he met, yet his percentage was not always that high with Brother Francis or some other Capuchins. At times, half in frustration and half tongue-in-cheek, Francis would call Solanus "that old fraud."[15] Other times he would chide Solanus about taking so much time with people that he would be late for meals. Often Francis would come into the refectory (dining room) saying that Solanus was "still talking, still talking." Bernard Burke, who sat at table with Solanus in his later years at St. Bonaventure's, bet Solanus a rosary for every time Solanus would be on time for meals. Fr. Bernard insists he never had to say a rosary. There were just too many people to see; Solanus felt their needs were more important than his need for food.[16]

Sometimes, the friars would half-tease or half-seriously chide Solanus about his high-pitched, low-volumed voice. "Nobody understands you"; they would say, "Open your mouth." He would merely respond, "Well, God understands me." And he would leave it at that.[17] To say that, at this time in his life, such remarks had no effect on Solanus Casey would be wrong. His was a personality that was sensitive to criticism; yet, while the comments cut, he neither showed it nor retaliated with negativity of his own.

For every negative remark some friars might have made to Solanus, there were many more positive words which indicated their support and genuine affection. This affection for him was reciprocated. Solanus never acted in an extraordinary way with friars; he just seemed to fit into their normal relational life. As Fr. Cosmas Niedhammer, of the present New York–New England Province recalled:

When I was with him in Detroit, I recall that he would come into the recreation room on Sunday nights. He would draw himself a glass of wine from the gallon jug by holding it over his shoulder and then he'd tell some humorous incidents. Fr. Solanus was very gifted in that way. He could spin out a story just like that, and become personally involved in it. He was always very simple as though he had no context of uncharitableness. Sometimes he spoke of some incident that happened in their family of 10 brothers and 6 sisters. And Fr. Theodosius would poke fun at him about when he used to be a streetcar conductor. He would say that Fr. Solanus was now doing penance for all the nickels he had taken and didn't ring up. Fr. Solanus would laugh and have another anecdote ready. He was really quite human in that way.

Other times he would come into the recreation room after the noon meal like the others. He liked to play pool or billiards. Often as not though, he would pick a cue and start to shoot and his call bell would sound. Then he would have to put it right back into the rack, but never with any expression of impatience. It was remarkable. And it meant that when he was called, he would be in the office until supper time. And sometimes he was so tired that we knew he would have to go into the last room of the office and lie down on the floor for a few minutes to take a catnap. He would just take off especially if he had an interruption. . .

Sometimes I would drop in the choir at midnight or one o'clock in the morning and sure enough Fr. Solanus . . . was there with his fiddle in front of the Blessed Sacrament. At other times when I thought I was alone in

> choir, a figure would rise up from behind the stall and Fr.
> Solanus would be there with a grin. He was just taking a
> little nap after a fatiguing day.[18]

Solanus' understanding and compassion for people experiencing pain was sharpened by his deep personal involvement in the sufferings of his brother, Fr. Maurice. Toward the latter part of 1928, Maurice visited Solanus from the Western missions where he had been ministering the immediate years before. He was disillusioned with his life as a diocesan priest.

Twenty-five years before, just before he made his final decision to go back to the seminary, Maurice had told Solanus that he would never become a diocesan priest. He entered a seminary in Berlin (now Kitchner), Ontario. From there he wrote Solanus, "I have found the grace again I looked for so long."[19] Despite his earlier resolve, he was ordained a diocesan priest in 1911. He spent much of his priesthood in individual parishes in the West. Gradually growing more melancholic and disillusioned, he used the occasion of his 1928 visit with Solanus to discuss with him and the Capuchin superiors his desire to join their ranks.

Maurice returned again to Detroit for Solanus' silver jubilee of ordination, acting as deacon for the celebration which took place on July 28, 1929. In September he returned to Detroit again. From here he went to the novitiate in Huntington, Indiana, on August 10, 1929.

Because of the increase of vocations and consequent overcrowding in the novitiate wing at St. Bonaventure's, the novitiate had been transferred from Detroit to Huntington the previous March 2. Maurice would be in the first new class in the new novitiate. He received the name Joachim. "Thanks be to God, he seems well and hopeful of making profession in September,"[20] Solanus wrote his sister Margaret in April 1930. But this time, (as it would happen more than once with Solanus vis-à-vis Maurice) Solanus' insights about someone were clouded by being too involved in the relationship.

Something in Maurice made the superiors concerned about his profession; they decided not to accept the sixty-two year old's request for vows. Instead they offered him the possibility of remaining part of the Province, but as a Third Order member. He would live the full Capuchin daily routine among the friars and accept regular assignments. He would be able to keep his own money, but would be under the superior of whatever house he was a member. He would also be under the Provincial. Fr. Maurice Joachim (as Solanus would call him) agreed to their alternative plan. Consequently, the superiors assigned him to Sacred Heart in Yonkers. He began what appeared would become a fruitful ministry.

During the tense period when Fr. Maurice was negotiating his entry into the novitiate, the deaths of their two brothers, John and Thomas, occurred. On their way home to Seattle from Tacoma where they had been trying a lawsuit, the two lawyers were killed in a car accident. With their death the Casey family had lost four of its members suddenly and tragically. John and Thomas in the prime of life and Mary Ann and Martha in their first years.

When Maurice was determining his future with the Capuchins, several significant things were happening at St. Bonaventure's. Because the novitiate was moving to Huntington, and because the novices needed to be fitted for habits, it was decided that the provincial tailor shop should be permanently housed there rather than Detroit. When the superiors observed what was happening in the front office, they decided that the Province could always get a new tailor; it could not that easily replace Francis Spruck and the effective way he handled the burgeoning crowds coming to see Fr. Solanus.

By this time more chairs had been added to the room. The people sat in them as in a doctor's office, waiting to talk to Solanus. The front entrance which had been locked in the past now was always open. Above it was a simple invitation: "Walk in." No matter how many people filled the room, however, it never seemed that anyone heard the dialog between Solanus and the person talking to him, even though the conversation was taking place in front of many others.

On Wednesdays, the front office was particularly busy. This was the day of the "St. Maurus Blessing of the Sick." It had been a regular weekly devotion at "The Monastery" long before Solanus arrived. However, with his arrival and periodic celebrations of the service, the numbers of people increased rapidly. For instance the crowd on February 29, 1928, was big enough that the house chronicle noted: "A very large crowd at the blessing at 3:00 P.M. Fr. Herman acted as traffic cop, while Fr. Solanus offered the relic to the people."[21]

The St. Maurus Blessing allegedly derived from a Benedictine by the name of Maurus (510–584) who had become famous during his lifetime for the gift of healing. After he died, the Benedictines continued to bless the sick and gradually developed a formula for the blessing which was approved May 4, 1882. Although they were Capuchins, the friars at St. Bonaventure's had received permission to use the blessing. This constituted the main part of the service.

Unlike the other Capuchins who gave no sermons at the Wednesday services, when Solanus presided, he always included a reflection. He would often mention examples from his Notebook, or other incidents where people were delivered from their problems through the Wednesday blessing. Fr. Marion, who lived at St. Bonaventure's at this time, recalls:

> His simple discourses in connection with this weekly devotion consisted in admonishing the people to strive to come closer to God through the frequent reception of the sacraments, prayer, and conformity to God's Holy Will in all the events of their lives. He insisted that penance was very necessary to make up for sin and for the salvation of their souls.[22]

Because Solanus spoke in such a quiet voice, the people came early so that they could get closer to the front. At times scores would be standing immediately in front of the pulpit from which he spoke. Invariably, his theme would be the same: trust in God and use the gifts of Faith and of Charity to show gratitude. After his talk, he would say the prescribed prayers, incense the relic of the True Cross, take it from its reliquary at the altar, and give the general blessing of the sick with the relic, saying

> through the invocation of the most holy name of the Lord may that faith, in which St. Maurus, by employing the words that follow, healed the sick, and in which I, though an unworthy servant, utter the selfsame words, restore your health as you desire. In the name of the most holy and undivided Trinity, and supported by the merits of the most holy Father Benedict, I bid you to rise, stand on your feet, and be cured. In the name of the Father, and of the Son, and of the Holy Ghost. Amen.[23]

After this general blessing, the people would process to the communion rail to receive individual blessings.

Because he could get so personally involved with the people in his office, Solanus was often late for the Wednesday service. As a result, Francis Spruck had developed a routine to get his confrere to the chapel on time. Fifteen minutes before the beginning of the service he would loudly call out "2:45." At five-minute intervals, he would insistently quote the time until at the very time the service should have begun. He would say sternly "Casey!" Sometimes he would just sarcastically say, "It's time." Solanus would sheepishly get up and go into the chapel for the service.

One time when Solanus went to the chapel one of the people left in the front office was Bernadette Nowak. She recalls:

> My sister, Geraldine Bieke, took me to Fr. Solanus. However, before I could talk to him, he rose and said it was time to go to the church for the blessing. I was disappointed, but went to church. As he passed before the people kneeling, he passed before me, gently touched my cheek and said softly, "Stop worrying now. You're going to be all right now," or words to that effect. I had not seen him stop to talk to anyone else and was surprised. That night I had the first sound good night sleep in over a month. From then on I was better.[24]

The chapel was generally filled with people of all faiths and races, as well as many skeptics. One of these was Casimera Scott. As she recalls it:

> I used to come to the Wednesday afternoon devotions where Fr. Solanus used to bless all who came to the altar rail. I went thirteen weeks not believing that he could heal others. I was a doubting Thomas until one Wednesday, I saw a Rabbi with his cap, long beard and a heavy cane. He used to come every week too. Now he had Faith and I was full of doubts. But when I saw him walk away *without* the use of his cane, then I believed. I was in excellent health then. Maybe I was blessed so because of going to Fr. Solanus for his weekly blessing.[25]

On October 29, 1929, the stock market crashed. The Great Depression started to infect the bones of the nation. Industrial cities like Detroit were especially hard-hit. Soon increasing numbers of people began appearing in the Front Office. They came not for healing but for bread.

Solanus listened to story after story. He could not help but be "moved to pity" at the sight of the crowds needing not only healing, but bread as well (cf. Mt 14:16–21; 15:29–38). Like Christ, his heart too "went out to the crowd." His growing mystical union with God was now being evidenced even more in charity, the height of the virtues. His contemplation of God bore fruit in his concern for the masses of people in need. Somehow, he saw in the pain and shadows of the poverty around him a reflection of the poverty within him—his own emptiness and need. His efforts to bring healing to others in their need brought further healing to himself in his own need.

Far from being overcome by his own brokenness, Solanus was able to direct it to bring a fuller healing and unification to others. Solanus, to use the words of the contemporary writer on mysticism, William Johnston, was

> . . . confronted with a cosmic reality, the evil in the world and all the suffering in it—([and] discover[ed]) what Jesus saw in Gethsemane. That's why I feel it's not fair to say that

contemplative people are running away from the suffering
of the world, from social problems and so on. If they go
really deeply into contemplation, they're facing these problems in another dimension.[26]

As Solanus took the myriad needs of the Depression to God, he
gradually realized that God's care, which he experienced meeting his
needs in contemplation, had to "go out to the crowds" as a deeper
manifestation of that care. Care thus became the basis of his experience
of God and his ministry to others. This realization did not happen
immediately or with a spontaneous insight. It evolved gradually,
through normal events. But his experience of God's care in contemplation was the basis for his ministry of care to those in need.

For as long as people like Fr. Herman Buss could remember,[27] the
Capuchins shared their own food with those coming to the Monastery
door. If some objected to this practice, Solanus would remind them that
"The poor have as much right to the food as we." This food-sharing
might be from the friars' regular meals, but most of it consisted of
coffee, a bowl of soup, and bread. Before the Crash, about 100 to 150
people came daily for such help. However, as the effects of the 1929
Depression deepened, more people were coming to the front door. Only
Solanus and Francis were there to meet their needs. When the numbers
reached 200 and 300 daily, the superior of the house concluded that it
was becoming impossible for the friars to continue giving out bread in
addition to their other work.

He asked Fr. Herman, the Spiritual Director of the Third Order
(known today as Secular Franciscans), if his fraternity might help. The
St. Bonaventure's Fraternity included hundreds of concerned women
and men who only needed an appeal from Herman to begin ministering
to those in need. On November 1, 1929, Herman shared the first cup of
coffee with a needy person. It had come from a pound he had bought
beforehand.

In the Third Order Hall, next to the chapel, a kind of restaurant was
gradually established. It became known as "The Soup Kitchen" after
its chief meal, a big bowl of thick meat stew.

The Soup Kitchen remained a special concern for Solanus, even when it moved down the street from the Monastery. He tried to involve many people who came to him for favors by asking them to do some kind of corporal favor for the Soup Kitchen. He got the rich and powerful to cooperate in the new project as well. Wealthy people from Grosse Point were tapped for cars to haul food. Tom Bresnahan, the mayor of River Rouge, a Detroit suburb, and Frank Murphy, the mayor of Detroit (and later a Justice of the Supreme Court) would often visit Solanus seeking his advice. He would use the occasion to get them involved by seeking funds for the free meals being served down the street.

When he had a few spare moments, Solanus himself would go over and get involved. He mingled with the people in the line as well as with the workers.

One of the volunteer workers with whom Solanus became well-acquainted was Arthur Rutledge, who worked for the Fire Department. Once, when he had been in the hospital for observation for a tumor in the stomach, Fr. Solanus passed him in the hall as he was being wheeled into the operating room. Recognizing Art, Solanus stopped the cart and asked: "Where are you going, and what are they going to do?"

Art replied, "They say I have a tumor and are going to operate."

"Where is the tumor?" Solanus asked.

Art explained that it was in the abdominal area. Solanus placed his hand on his abdomen and said, "Have them give you another examination before they operate." When the doctors made another check, they found no tumor. Art was discharged from the hospital the following day. He returned to the Fire Department and the Soup Kitchen to volunteer his talents. He never had a recurrence of the disease.[28]

From Herman's viewpoint, although Solanus was not always in the Soup Kitchen physically, he was present spiritually: "Even though he wasn't there all the time or directing the thing, through his holiness I believe he is the one who helped us to get help from Divine Providence. God was blessing the operation because we had a holy man right there." He recalled:

> One day I said, "Fr. Solanus, we have no more bread and two or three hundred men are waiting for something to eat."

He went over to the hall and told the men who were waiting in line, "Just wait and God will provide." Fr. Solanus said an "Our Father" after inviting the men to join him in the prayer. We just turned around and opened the front door to go out, and there was a bakery man coming with a big basket full of food. He had his whole truck full of stuff, and he proceeded to unload it. When the men saw this they started to cry and tears were running down their cheeks. Father Solanus, in his simple way, said, "See, God provides. Nobody will starve as long as you put your confidence in God, in Divine Providence."[29]

By this time, according to Fr. Herman, the Soup Kitchen was serving over 3,000 people daily.

At the height of the Depression, with more food needed, Solanus increased his requests of those coming to visit him. He also contacted bakeries for day-old bread and asked butchers to donate meat bones. At other times he would join farmers, helping to pick and load apples and also vegetables for use in the stew.

One of the trips to the rural area which Solanus made each year was to the Eagen Farm in Smiths Creek. Solanus helped load the truck, pitching gunny-sacks of vegetables such as potatoes. Heaving the big bags on the truck revealed a strong power that was hidden by his scrawny frame. This annual trip was relished by Solanus. He said it reminded him of the days on the farm in Wisconsin.

Such excursions into the country (like all trips) would be incomplete without the recitation of at least one rosary. On one such occasion, Solanus loved to recall, he was in the cab of the truck with Ray McDonough, the director of the Soup Kitchen. It was late afternoon when the truck came to the top of a little hill. Directly in front of them loomed a huge red sun, so overpowering that it seemed that they were about to drive right into it. Solanus could only utter deep thanks and praise for such beauty.

During the time Ray McDonough worked at the Soup Kitchen, his daughter, Rita, gave birth to a daughter in her home. According to Rita:

The doctor said Carol was born with a club foot. I became very upset about this. Then my father, Ray McDonough, brought Fr. Solanus over to see me. Father took the baby's foot in his hand and blessed it. He told me not to worry. Then when I took her in the next time for her checkup, the doctor said her foot was perfect. Carol grew up with no trouble in that foot and now is married and the mother of three children.[30]

While Ray might have had experiences like this to deepen his faith, the day-to-day routine of directing the whole operation of the Soup Kitchen could become very difficult. Occasionally, some of the poor can become as fussy as some of the rich, giving the impression that people should jump at their beck-and-call. On one such occasion, a woman at the Soup Kitchen wanted jellied doughnuts instead of sugared ones. The man in charge of supervising the distribution of food had a rough day and was not ready to debate her need. Exasperated, he came to the front office, complaining to Solanus about her insistence. In a manner that in no way made the man feel he was being insensitive, Solanus merely said, "If we have jelly doughnuts, then why don't you give them to her?" It was as simple as that; the poor have a right to what we have. This was the message of the Gospel; Solanus wanted to make sure that it would be translated in all activities in the Soup Kitchen.

In spite of dealing hour after hour with various traumas in the office, at the Soup Kitchen, and with family problems, Solanus maintained his joy and equilibrium. At his retreat in 1929, the year when all sorts of turmoil invaded his life and the world-at-large, the item receiving the most notation dealt with the importance of manifesting joy in the midst of adversity.[31] Such joy flowed from his depths. It gave Solanus the kind of confidence that the people needed to feel as they came to the office for help.

Although the people came to Solanus for help, he went to God for help. When someone asked for a particular need, Solanus would often find ways to sneak off to chapel for a few moments of prayer. He would also pray for extended periods late at night. These times of prayer evidently afforded him some unique experiences of God. He developed a personal and friendly relationship with the members of the Trinity. He related to God as friends do—sharing common interests and mutually desiring to be in each other's presence. One of the ways friends like to share is through leisure and entertainment. Consequently, late at night when he thought everyone was in bed, Solanus would go into the chapel with his violin and play before the Lord.

Even though he used different forms at prayer, Solanus had his share of distractions. While he admitted there were times he prayed without distractions and was able to do so from a power beyond himself, he didn't get upset when distractions came. He wondered: " 'Do such distractions displease the Good God?' For myself, I do not think that they do. Rather, I would answer, as I have occasionally done now and then to assure scrupulous souls: 'No, Jesus is no crank. He knows that we are not angels, but poor sinners.' "[32] Since all things were good, distractions themselves should become part of praying.

As the Depression continued, so did the lines of people unemployed. While at prayer, Solanus often brought the concerns of the people who were unemployed. With the Depression continuing, he brought them to mind during times of prayer and work. He also remembered the sick and the jobless when he personally fasted or did so as a Capuchin. Solanus tried to help the sick, poor, and needy as best he could.

Someone who continually made Solanus aware of the unemployed and those in need was William Tremblay. According to Tremblay:

> There was a cousin of mine, Henry Wargnier, a Belgian whose wife was French. They had eight children. He was a steam engineer, and was laid off from where he worked and was facing the loss of his home. Some of his children were big boys, but none were working. So, I said to him: 'Why don't you come with me and we'll go to see Fr. Solanus. Maybe through his prayers, he'll find you a job. So he agreed, and we went to the Monastery and he talked to Fr. Solanus.
>
> He told Fr. Solanus that he was looking for work and that

everything looked impossible. That was during the Depression in 1933. He told Fr. Solanus, "I have eight children, many big boys but none of them are working; they are all depending on me."

I'll never forget what Fr. Solanus told him. Father said, "You know one father can support eight children, but eight children can't support one father. I wouldn't worry about it now. You go to Mass and Communion every morning but don't go looking for a job. They'll probably call you."

Three days later, I talked to him and still nothing had happened. So I said, "Let's go back to Fr. Solanus."

"Well, I hate to bother him," he said.

"That's no bother; he'll be glad," I told him. So he went back and he told Fr. Solanus: "Nothing has happened."

So Fr. Solanus told him, "You know, sometimes the Lord goes to sleep, and the best way to wake him up is by more prayers, more sacrifices, more Communions. Do a little more and don't go looking around, something's going to come up."

So the man went back home, and the next morning a place called him to go to work. He got more money and a steadier job and was very thankful. He remained a friend of Fr. Solanus as long as he lived.[33]

To some observing him, Fr. Solanus' work appeared full of interesting people and excitement. Yet for himself there were times when the constant repetition of need after need became very monotonous. Solanus tried somehow to turn this tediousness into a kind of fasting that would draw himself and others closer to God's presence and power. He wrote to his friend, Br. Leo Wollenweber (who also was a porter):

Sometimes of course it becomes monotonous and extremely boring, till one is nearly collapsing, but in such cases it helps to remember that even when Jesus was about to fall the third time, he patiently consoled the women folk and children of his persecutors, making no exceptions. How

can we ever be grateful as we ought to be for such a vocation, to such privileged positions, even in the Seraphic
Order of the Poverello of Assisi? Thanks be to God that he
has such divine patience with us.[34]

While much office work could become "monotonous and extremely
boring," and while Solanus tried to enliven it with the perspective of
faith, there were also occasional experiences that broke the routine. One
of these outlets was the periodic rides he would take with others. These
outlets as well as trips to pick fruit and vegetables in the country supported Solanus' natural inclination to be on the move.

While Solanus worked long hours, he was not a workaholic; he
thoroughly enjoyed such outings and other forms of recreation.

"I remember one instance when Fr. Solanus and I were driving out
Gratiot Avenue and we passed a bar," William Tremblay recalled:

This was not too long after they brought the liquor back.
Fr. Solanus said to me, "Let's stop at that bar. There's a
man there that is very good to the Monastery. It will please
him to see me stop."

So we went in, and when the man saw him, he was
overwhelmed. He didn't know what to say when he saw Fr.
Solanus. He was so glad he brought out a table and a chair.
Fr. Solanus said, "Oh, no, we'll sit at the bar. Just give us a
beer." Of course the guy was surprised.

All the men in there kept looking at Fr. Solanus with his
beard, taking a glass of beer and talking like any other man.
When we left, the man handed Fr. Solanus something. I
don't know what it was; it might have been a check. But Fr.
Solanus said, "Oh, I didn't come for that; I came for a beer.
You have very good beer and you have a nice place here."

Somehow going beyond the canon law which stated that priests
should not frequent bars, Solanus either did not recall the law or felt that
the value of fraternal charity went beyond it. The result was evident in
the man's response:

> The man said, "Father, you don't know how proud I am.
> I get many customers but I never got one that I favor more
> than you. I hope you come back."
> I will never forget the reflection on that man's face. He
> was so glad to see Fr. Solanus come in and take a beer just
> like any other man. It just shows his humility and his good
> sense of understanding of good people, no matter where
> they are at or what job or what position. He was at home all
> over, you might say.[35]

Solanus' spirituality was a holiness-as-wholeness type. All things
were his (be it work or leisure, books or beer) but he was Christ's and
Christ was God's (1 Cor. 3:11–22). Therefore he looked for God everywhere, from front offices to working-class bars.

Because Solanus mixed with people of all economic backgrounds and
all races, he was able to better understand their inherent goodness and
facilitated that toward their further conversion. Because he sensed each
person's goodness, he was extremely patient with their failings. At the
same time, he never let them feel he approved of their actions if they
were sinful. He had known God's patience with himself; this enabled
him to exhibit an uncanny patience with peoples' most trying situations.
Even when people showed their impatience with God, Solanus kept
gently, yet insistingly, professing his belief in God's power to turn all
things for the good (cf. Rom 8:28). A case in point has been narrated by
Mrs. Mary Therese McHugh:

> It was in 1933 that my daughter Marianne (then two years
> of age) became very, very ill. The doctors said her tem-
> perature was 104 degrees and much, much too high for
> them to remove her to a hospital. She grew progressively
> worse and, after his house calls very late one night, the
> doctor stopped by again to see if it would be possible to
> remove her to the hospital. But she had slipped into a tem-
> perature of 105 degrees.
> After he left I called Bishop Murphy (then pastor of St.
> David's and a close friend of the family). He had seen

Marianne that afternoon. He said to call Fr. Solanus at once and do whatever he (Fr. Solanus) asked me to do. I called and Fr. Solanus told me to wrap the baby up in a blanket and bring her down to the monastery immediately—about a fifteen minute ride from our home. My mother and I were watching over her as my husband had fallen asleep. So I wrapped her up warmly, slipped out of the house and went to see Fr. Solanus.

When I got there he was waiting at the door for us. He took the baby from me and held her in his arms for some time, praying silently and smiling down at her. Then he carefully placed her back in my arms and took us to the car. He said, as he closed the car door after placing the baby on the seat beside me, "Therese, be sure to bring her back on Saturday" (three days later). I told him that the doctors did not expect her to live until Saturday. But he said, "Just do as I wish. Bring her to me; she'll be ready."

I drove home, feeling much at peace. I put her back in her bed and sat beside her, placing cool towels on her hot brow. About six o'clock in the morning she opened her eyes, smiled and said, "Mummy, I'm hungry." The sheets and pillow cases were soaking wet. The temperature had broken. I called the doctor and he came right over. When I told him what I had done, tears came to his eyes and he said, "I cannot help but think this was a miracle." Then Bishop Murphy came over an hour or so later and he could not grasp the change in the baby. But he repeated also that it was "another miracle by Fr. Solanus."[36]

Solanus often operated hand-in-hand with the medical profession in the way he dealt with people in their illness. As a result doctors considered him a true partner. Sometimes he would recommend people to go to a doctor. Other times, he suggested that people visit the doctor, but added that the doctor would not find anything. Still other times he said to some, "You don't need to go to a doctor." When Solanus told people that they did not need to go to a doctor, this response sometimes generated resentment or questions. Some became unsettled by such a seeming lack of support for the doctors' role in the ministry of healing. However, despite rumors to the contrary, at no time has it been shown that anyone was told not to consult a doctor who subsequently suffered as a consequence. Medical doctors were part of the healing process; but ultimately healing is God's power, Solanus reasoned.

Solanus himself had doctors throughout his life. He respected their powers. Yet he respected the healing power of God even more. Speaking of an experience she had with a doctor and Solanus in 1935 or 1936, Elizabeth Ann Maher wrote:

> At the age of six, I became ill. Many leading specialists in the city of Detroit were consulted. My ailment was diagnosed as osteomylitis.
>
> For six months, every other day, my dear mother took me to the hospital where the doctors would chip away the decayed bone in my shoulder. My doctor then decided to consult with the leading specialist in the city.
>
> A bone would be removed from my shoulder which would result in either making my arm shorter than the other or I would have a pronounced hump on my back.
>
> Two days before the scheduled operation, my darling Mother took me across town on one of the coldest days of the year to seek the guidance and advice of her dear friend Fr. Solanus.
>
> Fr. Solanus placed his loving hands on my shoulder, looked at me with those saintly blue eyes and said, "She will not have the operation."
>
> At the next day's appointment with the doctor, our visit to Fr. Solanus was related to him. Dr. Andrews (being a man of great faith) said, "Let's take a final x-ray." After reading the x-ray he said, "It's like a miracle. The operation will not be necessary." He put the arm in a cast for one year and the bones knitted together.[37]

Another woman noted a unique way Solanus responded sometimes to situations after doctors had diagnosed surgery or other radical forms of treatments to problems:

About 1936 or 1937, I had terrible pains in my right wrist. I was seeing my doctor who worked at Harper Hospital. He called in a bone specialist, Dr. Campbell. X-rays showed a tumor in the bone. It was badly swollen and for three months the doctors treated it. It continued to grow worse. Doctors were using radium. My doctor was the head of the radium therapy department at Harper Hospital. Finally, the x-rays showed the tumor spreading like a web. Doctors felt that it was impossible to operate on the tumor. It would only spread through the bones. The only thing possible was to amputate the arm at the elbow.

We lived in Precious Blood Parish at that time and a friend there told me to see Fr. Solanus. All my neighbors were concerned about me.

When the doctor said that they would have to amputate, we went then to see Fr. Solanus. He looked at my wrist and talked to me; he spoke very softly, so low I had to listen very carefully. I felt so awed, it was (like) talking to God, to Jesus himself.

Fr. Solanus took my hand, held the wrist, and his eyes were closed. He was praying like he saw a vision or something. When he opened his eyes, he said, "No, we're not going to let them amputate." I could just feel that he was seeing something like a vision, that he could see that I would not have to have that operation. After that was when the change began.

Fr. Solanus asked me to do something for the Dear Lord on my own. I promised then that I would say all three sets of the Mysteries of the Rosary, that is, fifteen decades every day as long as I was able. I also promised to offer one extra day a week (other than Friday) without meat. I prayed if only I could do my work, care for my children. I made a promise to bear the pain and offer it all for the Poor Souls.

The change started after I saw Fr. Solanus. I continued the treatments for the next three months, but they did not have to amputate; the tumor no longer spread. The doctors' minds were directed. They no longer spoke of operating. They were so amazed that my arm was saved.[38]

Around the time this letter was written (1936), Fr. Maurice Joachim was becoming increasingly agitated and depressed. He had written his brother, Edward, now a monsignor, (who had left his teaching job at St. Thomas in St. Paul to become a missionary in the Philippines) about his displeasure with certain Capuchin superiors. Solanus began to sense the depth of Maurice's feelings when he went to visit his brother at Our Lady of Sorrows to celebrate Maurice's priestly silver jubilee. Subsequently, Maurice's negativism grew to such an extent that it was decided that he should be removed from regular parochial work and be sent to the Capuchin seminary at Marathon, Wisconsin (which had been built in 1917 as a theologate).While suffering this depression, Maurice was not so sick that he could not be concerned about others.

In June 1937, St. Joseph's Church in Prescott, Wisconsin, would celebrate its seventy-fifth jubilee. Maurice persuaded Edward to come from the Philippines and Solanus to come from Detroit. Both joined Maurice in a reunion of the Casey brothers in the Prescott area where Solanus could return to his roots and try to bring peace to Maurice.

The delightful experiences Solanus had those days became the basis for his longest letter extant, a seventeen page itinerary to his brother, Jim. For the most part, it describes the different people met and places visited in and around Prescott, "The Trimbelle," and Superior.

The letter shows that Solanus was not afraid to preach conversion in "his synagogue in Capernaum." He gently urged his family, former peers, and parishioners to change their practice of infrequent reception of Holy Communion. Speaking of himself in the third person, he notes that at the Solemn Jubilee Mass at Prescott:

> Fr. Solanus had been about the same as appointed several months before the sermon. If it was satisfactory or no, I could hardly say. For him it was far from what it should have been. Perhaps it was fortunate that he did not foresee what caused him quite a disappointment before the Mass was over—not a Holy Communion received save that of the Celebrant. Of course, we hoped they had received at earlier Masses. . . .
> The funeral the next day drew quite a crowd, having been

announced the day before as to be solemnly conducted by the three brothers. It went off quite satisfactorily, save one feature, however. Fr. Solanus gave them a sermon in which he told them of his lamentable disappointment at the celebration the day before—not a single person to come up and receive Holy Communion![39]

As he visited with old friends and family, Solanus' awareness of people's needs was not limited to the spiritual dimension. Many still suffered the effects of the Depression. He heard much about their doubts and fears. Many of these concerns dealt with the economy and politics. Faithful to his Irish heritage of love for politics, Solanus was not shy about sharing his ideas.

To a strong degree Solanus had been influenced by his friend, Fr. Charles Coughlin, "The Radio Priest." At this time he considered the controversial priest "a prophet."[40] During this period as well, Solanus also identified with many of Coughlin's political opinions (although his ecumenism could never find Solanus categorized as anti-Semitic in the way Coughlin was). One of the opinions of Coughlin which Solanus shared dealt with President Franklin Roosevelt. Originally Coughlin was a great supporter of the champion of the "New Deal" which put people back to work. But as Coughlin gradually "soured" on Roosevelt, so did Solanus. Writing a letter after his return from Prescott to his sister, Margaret, he said:

> As for being for Roosevelt: Well, I say God bless him, too, though my enthusiasm for him is almost, or fast becoming ancient history. If he were a practical friend of the laborer or of the poor, considering the billions he's been demanding and having spent, you and your class would hardly need worry for a decent employment. It seems to me he is simply of the bankers.[41]

In Solanus' eyes, many of the rich simply were not concerned about the poor. To this degree he rejected their behavior. Roosevelt would be no exception.

Ever-concerned about the poor and eager to help involve others in ways that would alleviate their needs, Solanus accepted an opportunity in 1937 to give a radio speech to the people of "on both sides of the river" (i.e., Windsor, Ontario and Detroit, Michigan). The talk was scheduled in conjunction with these cities' "thank you" for the work of the Capuchins among the poor.

Solanus recalled how the Capuchins were able to respond to the needs of the people during the days of the Depression (which were now beginning to bottom out) precisely because of the countless people who had been showing their care *along* side the Capuchins. In the five minute radio talk he addressed his friends on both sides of the Detroit River:

> Good Afternoon, My Brethren:
> An opportunity was offered to me today to speak to you on the radio. The occasion is the benefit party which some of our friends have arranged for us this evening at the Naval Armory on East Jefferson Avenue. We have always known that many of you have been our friends, but since the preparations for this beautiful party have been in progress, we are convinced of it. From all parts of the city men and women came to us asking how they might help. We Fathers are told that the city of Detroit wishes to show itself grateful for the help we have given during the days of the Depression. We admit that we have tried to be of service to the poorest of the poor, but must add that it was simple duty.
>
> St. Francis, our Holy Founder, impressed it upon his brethren that they must labor for their daily bread. And he added, "should the wages of our work not be given us, then shall we have recourse to the table of the Lord asking alms from door to door. . . ."
>
> Our lot has been cast among the simple lives of the poor and our object is to give them spiritual aid and, if possible, material help as well. When speaking of those days of depression, we cannot forget that our work in relieving the misery and poverty was made possible only by the willing

cooperation of such men as the bakers, who supplied the bread, the farmers who gave us the vegetables, and our numerous friends who made donations from their fairly empty purses.

It is to these generous souls that we want to pay tribute today. May the all-bountiful God, who leaves no glass of water offered in His name to pass unrewarded, recompense the generosity of our friends with true happiness—the peace of the soul.

Our gratitude extends to them and to all those who are now helping make this benefit party a success. We are deeply appreciative of all they have done for us, and, in return, assure you that you are remembered in all the prayers and good works of our numerous brethren.

It is our sincere hope that this harmony of interest and action may never be broken. Our community is at the service of those who may require it. And as long as we are among you here at Detroit, we will have the needs of the poor at heart and will relieve their misery as best we can.

Once more, let me thank you, my brethren, one and all, in the name of our Capuchin community. May mutual appreciation be the soul of our relationship in the future as this party in the Armory tonight seems to prove it has been in the past.

God bless you all.[42]

Father Edward stayed in the United States several months after the priest-brothers' reunion at Prescott, making appeals for his Philippine missions. He used part of his time in the United States to come to St. Bonaventure's in April 1938 to visit Solanus. Much of their conversation resolved around their concern for Maurice. By now Maurice had become dissatisfied at Marathon, even more so with the Capuchin life, saying he wanted to return to the St. Paul Archdiocese.

As the months developed, so did Maurice's thoughts about being reinstated in the Archdiocese. Solanus argued against Maurice's rationale. He rejected strongly the direction Maurice was taking. A December 15, 1938, letter to Maurice showed Solanus' prayerful concern; yet it also made his disagreement quite clear:

I offered my rosary this morning out in the crisp, moonlit air for your intentions and your guidance. I am confident that though, like the rest of us poor children of Eve, you have your difficulties, your temptations, your falls even, and your occasional little triumphs, our dear Lord will keep you from serious blunderings. In fact, not only this, but notwithstanding our very sad blunderings in the past—possibly worse than my own, possibly not so bad—I still hope and pray that in the few years left us, you may do something to make up for lost time; something to save your soul and gain the one victory, the one crown, the one triumph really worthy rational creature's effort.

"The few years" did I say??? Who can tell? We hope so, of course, if it be God's holy will. But, oh, how uncertain (it is)! It may be tomorrow they'll say of you or me or of each of us: "He is gone."

If either of us lives ten years longer it will be passing the old-age mark for our clan. And after all, what's the difference if we only be ready? Nay, if it be tomorrow or fifty years hence, if we only save our immortal souls? What's the difference?

But dear Fr. Maurice Joachim, I hardly know what to say or to think of your present proposition to write back to your old diocese, to a prelate you've probably never met and who has possibly never heard of Father Joachim. Naturally you would hope to be received with open arms, dreaming as you probably do, of some cozy little place just smiling across the Wisconsin hills at you. Ah, dear Fr. Maurice Joachim! You may be sure, such would be only dreaming. Our age and your experience should rather exclude such dreams as belonging to the long ago. This we might think especially, considering your years of dreaming when and how you might get away from the world to a monastery. Think of it, Fr. Joachim. . . .[43]

While he asked Maurice to "think of it," it might be argued that in a close family case such as this, Solanus himself did not think objectively. As had happened before with Maurice, it might be questioned if Solanus was not being too hard on his brother, especially if it is true that Maurice was suffering from some kind of nervous disorder. The strength of his letter to Maurice might be another case where Solanus' "confidence" about a positive outcome did not apply, especially regarding his own family—blood or religious.

Although he received Solanus' letter Maurice did not find Solanus' suggestions resolving his problems. Furthermore, his difficulties were being aggravated by a very painful carbuncle on the back of his neck. When the local doctors around Marathon could not help him, Maurice was sent for treatment to another Wisconsin city, Fond du Lac, which was about twelve miles from Mt. Calvary. Nobody there seemed to know how to treat him either. From Fond du Lac he appeared in Detroit, increasingly bitter toward his Capuchin superiors and Capuchins in general. His negativity was evident by the fact that he stayed with Fr. Charles Coughlin in Royal Oak rather than at St. Bonaventure's with Solanus and the other Capuchins. Coughlin finally persuaded Maurice to call Solanus. When he came to the telephone, Solanus didn't even recognize his brother's voice, so serious was the tension Maurice was experiencing. A visit with the provincial was arranged. The visit ultimately resulted in Maurice's "letter of exit" from the Order.

After leaving Detroit, Maurice wandered around the East Coast. Finally it was discovered that he was a "guest" at Mt. Hope Sanitarium in Baltimore; he was a broken-down old man. Knowing how much a visit would buoy him up, Solanus visited Maurice from July 20 to August 5, 1940. It was a break that Maurice and Solanus needed.

These difficult days had taken their toll on Solanus as well. For almost a month—in late Spring the same year—he suffered from almost continued bouts with colds and flu. While his ailments could have resulted from the drafty window above his head in choir, it is not unthinkable that the tensions of dealing with Maurice and so many others were working themselves out psychosomatically through Solanus' various illnesses.

While he suffered his own inner pains, the people coming to see Solanus would never have known it. Ever kind and patient, he continued to touch people in ways that brought them a deep sense of restoration and peace. "Although there were always many people waiting to see him, he had infinite patience with each of us," one woman remembers. "He never let us feel he was hurried, giving each person as much of his time as we desired. Also, the meekness of his manner and his extremely low voice and sincere desire to help each of us, are things I remember."[44]

The only time that Solanus would not speak in a low voice was in these situations where people lacked faith in the "good God." And even then, only those close to him could detect an increased intensity to his already high-pitched voice. In such cases Solanus was ready to spend more time and effort with people if it might lead them to faith.

Whatever the situation, Solanus gave sufficient time to people who needed it; yet he also knew how to deal with people who often unwittingly, or even knowingly, monopolized his time. Many times, he used his wisdom—as well as his humor—in dealing with such situations on the telephone.

At that time, St. Bonaventure's had but one telephone line; it came into the friary through the front office. This was just the way the front office was operated; people did not expect things to be different. As porter, Solanus would answer all calls, even when he was in the midst of counseling people.

A particular person called Solanus regularly, often speaking at great lengths about her concerns. Many times she extended her conversations to discuss her feelings about life in general. Br. Leo Wollenweber, who came to help relieve Br. Francis Spruck in 1940, recalls that the woman telephoned one day when the office was particularly busy.

After listening to the woman for quite some time, Solanus gently put the receiver down and continued to talk with the person at the desk. Every now and then he picked up the telephone and made a few sounds of recognition. Once as he picked up the telephone, he realized that many of those in the front office were watching this routine. He placed his hand over the mouthpiece and whispered to them with a wink in his eye, "She's still there!"[45]

In situations unlike this, however, Solanus gave callers his undivided attention when he talked with them. Because their concerns were God's (cf. Mt 7:11), their concerns affected him as usual. "When he was speaking with you," one of his fellow Capuchins recalls, "you felt that he was constantly God-centered, on fire with love for God, and constantly God-conscious, seeming always to have his eyes on God. He seemed to see everything as flowing from God and leading back to God."[46]

While the ability to "see everything as flowing from God and leading back to God" is a definite characteristic of the mystic, Solanus was far removed from a popular notion about mystics—i.e., that he was uninvolved in real life. In many ways, the sign of authentic mysticism—which is equated with union with God—is synonymous with union with God's will, which is to extend God's reign to all people.

Many of his fellow Capuchins experienced in Solanus this God-centeredness and were spiritually edified by it. However, one thing that his fellow Capuchins did not experience in Solanus' presence was personal healing for themselves. Solanus simply believed that, in general, Capuchins, like all religious, were "called to endure suffering."

Possibly because he had not professed vows as a Capuchin, an exception to this rule was made in the case of Br. Daniel Brady. He was in the Brothers' Novitiate in Detroit. He recalls:

> I had a front tooth that had root canal work done on it about 1930. It never gave me any trouble until I was in the Novitiate in 1941. When I went to the dentist he opened it and found it infected. It had even infected the jaw bone and was filled with pus. He said I should come every week so that he could drain it; but his efforts were to no avail. After many x-rays, he saw that the infection was deep in the jawbone; the only remedy was to remove the affected part surgically.
>
> When I came back to the Novitiate, I met Fr. Solanus in

the sacristy. He had just finished the usual Wednesday afternoon devotions. He said to me, "What ails you? You
look so downcast."

I told him my problem. Then he scolded me for my lack
of trust in God. But I told him my concern was more with
the operation. It was more-or-less major, and being only a
novice, it meant I would have to leave the Order (as was
sometimes the practice at that time).

He then said, "Kneel down, and I will give you my
blessing. When you go back to the dentist, he will be surprised." As he did so, he touched my cheek and when he
did, I knew I was healed. I could feel it tighten up.

The dentist was surprised. He thought I came to arrange
for the operation. He had me come back four or five times
before he would even put in a temporary filling.

The dentist worried that the filling would surely have to
come out and told me that anytime I got pain to come in.
Then he would take it out. It never did flare up again; it was
healed for good.[47]

On the last day, after getting the final "okay" from the dentist, Br.
Dan came back to the Novitiate through the front office where he told
the good news to Solanus. "That calls for a celebration," said Solanus.

With that he opened one of his desk drawers and produced two ice
cream cones. Somebody had brought them in about a half hour before
and Solanus had put them in the drawer. When he pulled them out, they
were as good as new.

Whether with his fellow Capuchins or the laity, Solanus Casey was
simply a warm, kind, and caring person who not only helped them; he
was a friend who loved them very much. One of these people was
Casimera Scott. She recalls:

He and I were friends. I was a Grey Lady at Deaconess
and I inevitably was always donating for Masses. Also, my
nickname is Casey and his last name was Casey. Believe it
or not, he had a most delightful sense of humor. He used to

say, "To those who don't understand, no explanation is sufficient and to those who do understand, no explanation is necessary. . . ."

He used to say to me, "Life is to live and life is to give and talents to use for good if you choose. Do not pray for easy lives, pray to be stronger. Do not pray for tasks equal to your powers, pray for powers equal to your tasks. Then the doing of your work shall be no miracle but you shall be a miracle. Every day you shall wonder at yourself, at the richness of life which has come to you by the grace of God. But, everyone needs someone, knowing that somewhere someone is thinking of you."

I remember crying when he told me one time, "I am a lantern along the feet and I shall shine the lantern to guide you. You shall work in the house of the Lord and you shall keep his house clean and my blessings will fall upon you my child. Only goodness and mercy shall follow you the days of your life."[48]

From the recollections of someone like Casimera Scott, it would be safe to say that Solanus exercised various prophetic gifts before people called them such in the Roman Catholic tradition. While some of the prophecies took the form of encouragement such as the prophecy to Casimera Scott, the prophecies of Solanus served other purposes as well. Sometimes they would challenge, as the time he told a woman that she was practicing birth control.[49] Other prophecies told people they would get better. In the case of Sr. Joyce Pranger his prophecies took the form of foretelling the future.

Sister Joyce wrote at length about a visit she had with Solanus while he was spending some time resting at Huntington (where he would go periodically to get a break from the usual routine in Detroit). Since her reflections are so significant about Solanus' gift of prophecy, they deserve to be quoted at length:

Every now and then we come across a person who deeply influences our lives. I can recall many people in my life who have been such a powerful force in my own spiritual formation. There were the nuns, my grandmother, my pastor, spiritual directors I have had along my pilgrimage of life. But one of the most powerful ones was a dear old Franciscan Capuchin priest. His name was Fr. Solanus Casey!

I was only thirteen years of age when a friend of mine, Frances Harrison, invited me to go with her to visit the Franciscan monastery in Huntington, Indiana, where he was then acting as porter or gate keeper. It was a different kind of experience for me to go to the monastery; but since I planned to be a nun, I accepted.

I watched this brown-robed friar from the long line of people waiting to see him. He wasn't a striking figure, but there was something that was different. What was it?

Soon it was my turn to go into the monastery parlor. At first, my heart was beating very fast at the prospect of being alone with this servant of the Lord. But it didn't take me long to be perfectly at ease.

His warmth and joy were contagious. He talked to me of the love of God and what a joy it had been for him to spend his entire life dedicated to him. Father's eyes were crystal blue like a mirror in which I could see the depths of eternity.

It was growing dark in the room and he spoke, on and on, of the love of God. It didn't seem to phase him that a long line of people was still waiting outside to see him. He remained unruffled. He counseled me lovingly, as a Father of the desert counseled his disciples. For him, man's greatness lies in being faithful to the present moment.

As we rose to leave, he took my hand gently, and whispered in my ear softly, "God has great designs for you in your life. Through you, many people will come to the Lord Jesus. You will enter religious life eventually. During that time you will have much to suffer. Then the Lord will bring you out, into a ministry entirely different from any known to Sisters at that time! Through you, the Lord will heal many people of various afflictions. But you must remain faithful every moment or you will frustrate the plan of God for your life!'' He blessed me and the door closed behind me. Never again in this life would I see this servant of God.

The visit and the prophecy all seemed to fade away in my memory until one day about twenty years later, when I was browsing in the community library looking at new books.

Among the publications I came across a book entitled "The Porter of St. Bonaventure's." I stood aghast. I couldn't believe my eyes. Here this man with whom I had prayed was considered a likely candidate for sainthood. His counsel to me, "a little act of fidelity may open the door to great graces," was truly a lived reality in his own life.

I feel that the life of Fr. Solanus was a life lived moment by moment in utter fidelity to his vocation and God. To live for God is truly a noble vocation. Fr. Solanus' greatness came from his spirit of utter dependence on God every moment of his life.

According to his biographer, he was ordained, but without full faculties. He did not preach the word or hear confessions. This must have been a great humiliation for him, but he accepted it with love. His superiors represented the voice of God for him.

By re-orientating his life totally to God, he was able to take a new stand in his approach to life. He became the humblest of God's servants! And as a result, his very humbleness drew forth the glory of God within him.[50]

What was the origin of Solanus' various forms of prophesy, such as this in the case of Sr. Joyce Pranger? His ability flowed from his depth, from the "glory of God within him." At this time in his life, Solanus' handwriting shows that he was making little or no use of those intuitive abilities that had been with him in earlier years; thus this form of prophesying came not from his intuition, but from a power beyond his own abilities. It originated from another source, namely God. Having longed to be in touch with that source of his life and gifts and having sought that God's face, Solanus was becoming an instrument of God's Word and glory to others.

Although Solanus was extremely busy responding to the needs of his family and the people at the front office, this period reflects a time of great concentration on his internal life. And while he also did a lot of analyzing of the people's needs, his analysis too was more introspective. Solanus Casey was concentrating on being in touch with that God whose glory and presence dwelt within him. Having developed a contemplative attitude toward life, he coveted those times when things would become quiet so that he could be still and know the Lord's presence within and about him. When those quiet times were not immediately available, given the busy pace in the front office, Solanus learned to develop a way of reflecting for a few seconds after people presented their problems or requests to him. Often gazing off as though he was entering into another place, or being present to another reality, Solanus seemed to touch that power of God's glory within him. Then he would make a response to the person in front of him. By "dipping into" his depths, he was able to be formed by the word in such a way that he could be empowered to make the various prophetic declarations that he did, as with Sr. Joyce.

Although Solanus brought people into contact with the prophetic and healing power of God and even though he was beginning to suffer more and more ailments, he did not try to "heal himself." To do so would have been tempting God, he believed. He did not believe it was part of his vow to be free of pain.

On September 13, 1942, the *Chronicle* of St. Bonaventure's notes: "Father Solanus was sick in bed last night; he was unable to go to his help-out at St. Paul's. Fr. Solanus was taken to St. Mary's Hospital with 104.5 degree temperature."[51] Belying the *Chronicle*'s brief comment, what actually happened to Solanus was quite serious.

Trying to get a little relief from the chronic eczema on his legs, which sometimes looked like "raw meat," Solanus would often try other people's remedies to relieve the pain. This particular cure was to have come from the heat of an electric light. The remedy backfired. From his hospital bed he explained what happened: "I had been fighting the grippe for about five days," he wrote his sister Margaret, "when on September 13, I awoke 'doubly downed,' having forgotten the night before to apply ointment or salve to my feet after using an electric light on my varicose veins and eczema around my ankles."[52]For his effort at self-medication, Solanus had to spend "a novena of weeks"[53] in the hospital.

Psychologically speaking, this time of his sickness in 1942 seems to have resulted in greater-than-usual introspection. The hospital afforded him opportunity to respond to his growing desire for more inwardness, reflection and prayer. It provided the time and space he desired for fuller integration and more profound depth, despite the suffering.

While he was in the hospital, a rumor spread that Solanus had died. To counter the many calls and to keep the people from coming once they knew he was still quite alive, the "hospital sisters had to make strident rules regarding visitors since most of the people wished to see him about their troubles, having little consideration for his worn condition."[54] These rules were just what Solanus needed. Away from the people, he could nourish his own inner life and spend more time in personal reflection. His energies and intensities were able to be focused on this level of his being. He was now at a point where the most important thing that he wanted was to be still and be with God.

Despite his pain, Solanus realized it was also a time of great grace. True to the way he advised people in their pain, he tried to use the time to give God greater glory and to thank God for the gift of health given him in the past and in the future. While he was recuperating in Huntington, Solanus reflected on his experience in the hospital. He wrote his brother James:

> While a number of my friends both in the hospital and outside, seemed to have considered my case a close call, I never felt that there was any immediate danger of collapse. Thank God. To me it seemed about ten days of the really

best penance that the poor sinner Solanus had ever gone through. Therefore, since by God's grace he persevered and lived through it without complaint, we have a reason to thank Heaven for the wonderful experience.[55]

The recuperation was slow. As time wore on, Solanus was able to begin to move around, but not without some degree of pain. He mentioned to his sister that he was able to offer Mass only with some difficulty.

Of course I had to limp around the Altar pretty much, but thanks be to God [I] got through without any serious difficulty. The old foot is still stiff but by keeping it raised and rested, it causes very little pain. I'm resting it on the bed now and it gets tiresome sitting in one position. Well anyone over sixty need not be told how the "rear fenders" cry for better padding.[56]

In the earlier *Chronicle* notation indicating that Solanus had been taken to the hospital, it mentioned also that "he was unable to go to his helpout at St. Paul's." Capuchins called "helpouts" the weekend ministry they supplied in surrounding parishes. Solanus had taken regular helpouts from 1925 until this time. While he had a regular summer helpout for a week or two at Brighton from 1933 to 1940, his weekend helpouts took him all over the Detroit Metropolitan area.

From 1938 until 1945, Solanus supplied at one parish, St. Paul's Maltese Church on Fourth and Plum Streets in Detroit. Michael Z. Cefai was the pastor. The way Solanus began at St. Paul's is a story in itself. According to Fr. Cefai:

I needed a priest to help at the parish and went to Fr. Marion, superior at St. Bonaventure's monastery asking for this kind of help. He told me he had no one that he could send. All the priests already were assigned. He said he had some old priests. He also said, "We have Fr. Solanus, but he is not allowed to go out. He does not hear confessions; he can't speak Maltese."

At that moment Fr. Solanus came in. He fell on his knees . . . and asked for his blessing. I told Fr. Solanus why I was there and asked him if he would be willing to come if his superior approved. He said, in his high-pitched voice, "Father Superior, can I go?" Thus, it worked out that Fr. Solanus came to my parish weekends.

On those weekends, many, many people came to talk to Fr. Solanus and to ask his prayers. Men and women, young, middle aged, old, and very old, Catholics, non-Catholics, Jews, all sought him out. Officials of the government, thirty-third degree Masons, etc. came to see him, sometimes talking to him on his way from the church to the house where I lived. He had as much of a following among non-Catholics as among Catholics.

When people asked his prayers, he would say Yes, he would pray, but they would have to pray too. As a priority he always sought the return of the person to God. He told people directly that God does not hear the prayers of sinners unless they are repentant and are converted to Him first. He used to ask the Catholics how often they went to Holy Communion. If they said three times a year, Fr. Solanus would tell them that was not enough; they should go every month. If they went every month, he would urge weekly Communion. For weekly communicants he would sometimes suggest that they receive daily. He told people, "Faith alone is dead" and urged them to supplement their faith with good works.[58]

Fr. Cefai was indebted to Solanus not only because he was so popular with his parishioners; he also believed that Solanus had healed his father. The two got along very well, swapping stories and telling jokes. Solanus loved recalling events of the past, not just for their own sake, but to be conscious of how an awareness of these events and their meaning might affect present and future situations. Fr. Cefai was a ready audience for Solanus' recollections and his ability to bring a faith-perspective to them.

While Cefai had genuine admiration for Solanus and respected his opinions, one of Solanus' activities did create for him great anxiety. It revolved around Solanus' devotion to and promotion of Mary of Agreda's *Mystical City of God.*

Shortly after ordination, Solanus discovered the writings of Mary of Agreda in a condensed volume. Her reflections resonated with his own spirituality, which, like much spirituality of that era, was reinforced by private revelations. Because he was convinced about the spirituality articulated in the writing, Solanus began suggesting to more and more people that they read the four volumes of her *Mystical City of God.* This was often part of their "work" or sign to God of their sincerity in response to requests for prayers and blessing.

As he increased his suggestion that people begin reading the volumes, more and more concerns began to be raised. Some criticism revolved around the price of the volumes; others noted that the average person was "not ready for such writing"; still others debunked the authenticity of the *Mystical City of God* itself. For every charge against the book, Solanus offered a counter charge. Always ready to defend what he considered was truth and justice, Solanus argued that the book had been endorsed by popes and theologians and saints of the holiest reputation. He was quite aware of the criticisms and tried to explain the rationale for devotion to Mary of Agreda's writings. One of the people to whom he tried to explain his position was his brother Edward. He wrote:

> It ought to be self understood that no simple reading of any book is going to move the Heart of Heaven in our favor. Only inasmuch as any book can serve to raise the heart to God and thus draw his blessings to us can it be said to have any quality or prayer about it. . . . Now in my opinion, there is hardly another book written, outside the Bible itself, more inspired-like and more inspiring than this wonderful work, *The Mystical City of God.* Its introduction alone, if

read with prayerful attention, will hardly leave a doubt as to its supernatural origin.[59]

Even though some seriously questioned the merits of the four volumes or his perspective, in his determined way, Solanus felt these people were just plain wrong. After all, hadn't amazing signs often occurred after people began to read the works? He himself could attest to a very important sign in his own life, as he noted to his sister Margaret:

> About New Year's Day, 1941, inclined to be discouraged in regard to Fr. M. Joachim's condition, I made up my mind, notwithstanding the fact that it had taken me nearly eight years to finish four books before (the *Conception*, 610 pages, the *Incarnation*, 608 pages, the *Transfixion*, 790 pages, and the *Coronation*, 610 pages) that I'd pray them this time on my knees.
>
> I had hardly started when Fr. M. J. wrote the letter to Fr. Edward which I received back from the Philippine Islands with his comment: "This is the best letter I've received from him in years." And before I was half through with the first book, he was saying Holy Mass. . . . Deo Gratias! On October 16th, I finished the second book and that day I received about the most encouraging letter from him of any yet.[60]

In time, Fr. Solanus' enthusiasm for *The Mystical City of God* led him to some difficulties through the activities of his friend, Ray Garland. Solanus had met Ray around 1927. Ray often visited Solanus asking for help and counsel in various difficulties. In turn, Solanus enlisted Ray for drives into the country to get vegetables for the Soup Kitchen. When Ray was "dropped from the employ" of a certain Charles H. Chisholm, Solanus had gone to bat for him: "I have known Mr. Garland for about ten years," he wrote Chisholm, "and I can honestly say that I doubt if I have ever met a person more solicitous to do a labor or more practical in suggesting remedies in time of difficulties."[61]

About five years after he had first met Ray, Solanus urged him to write the publisher of the four-volume work of Mary of Agreda, asking to work as the books' Michigan representative. Ray received the job. For fourteen years he devoted his leisure time promoting the volumes. He sold a little over 200 books a year. Whether Ray benefited financially is not known. His widow has stated that the publisher always got the full amount. Neither Solanus nor the Capuchins received any remuneration.

When Solanus began his Sunday helpout at St. Paul's Maltese Parish, not only Ray Garland but a whole band of devotees of Solanus and Mary of Agreda started to come to the Parish for his Mass. These people were given permission by Fr. Cefai to hold breakfast meetings in the church basement after Mass on Sundays as long as Solanus attended. Fr. Cefai insisted that Fr. Solanus be present because he sensed an excessive piety in some of the group's members. His conclusion was reinforced when he received reports that some members of the group were taking petals from flowers in the church to be blessed by Fr. Solanus. After his blessing, some insisted that they saw images of Christ in the petals.

Later, when Fr. Solanus was hospitalized for some time, the group continued to hold their meetings at St. Paul's without Fr. Cefai's permission. This upset Fr. Cefai. He finally told them to leave. The meetings then moved to the Garland home. From there they would phone Fr. Solanus in the hospital asking for his prayers, his comments and his blessing upon their various concerns and causes.

Once Solanus returned from the hospital his superiors became aware of these things as well as Ray's frequent contacts with Solanus. Although Ray and the group may have had the best intentions, the superiors now felt they should intervene. They simply told Ray to stop coming to the Monastery.

He complied with their request. He stopped coming; yet he continued to contact Fr. Solanus by phone. All through this difficulty Solanus remained steadfast in the support of his friend. Because he had such simple faith in the goodness of people, Solanus just could not believe that anyone would try to manipulate him.

Around the same time some complaints had come to the Chancery of the Archdiocese of Detroit concerning the four volumes of Mary of Agreda. A few people complained about Solanus' request that people buy the books which some could ill afford. Hearing this, Theodosius Foley, the Capuchin Provincial, felt it necessary to act more decisively with Solanus, who also was his dear friend. According to Fr. Marion Roessler, St. Bonaventure's local superior at that time:

> . . . Fr. Theodosius, the Provincial became very firm with Fr. Solanus and forbade any connection with this man (Garland). Fr. Solanus told the Provincial very simply that the man was being misunderstood. Then he begged Father Provincial to give him a different position, even working in the kitchen. Fr. Theodosius told him he didn't want to take him out of the office, just to sever all connections with that fellow.[62]

Around this time (by now it was mid-June 1945) Msgr. Edward Casey had been released from the prison camp where he had been interned by the Japanese during the second World War. This release provided the occasion for a family reunion. Edward, along with his brothers Owen and Patrick, came to St. Bonaventure's to convince Solanus he should take a vacation and visit "The West." After hearing their ideas about the trip, Solanus asked, "Is Fr. Maurice going too?" When they said he was not, Solanus responded that unless Maurice went, he did not feel that he should go either.

When they realized that Solanus was serious about Maurice attending as well, the three brothers went to Baltimore and achieved the release of Fr. Maurice. They returned to Chicago where they met Solanus and headed West. The superiors were glad to have Solanus go; it would give him a respite from the long hours at the office as well as the controversy.

By the time he reached Spokane and Seattle, the word was out that Fr. Solanus Casey was in town. All during the reunion, the Casey family was besieged with phone callers seeking to talk with Solanus. Mrs. John Cunningham recalled, "Our home was packed until his departure. I don't know where all the people came from."

As various relatives cajoled Solanus to visit their homes throughout Washington, the California relatives were feeling slighted because he had not planned to visit them in their homes. After a good deal of coaxing, Solanus decided to visit them as well.

He had received permission only to visit his relatives in Washington. However, Solanus figured that the purpose of his trip and permission for it was to visit relatives. Whether they were in Washington or California did not really matter. Even though it was not strictly part of his "obedience" or permission to travel to California, he went.

Unfortunately, he did not anticipate the consequences of traveling in postwar time. The trains were very crowded. He soon discovered that he was not going to be able to return to Detroit by the deadline indicated on his "obedience."

He wrote Fr. Marion about his dilemma saying that the Capuchin superior in Los Angeles tried to get him reservations on his clergy pass. He wrote of the superior:

> . . . that the very best he could do—in regard to transportation, was to get 'reservation for next Thursday (July, 12th) instead of yesterday (9th) for Seattle, so that I may use my "pass" to St. Paul. To get on the train as I promised, without reservation, he stressed, would be foolhardiness. So here I am still—hoping to make the best of missing the privileges of the Chapter.[63]

Solanus finally arrived in Detroit, on Saturday, July 21. Almost immediately he was informed by Fr. Bernard Burke, the newly appointed superior, that it had been decided during the Chapter that he should be transferred to St. Michael's in Brooklyn.

Bernard recalls that Solanus received the news as if he had been told that it was time for the next meal. It was just a matter of fact. Transfers were just part of God's blessed design. Without registering any surprise, complaint, or question about the continuance of his front door ministry, Solanus immediately began to pack his bags. He arrived in Brooklyn the following Monday.

Shocked Detroiters had great difficulty accepting that their "Father Solanus" had been transferred. Their friend had been with them "in good times and bad." He had arrived in the peak of Detroit's prosperity and power, in the early and mid-1920s. With them he had watched the auto industry grow, spurred by the toughness of Henry Ford and the Dodge brothers. He had supported the immigration of blacks from the South who came looking for work. He was with these blacks—and all the people of Detroit—when the Depression came, when the impact of unemployment throughout the United States struck Detroit first and hardest. He watched the closing of the banks, which seemed again to begin in Detroit. After sharing the happiness of the gradual recovery in the 1930s, he experienced the mixed emotions that came with World War II when Detroit became the "Arsenal of Democracy."

During his time in Detroit Solanus had made friends in strategic places; he had been able to call on them when he needed their resources to obtain jobs and other help for those who came to him in need. Whether it was with these people in high places or with the countless thousands from lower places, Solanus' universal care of Catholics, Protestants and Jews had become known throughout the city. Many people said he was the best-loved person in Detroit.

Now their friend was gone.

CHAPTER SIX
Brooklyn
July 23, 1945—April 24, 1946

One of the reasons for the seeming abruptness of Solanus' transfer from St. Bonaventure's in Detroit to St. Michael's in East New York, or Brooklyn, was that Solanus was vacationing when the transfers were published. In those days a friar might get three weeks for a vacation, but Solanus Casey extended his visit to the West well beyond that. Solanus had left Detroit for his vacation on June 15. Ordinarily he would have returned to the Province in time for the Chapter, July 12, as was the custom.

The St. Bonaventure's *Chronicle* notes for its July 15 entry (a month after Solanus left for his vacation): "The results of the Chapter were published at 10:00 A.M. Father Solanus, traveling in California at the time of the Chapter was transferred to St. Michael's"[1] (in Brooklyn, New York). The effective date of the transfers seems to have been ten days from the July 15 announcement. Ordinarily ten days would have given enough time for the friars to settle their affairs, say their good-byes and transfer to their new assignment. Because he was so late in returning from his vacation, Solanus only had time to pack a few things and leave immediately if he would make the ten-day deadline.

Within the generally accepted notion of obedience as it was practiced in the Province at the time, there would be no exceptions simply because Solanus was away. For its July 21, 1945, entry the *Chronicle* of St. Bonaventure's states: "Father Solanus returned after an absence of five to six weeks. He left the next day for his new destination, St. Michael's."[2]

"I know he was simply told to go, and he went," Cosmas Niedhammer recalled:

> I know the rest of the community hardly noticed either. He was just transferred. That was it. I don't know much of the reaction on the part of the people. But I imagine, they might have been disappointed to hear that he was not in Detroit anymore. Certainly people were surprised and I think most of the friars felt that this transfer would relieve him from all this pressure and it was explained to people in that way. He was moved in order to give him a well-earned rest.[3]

While many friars had the same reaction to Solanus' transfer as Fr. Cosmas, others interpreted his change from Detroit to Brooklyn differently. Probably because they did not review the dates and the actual constraints placed on Solanus by the way transfers were handled in those days, the impression among many of them for a long time (including two subsequent provincials) was that Solanus was transferred to St. Michael's as some kind of punishment for being so overdue in his vacation and for having gone to California without explicit permission.

Although he was overdue, Solanus was hardly the technical "fugitive" (one who was away from the Province without permission) some made him out to be. In the first place, while he was in Washington, Solanus had been in communication with his superior in Detroit. He had indicated his situation as well as the fact that he had received invitations to extend his stay. One of these requests even came from the local bishop in Seattle. Fr. Marion, the superior, had telegraphed back to Solanus in Seattle: "Stay to see Bishop. Return as early as convenient and as traveling accommodations permit. Let us know when to expect you. God bless you and yours. S/ Fr. Guardian."[4]

Whether or not Solanus received the formal permission to extend his travels from Washington to California may never be known. But it is now clear that the real reason for Solanus' transfer was primarily to alleviate his physical ailments and to give him space from the situation with Garland and his group. Certainly it was not a punishment because he traveled on to California.

In his reflection on the matter, Clement Neubauer, elected Provincial Minister while Solanus was away, noted:

> I was the Provincial Superior at the time of Father Solanus' transfer from Detroit to New York. There was talk that he was transferred as a penalty for overstaying his visit on the West Coast. This is not so. The reason for his transfer was to relocate him at a distance in order to avoid the harassment of a particular layman. His lengthy stay on the West Coast was not considered by his superiors as an act of disobedience.[5]

While some considered Solanus' transfer a kind of sanction, Solanus merely accepted it as something that was a part of his Capuchin-Franciscan life. Many friars had come and gone during his twenty years at St. Bonaventure's; now it was his time to move on—even though he was already seventy-five years old.

Far from being upset by his change, Solanus seemed quite accepting of the decision. Detroit had taken its drain. Brother Ignatius Milne recalls his writing a note in a moment of confidence that said he was tired out and would like to get away.[6] Now that he had been transferred to Brooklyn, he not only seemed relieved, he prided himself on the cross-country nature of his transfer, noted in a letter from St. Michael's to his sister, Margaret:

> We'd come in from Los Angeles the night before (July 12) and offered Holy Mass in the Cathedral—and had a nice conference with the Archbishop. At 1:30 P.M. Owen left me on the train for Seattle. That was Saturday. Sunday and Monday I had Holy Mass at the Convent (in Seattle). Fr. Joachim served. I stopped over 24 hours in Spokane. We

were on the train all day Wednesday from 7:20 A.M. until Thursday at 10:30 when we arrived in St. Paul. I said Holy Mass Friday in St. Paul, got to Chicago on Saturday, Detroit on Sunday, New York on Monday and Tuesday in Brooklyn. I missed two Masses from Los Angeles. Thanks be to God for all things. Praised be Jesus![7]

From his letter to his sister, the only thing that seemed to bother Solanus was not his transfer or that he would miss the people in Detroit or they him; his only concern was that he missed offering two Masses.

Once he arrived at St. Michael's he realized he had to retrieve things left behind in his rush to arrive in Brooklyn on time to meet his "obedience" deadline. In writing Br. Leo Wollenweber about getting some of his personal belongings, he also wrote that in Brooklyn he could afford himself a much needed rest from his busy schedule. In what probably is the first letter (extant) written from St. Michael's, he wrote his friend Br. Leo Wollenweber at St. Bonaventure's:

God bless you and yours. I hope you keep well. Thanks be to God, I am here in this new assignment of privileged duty just a week. Tomorrow will be the forty-first anniversary of my first Holy Mass. Deo gratias. The next day (will be) the 21st (anniversary) of my arrival from Harlem, Our Lady of the Angels, back to St. Bonaventure's, 1924. How grateful we ought to be for so many graces and privileges. Praised be God in all His works and ways!

Now I hope you have not found that middle cell that succored me so long is in too hopeless a disorder. I rather fear having left you a difficult job when I asked you to pack up and forward things here. They would be of no use to anyone else and might be of quite a little convenience to me. I am not certain if I brought a trunk with me from Harlem twenty years ago. If I did, it must have been worth next to nothing, so any old box you might find would do. A box may perhaps be better than a trunk.

The "Letter" box on top of the "wardrobe" contains Fr. Edward's letters. These are good. The others are not important. I would like to have those few unfinished pieces in the clipper on the side next the desk, if you've not thrown them away.

I would also like to have that little prayer on modesty that we were figuring on having in the office. I started over to bring it for Fr. Provincial's approval but he was not in and then it was neglected. I hope to get a little more time for such things here at St. Michael's, although so far—what with getting acquainted, etc., I've not had much surplus time. One thing, however, I've taken a little more sleep under the great archangel's wings this past week than perhaps in three weeks before my arrival.[8]

While Solanus was able to get a much-needed rest, the people never let him forget that there were needs which had to be resourced with the healing power of God's love and concern.

Around the same time that he wrote to Brother Leo in Detroit, another Michiganer tracked down Solanus to Brooklyn. Mrs. D. Edward Wolfe of Brighton (where Solanus had gone for many years to act as summer chaplain at St. Vincent's Home for Children) telephoned him saying her infant daughter, Kathleen Ann, was dying from "early" celiac disease. Feeling that the doctors were not helping her baby get any better, she called Solanus saying she wanted to bring the baby to Brooklyn for his blessing. Solanus would hear none of it. Not only was the baby deathly sick; the expense was too much to consider.

Contrary to all rules he had been taught in Canon Law and morals classes about "transmitting" blessings through mediums more than fifty feet from the hearers, Solanus said, "Kneel down with the baby and I will give you my blessing over the telephone." When he had finished praying, he suggested that Mrs. Wolfe use the money that she would have spent coming to Brooklyn to "do something for a poor family."

Kathleen Ann recovered.

Solanus used the first, quiet days of his time in Brooklyn to make his annual retreat so that he might "try again to be converted for another year."[9] He went the fifty miles to "Beautiful Immaculate Conception

Monastery at Garrison on the Hudson,''[10] that he might go apart and be with the Lord. In his retreat notebook he began: "Thank God! First day: Busy day; weather ideal. Arrived at the station about 5:00 P.M. (for the retreat from New York). Had a good hike from the station." The theme of the retreat, preached by Fr. Norbert from the Pennsylvania Capuchin Province was: "To imitate St. Francis who so perfectly followed Jesus, our Divine Model."[11] Either the retreat provided many insights or Solanus began a new practice at Garrison; he wrote more retreat notes there than he had for years previous.

His notes, containing reflections on the vows, the beatitudes, and the "last things," filled nine pages. Elaborating on the conference on penance, which has as its theme: "Unless you do penance you shall all perish," Solanus made the following observations:

> God knows as no one else knows that we all and each need penance. God knows we need humiliations whereby we can foster humility. Hence in His love, He never fails to provide occasions for each one to practice penance, which means in other words to check self-conceit and, with God's help, to get somewhere in humility. Hence for a religious, the most practical penance is that naturally and logically connected to the Rule.

"Of course," Solanus added, "private penance is good and often practical. But," he added, recalling a poem of his priest-brother Edward:

> Too often, penance self-imposed
> May hold to seeds of pride enclosed.
> And the Devil—blast his skill
> Brings back with sleight-of-hand, self-will.
>
> But pains most fruitful recompense (the best penance)
> Is won by glad obedience.
> Obedience that looks to God
> To kiss humiliation's rod.

Oh, this (is) the sword that wins the strife
For God in many a wavering life.
Oh, this (is) the secret, happy way
To cure sinners—heaven's hay![12]

While he was at Garrison (where the young Capuchins studied philosophy), Solanus picked up some postcards of the seminary. A week after retreat he sent one of the postcards to an acquaintance in Michigan. He noted that already he was quite busy. "You've been on my mind frequently these days. I wanted to write you but getting acquainted in a new place keeps one on edge pretty much."[13]

In the same postcard Solanus mentioned that he had quite a stack of mail lately. It seems that some of the correspondence was coming from Ray Garland and others in his group. They were relating their activities and promotion of the insights of Mary of Agreda in her *The Mystical City of God*.

In an October 1945 letter to Ray Garland[14] Solanus commented favorably about the "interesting meeting" which the group had held a few weeks before. However, the letter also alluded to the controversy surrounding Ray and the group and implied that it was giving Solanus some concern. "Now I must tell you something that, in a way, I do not like to do," Solanus wrote:

> It is this. The arch-enemy of our Blessed Mother and of immortal souls—at all times on the alert—must have received an extra length of rope these days. I have been reported as having been phoning long distance to you and the "Agredan Society"
>
> Whatever the source, it seems to have given important offense, if not scandal.[15]

It is likely that Solanus was told by his superiors not to be in communication with Ray or the group. This was very difficult not only for Solanus to understand but to accept as well.

He firmly believed that Ray and the others were in the right. He fully believed in his mind Ray was being unduly maligned by well-meaning but ill-informed people inside and outside the Order. Despite his own feelings and his belief in this cause he followed the wishes of his superiors.

He told his friend Ray that he should not be involving himself (Solanus) in the very project he had helped begin and sustain. "Therefore, I wish that, for the present and until you be better known and your efforts recognized, you leave me out of the picture."[16] If the ministry was part of God's work, it would be exonerated, along with all its zealous workers. In this light he concluded:

> After all, if Venerable Mary of Agreda is a saint, about which I find it personally unreasonable to doubt, then in my way of thinking, it is high time that she get active in working a miracle of some kind. She needs to clear away the prejudice or jealousy or at least misunderstanding that has hampered her work—which is not hers but God's work—which has pressed on your shoulders for three years and on mine for at least seven.[17]

Ray Garland was not the only Detroiter who had communicated with Solanus after he arrived in Brooklyn. Almost immediately, letters and phone calls from Detroit started to come to St. Michael's. Solanus tried to respond to them all.

What happened to the people after he wrote his faith-filled replies will never be fully known. However, if the replies were similar to the one received by Mary Kenny of Detroit, they were filled with both words of consolation and hope as well as thoughts about God's loving care:

> Dear Mrs. Kenny: God bless you and yours.
> I came down from Retreat in Garrison a few days ago to find quite a stack of letters awaiting opening. I just came to yours of the 23rd and sure do sympathize with you and your family. However, we've had so many decidedly worse re-

ports than that about your Pat which turned out most reasonable after several months of suspense and anxiety, that I
shall still hope for a good word about son Patrick.

At all events, I have just enrolled him in the Seraphic
Masses as requested and we shall not be surprised at any
favorable report to come. We'll pray and hope, trusting in
God for the best. After all, if we look at things in light of
faith, the worst (as the world considers things) is only our
victory, according to our dear Lord's words: "Greater love
than this no one has that a man lay down his life for his
friends." I think that this ought to buoy us up as it is needed
in millions of sad bereavements these days. God bless you
again and give my love to all the family and friends.[18]

Asking to have his love given to the Kenny family and his friends was
typical of the way he related to people. People actually *felt* his love for
them. They felt his love in the way Solanus showed them his concern,
interest, and sincere effort to pray for their needs. Whether it was a
simple note or a telephone call, he knew that people would be nourished
knowing that their friend was prayerfully remembering them.

Solanus not only tried to show charity and friendship to people like
the Kenny's. If, for him, religion was the "science of our happy relationship with God and neighbor," and if charity begins at home, Solanus realized he had to show expressions of his love for his brothers at
St. Michael's. Thus he tried to share his life and love with his Capuchin
brothers.

While not all his expressions of fraternal charity were always appreciated, the friars there genuinely respected and even revered him. An
exception to this arose from one thing which Solanus did that got on
their nerves. Soon after he arrived in Brooklyn (according to Fr. Walter
O'Brien):

Solanus decided to entertain the friars at their regular Sunday recreation time. So he came in with his violin. The
friars thought, "Well, he is an old man trying to entertain

us.'' So they put up with his squeaking on the violin. Their reaction seemed so positive to Solanus that he thought he had done very well. The next Sunday night he showed up with his violin again.

As he began to play, one of the men went to the radio and kept turning up the volume. Without saying a word, Solanus left the room and went down before the Blessed Sacrament and continued his playing.

Each Sunday night after that he would go with his violin and ''play before the Lord'' for a half hour or so and play various hymns.

One Monday morning, after Sunday night Holy Hour, the sisters went up one side of me and down the other on the misbehaving of the altar boys in the sanctuary. (I was in charge of the altar boys). We have a big swivel window that separated our choir or chapel from the main altar of the church. Then I talked with the altar boys about their antics; ''Oh, Father, there were some squeaks coming from your chapel that we couldn't help but laugh.'' There was Solanus, it seems, oblivious to everything, playing before the Blessed Sacrament. All I would say to the altar boys was, ''The next time it happens just try to control yourself!'' And it did happen every Sunday night.[19]

In the early days at St. Michael's, Solanus had more time to write. He not only composed letters to his family and friends; he used the Christmas of 1945 to extol the birth of Christ in verse. Poetry helped him communicate the meaning of Christmas in the world and in the hearts of God's people. One of these poems (written perhaps as early as 1934), he now sent to his niece Helena Wilhite. It was entitled *Always Christmas Eve*[20]:

With love and Christmas greetings to all
Comes the Infant once more to free us from sorrow
Whose smile and whose power and whose gentleness call
To each heart and each soul for a manger tomorrow;

Whose love and whose goodness—whose wonders proclaim
Him, the Son of the Virgin, as promised of yore.
Oh, may he estrange us from sin and its shame!
And reign in our hearts, as his crib evermore!

. . . Ah, the rest of us, on Calvary
Mary conceived under the Cross
Thirty-three years later. Glory to God!
Peace to men of GOOD WILL.[21]

Even though many people from Detroit with relatives in New York came to see him, or told their relatives about him, while many people from his former Yonkers and Manhattan days gradually learned of his presence in their midst, Solanus still had more time to reflect and write than he had in Detroit.

Some of the letters he did write contained his reflections on past incidents of God's healing power that had been manifest toward the people who had come to visit him. In a letter to his niece Helena, Solanus reflected on one such incident that took place in his latter days in Detroit and early days in Brooklyn. Relating what happened almost as though he were an innocent bystander, Solanus noted that the power of healing came to people through the Seraphic Mass Association:

Now I am going to give you briefly something from my "NOTES ON CASES THROUGH THE SERAPHIC MASS ASSOCIATION," that for several years I was making and—while in Detroit. Just one case in perhaps more than a thousand—a number of them not only fearful tumors but of most positive and threatening cancer:
May 25, 1945. Mrs. Catherine Nagle, 45, a mother of eight children. She was opened up for an operation two weeks ago (May 9) in Providence Hospital. She was

found to be so hopelessly full of cancer that the doctors simply closed her up again saying she would "never leave the hospital alive." She has been enrolled in the Seraphic Mass Association several times. Today her husband enrolled the Poor Souls. The whole family is storming heaven by daily communion. Mother comes home today unable to take any nourishment.

May 29th. Mrs. Nagle as above May 25th. Thanks be to God. The fearful pains and swelling (are) gone from (her) abdomen. She has a good appetite and is eating fine. Husband enrolls Poor Souls again in thanksgiving.

Sept. 14th. Brooklyn, N.Y. Mrs. Nagle as noted above May 25th and May 29th (was) here today in perfect health. . . .[22]

Moving from this concrete example of the power of God's healing which he had witnessed, Solanus theologized on the need for confidence in the face of human suffering. In the two paragraphs which followed, he stressed the need for childlike trust in the face of suffering. At the same time, he also showed his continued support of the writings of Mary of Agreda:

But why worry? "To worry about anything," St. Theresa, the little Flower claims, "is to indicate a want of confidence in God." She very likely speaks of excessive worrying. But why should we worry about anything? Tumors? Cancers? Death? Why not rather turn to God, whose solicitude for our individual welfare, temporal as well as spiritual puts all created solicitude out of the picture. Why not foster confidence in his Divine Providence by humbly and in all childlike humility venture to remind him in the person of our divine Brother Jesus, that we are his children. We should remind him that we are, and at least want to be reckoned as among his "little ones." Therefore, we should thank him frequently for, not only the blessings of the past and present, but thank him ahead of time for whatever he foresees is pleasing to him that we suffer. We should do this not only in general but in each particular case. We should leave everything absolutely in his divine disposal, including with all its circumstances, when, where, and how he may be pleased to dispose the event of our death.

Try something like this and see if it doesn't bring you a big increase of peace and contentment. In my opinion there is hardly anything else that the enemy of our souls dreads more than confidence—humble confidence in God. The lives of the saints abound with examples of this virtue. Perhaps nowhere more beautifully than in the example of St. Joseph with Mary, God's Living Tabernacle seeking an abode wherein to give us salvation. What an example of confidence it must have been to their thousand guardian angels, as Venerable Mary of Agreda was instructed to inform us, did Mary have from the day of her Immaculate Conception. What an edification! And again what a surpassing reward that followed! What a HOLY NIGHT for them indeed! A HOLY NIGHT, the positive dawn of humanity rescued.[23]

It seems that one of the reasons why Solanus wrote such a long letter to his niece was to help her cope with two specific situations which were troubling her: the sickness of her husband, Edward Wilhite, and the fact that it did not seem she would be able to have any children. Reiterating one of his themes about "surprising the doctors," Solanus also invited his niece to do something concrete to show her confidence in God. Possibly she could bring life into the world in a new, creative way:

There has been something else in my mind, however, that I wanted to bring to your consideration. How about proposing to adopt one or more little ones, of whom Jesus assures us: "What you have done for the least of my brethren, you have done for me," and what if Edward would give the doctors a surprise and get well?

I find it always practical, especially in cases where all human scientific help is despaired of, to just turn to the divine author of all good—always solicitous to be asked for favors—and with all the confidence we can muster, to promise something that we are assured is pleasing to him if we might only be spared (or be granted the certain favor). But to even raise children for God and society is manifestly pleasing to God. This applies to cases whether they are procured by natural generation or by adoption (which seemingly is quite a matter of indifference to him), that he has given a specially beautiful coloring to the love of those whose privilege it is to have become earnest faithful parents. In this song of the psalmist it can be quite appropriately applied: "Oh, the depths of the riches of the wisdom and of the knowledge of God! How incomprehensible are his judgments and how unsearchable his ways!" (Romans 11)

I am herewith enclosing a letter of Fr. Edward's . . . that will speak for itself. I wish to address the verse I have underlined: "God condescends to use our powers, if we don't spoil his plans by ours." Because he is always planning wonders for the patient and the humble. Hence his own blessed words: "Unless you be converted and become as little children. . . ." Now I'll have to say GOOD NIGHT.[24]

True to his practical-bent, Solanus not only tried to be concrete in offering ways someone like his own niece could promote life in the world, he used the same approach with others who came to see him. For him God really doesn't care if people become parents by generation or adoption. Such a conviction might enable husbands and wives to cut through cultural biases and fears to understand the heart of true parenting.

Another woman who was helped by Solanus' insight was Asteria Mahoney. As she recalls the incident:

I met Solanus Casey in 1945 while I was a Girl Scout Leader at St. Michael's Church, 225 Jerome Street,

Brooklyn, N.Y. I was 27 years old, married 8 years, having no children.

When my husband returned from service, W.W. ii, we decided to find out once and for all the cause and the reason for our not producing a family. I was recommended to a well known gynecologist, Dr. O'Leary, and he in turn sent my husband to Dr. Griffin. The findings were that it would be very unlikely that we would have children.

This was heartbreaking news to me, having come from a large family. My husband then suggested that we could adopt a child. I was very hesitant, and it would be a first in both our families and I wondered if our children would be accepted and loved as the other grandchildren, nieces and nephews.

It was not generally known, but I had heard that Fr. Solanus was in our parish, that he was a very saintly man, well loved and sought after for counsel and advice by the people in Detroit from where he recently served.

One afternoon after a Girl Scout meeting, I rang the Monastery bell and asked if I could speak to Fr. Casey. Brother asked me no questions and ushered me to a small conference room when very soon Fr. Casey came in with a friendly smile. I told him about my marriage, how much I wanted a family, and my fears about adoption. His answer to me not only answered my questions, but will remain with me forever. He said, "If it wasn't for people like you, who would take care of the unfortunate ones?" When I left him, I was happy and convinced that this is what I was meant to do and shortly applied to the N.Y. Foundling Hospital to adopt a child.

On June 12, 1946 we brought our first son home. He was exactly two months old.[25]

For someone living in the 1940s, Solanus was far ahead of his time in cutting through cultural biases and barriers. Whether it be with the Mahoneys whom he helped break through stereotypes about adoption, with non-Catholics, or people of other races, Solanus cut through countless externals to get to the core of people and their basic needs.

In a letter written in early 1946, Solanus recalled an incident in his ministry that had taken place at St. Bonaventure's. The incident involved a married couple who were neither Catholic nor white. And while his letter shows he was not totally free of some of the terminology that white people used (which later revealed a bias), it was certainly unintended and was believed to be quite sympathetic to people who used such stereotypes. "We've had several cases similar to yours, and some of them altogether more tragic and hopeless, which have turned out to have been real blessings in disguise," he wrote a woman who wrote him complaining of serious headaches:

> A single example: It must be ten or more years ago that a certain modest lady, having waited close to an hour, until all else had gone, introduced herself: "I's not Catholic, but I would like to get a blessin' too. I's always had headaches." Her accent rather then her color indicated something of her particular origin.[26]

Just her southern dialect was enough to coax the literary bug in Solanus Casey. He tried in his reflection to recapture the context of their dialog, much like Faulkner was doing in his writing at that time. Solanus continued:

> About three hours later a well-featured but very dark visitor of the same name and identical accent asked for a rosary. I told him of his namesake who had been in about 11:00. "That's my wife." He went on to explain that she had come home without any headache. Glory be to God!
> They had been praying for a family for thirteen years and were naturally discouraged, or were becoming so. They believed in Christianity but had never been baptized. . . . It is next to "unbelievable," what difficulties they met with and, by God's grace overcame, before being received into the Church—and even for months afterwards. All Hell just seemed determined to keep them from their purpose.[27]

He told the woman receiving the above letter about his effort to get people to deepen their faith, or investigate the "claims of the Church," or for others to "get ahead of the Good God in generosity if possible." Then he concluded:

> I almost forgot to tell you that, having left Detroit, the convert darkies returned after more than three years. There were three of them instead of two. The good God blessed them with a decidedly promising youngster, the picture of his appreciative Daddy.
>
> I hope that this may offer you an example from which you might draw a practical lesson—one case in thousands. Thanks be to God.[28]

The more people heard such stories as the above, the more people came to St. Michael's ringing the front office bell. However, even with the growing numbers, it was nothing like the droves at Detroit. After eight months, Solanus wrote his brother Edward that his coming to St. Michael's had been a "decided relief" compared to the drain and strain of difficulties brought to the office for twenty years at St. Bonaventure's in Detroit. He noted, "I do have perhaps hours as long but it's a change. Here it's correspondence that takes most of the time. There, I simply had to leave most of that to others. And while I meet with pathetic cases to solve or try to alleviate, the strain and tension is by no means so pressing."[29]

Because he kept long hours either seeing people or answering correspondence, Solanus did not always get the hours of sleep that his body needed. So he devised a unique way to take catnaps while he was portering. He would push his chair back from the desk and crawl under it. Then he would snuggle up like a little child and take a quick snooze. He'd stay there until he was relaxed, or until a phone call or doorbell rang. Then he'd get up, brush himself off, put his hair in place, and, according to Fr. Walter, "look fresh as a daisy." It was always important to this Irishman that he looked dignified.[30]

With time the catnaps became less as more people from the parish and beyond were coming to see him. As had happened in Detroit, some people had to wait in line. One of these was Ruth Keck, who had a son at the Capuchin seminary at Garrison. He later became Fr. Barnabas Keck, the director of the Solanus Guild at St. John's in New York. According to Fr. Barnabas,

> When my mother still lived in St. Patrick's (Brooklyn), she had been in a hospital. The doctor wanted her to go home and then come back for surgery. She asked him, "If I ask you straight questions, will you give me an honest answer?"
>
> He said, "Okay."
>
> "Do I have cancer?" she asked. At that he turned and walked out of the room. So my mother turned to the woman next to her and said, "What's that supposed to mean?"
>
> She left the hospital and told my aunt Agnes what happened. "Ruth," she said, "let's go over to St. Michael's and see Fr. Solanus." So she went to the friary and waited in line. When my mother's turn came, Fr. Solanus said, "And what's your problem, dear."
>
> "I think I have cancer," she said.
>
> All he said was, "Don't you know God can cure cancer just like a toothache?" So she knelt down and he put his hand on her and blessed her, praying over her.
>
> She went home and never went back to the doctor and was eighty years old when the story was repeated in 1983.[31]

When the sick were not able to visit Solanus, others brought Solanus to visit them. Sometimes the process of getting him to these places created humorous incidents for his drivers. One such incident has been told by Art Lohrman. It seems that his wife knew Solanus and asked him to take Solanus to the houses of various people in the metropolitan area. One time they went somewhere which took them over the Triboro Bridge to the Bronx. Coming back, Mr. Lohrman wanted to have a little extra time for conversation with Solanus. So he acted as though he couldn't find the Bridge.

"Oh," Solanus said, "Let's say a rosary to the Mother of God that you find it." By the time the rosary was said, they had found the bridge. "Now in thanksgiving to the Mother of God," Solanus said, "Let's say another one." Finally, after three rosaries and no conversation with Solanus, Art made a decision: "From then on, I never opened my mouth whether I was lost or not."[32]

When he drove with people, Solanus did do other things besides pray. He used the time to talk about mutual ideas, listen to people's concerns, and to share stories about his youth or friends. He considered relationships with his friends and relatives very important and tried to cultivate them, especially through letters and occasional visits.

Besides these ways of cultivating friendships, Solanus made a real effort while at St. Michael's to stay in contact with his old friends and acquaintances inside and outside the Order. He went to Garrison to swim in the pool; besides leisure time, it gave him the chance to get to know the young friars better. He made sure he didn't miss the annual Labor Day Festival at Sacred Heart in Yonkers. He loved the excitement of the children, to watch the games being played and to eat the food being served. He especially enjoyed hot dogs with onions—hardly the kind of diet that reflected his later concern for eating healthy foods. While hot dogs might not be the best nourishment, they were part of the American scene of a parish festival, which Solanus fully enjoyed.

It was not long, however, before Solanus' presence began to be known by more and more. The more visible Solanus became at events like this at Yonkers, or just by being available at the door of St. Michael's, the more the superiors began to realize that well-meaning people were not going to be giving Solanus the rest they had sent him to St. Michael's to get.

Looking around the Province for a place that would be far enough removed from the major cities the Capuchin-Franciscans served (i.e., New York, Detroit, and Milwaukee), as well as having enough community presence to nourish Solanus in what they thought would be the twilight years of his life, the superiors chose Huntington, Indiana.

St. Felix in Huntington served as the Province's novitiate. In a rare move for that time (which generally found transfers coming only in connection with the triannual Chapter or convention), they transferred Solanus again from St. Michael's to St. Felix Friary. At the end of April, after just nine months of combining his portering with "semi-retirement," Solanus was given the official status of "retirement." He was 76.

His time in semi-retirement at St. Michael's had made Solanus more aware of people's strengths and weaknesses, largesse and pettiness. He also realized that some people seemed more interested in him and in what he could do for them than in what he stood for and the Power that enabled him to touch people's lives. Although he realized how such people were trying to manipulate him, he did not try to control them in turn. Rather he sought to deal with this form of control in a spirit of understanding and gentleness.

One such incident occurred during his last days at St. Michael's and his first days at St. Felix. It illustrates how Solanus responded to people who seemed to have a real need to be identified with him rather than what he represented. The cause of one such incident dealt with his "rubber stamp."

A rubber stamp had been made which reproduced Solanus' signature. The friars thought this would make it easier for Solanus to handle SMA enrollments and sign checks. They knew his arthritis made it very difficult for him not only to write and type his letters but even to sign his name. Thus the stamp with his signature. However, for at least one person, receiving Solanus' signature by means of a rubber stamp rather than his own hand, was an affront. She complained quite strongly.

The complaint reached Br. Leo Wollenweber in Detroit. So he wrote his friend Solanus about the displeasure he had "caused" the women when he used the rubber stamp at St. Michael's. Receiving Leo's letter, Solanus immediately wrote to the upset woman, trying to placate her. He made a copy of his letter and enclosed the following letter to Brother Leo.

The letter reveals the nonviolent way Solanus Casey tried to deal with anger, impatience and tensions of others. It also reveals that he was beginning to be plagued by various ailments, especially with his legs.

These "sentinels" were letting him know that he did need to slow down, if not retire altogether.

Dear Brother Leo:

God bless you and all at St. Bonaventure's.

I am sending the original of this carbon to Miss Lyke. I hope it may smooth the thing off in a manner; though I am not just clear to what she really complains about. Perhaps she expected a personal acknowledgement of some kind rather than just a rubber stamp.

I've been getting so many checks—both here at St. Felix and at St. Michael's—that I would have to possess an extraordinary memory to recollect particulars like this little mixup might require. One thing I do remember, that during the nine or ten months I was at St. Michael's it was very seldom, if ever, that I was without letters to acknowledge, even though I sometimes worked on them until after midnight.

God be praised, however, I did not mind it and my health kept fine. Sometimes my two faithful old sentinels would threaten to go on strike and to quiet them down I felt I'd have to give it up.

Well, she will possibly write again. After all if she got her checks back, she ought to know that things were okay.

We'll hope for the best anyhow and pray for the dear Lord's gentle guidance.

Praying in the meantime for one another's conversion, till someday we can sin no more and the angels will be able to bear us off to eternity. There, forever, really and truly

CONVERTED, we'll be able to sing on with the angels awaiting that blessed day: "O all you works of the Lord, bless the Lord, praise and exalt him above all forever."

Fr. Solanus Casey, O.F.M. Cap.
Praised be Jesus Christ![33]

This letter (from Huntington) would be one of the first during a period that would become that of Solanus' greatest volume of writing—at least in terms of those letters that are now available.

CHAPTER SEVEN
Huntington
April 25, 1946—January 12, 1956

The novitiate at St. Felix Friary in Huntington, Indiana, was ideal for Solanus Casey's "official" retirement. It was built just before the Great Depression of 1929. The novitiate in Detroit's central city had been too small and too urban. The large expense, $306,668.59, (in 1929 dollars), had been justified because the Province was entering into rapid growth. With 30 acres on the outskirts of the city, the professed friars and novices could have plenty room to roam and reflect.

When the novitiate site was purchased, the original property was flat and barren. However in the seventeen-year interim between the erection of the large building and when Solanus arrived, there was a transformation. Within a few months of their arrival, the original novices had planted an orchard of 170 apple trees behind the friary, as well as hundreds of other of trees and shrubs. Now the fruit of their work added a reflective and contemplative environment for future novices who would go there to begin Capuchin Franciscan living.

Solanus took full advantage of Huntington's atmosphere of serenity and peace. Here he could experience an environment that facilitated his contemplative attitude of gratitude and thanks. After an entire life spent in the busy urban area of Yonkers, Manhattan, Detroit, and Brooklyn, the fact that Solanus could walk just a few steps outside the friary and be in the middle of nature's beauty made him all the more sensitive to the abiding presence of God. Such strolls did not find him melancholy, brooding about the past; the very environment elicited a spontaneous

175

thanks. He was grateful for his past and for the present favors of God, as a letter to his sister shortly after his arrival attests:

> Oh the Faith! How little it is possible for us in this world to appreciate it! I was strolling in the orchard and vineyard this morning. They were bountifully loaded. Deo Gratias. I knelt for a while in the little Capuchin cemetery. All of these are behind this ideal monastery. I was thrilled by the chimes of SS. Peter and Paul in their tower smiling at me less than two miles away. Thoughts multiplied of the wonderful past. Wonderful indeed to muse over! Thanks be to God. Still how comparatively melancholy they are when, from the anchor of faith, we can turn to the spring of eternal blessedness that is assured those who persevere.[1]

After seventy-six years such a contemplative approach to life—where the beauty of nature enabled him to penetrate further to the very author of that beauty—came quite easily to Solanus. He could only conclude: "Indeed, what is all the past, aside from the privilege that ought to be our supreme aim, to have fostered and to foster appreciation of our being children of our heavenly Father and of our Blessed Mother Mary?"[2]

While it is not easy to define just what mysticism is, reflections such as this one from Solanus reveal elements of a true mystic. His openness to the sights of abundant orchards and vineyards, the sounds of faroff church bells, joined with the feeling of reverence and kinship for the reality that met him in his environment—including the world of nature and of persons—speaks of an intimate rapport with the very heart which that reality has as its source.

Solanus' reflections reveal what F. C. Happold calls "the mystical interpretation of reality." According to him,

> The mystical interpretation of reality is based on a world-view that the phenomenal world, i.e., the world as we know it, and individual consciousness, i.e., the self we know, are

only partial realities. Both are the manifestation of a Divine Ground (which is the Totality of God) which contains within Itself all partial realities.[3]

Solanus' identity with the God of all creation, who was the ground of all being, including his own, established a relationship with all of creation. The power of God in him could be extended into people with healing as well as into creation.

Soon after Solanus' arrival, the friars learned what this power over creation might mean. On May 13, the Huntington *Friary Chronicle* noted without further comment:

> Last Saturday when the daily papers announced the approach of frosts, the friars thought of lighting a smudge to save the tiny apples. Father Solanus volunteered to bless the orchard instead with the oration ''Ad Omnia'' and one to Blessed Ignatius, a Capuchin Brother. Now it appears that only the grapes froze. When all around us the neighboring apples were destroyed—ours were unharmed.[4]

The very fact that the chronicler did not elaborate on this unique event seems to indicate that, by now, the friars were taking as a matter of course the unique powers over people and even nature ''that went forth from'' this follower of Jesus Christ.

While others might consider God's power uniquely at work in him, as far as Solanus was concerned, it was *all* God's work. He never saw himself the way others did, a sign of his genuine humility. One of the friars who lived with Solanus around that time, Fr. Ambrose de Groot, noted:

> I am convinced that he was not aware that others held him in such high esteem. If he did, then all I can say is that he was a very good actor. But no one can put on an act for such a number of years without giving himself away. I just know he was not aware of the esteem in which others held him. Nor did he care.

He was not the kind of man who put himself on trial
before anyone, nor did he reveal he was on trial. He was on
trial before his God. And he loved his God and he knew that
God loved him. That was all that mattered. His whole conduct showed that this must have been the case. I cannot help
but marvel how God can hide such mass esteem for a person
without that person being aware of it. But God does. And
I'm convinced he did it in the case of Father Solanus. He
was genuinely humble—without any pretense.[5]

The early days at Huntington, where he was comparatively unknown,
afforded Solanus much more leisure to deepen his reflections about the
way God was working in the world. He shared many of these reflections
in letters to his friends and those people who were "promoters" of the
Seraphic Mass Association. These early years at Huntington found his
apostolate of the pen taking more time than front office calls. Where
previously front office visits created problems, now having time to
respond to peoples' letters was the difficulty. He noted to one correspondent who commented that he was late in answering: "It is not
audiences with callers now but answering letters that is my problem. So
please have charity to overlook my tardiness" in replying.[6]

While Huntington might have been his "official" retirement, Solanus was not one to rest on his past. Something in him never let him
dwell in the past in a controlling way; life was for the fulfillment of
dreams and visions, not to be controlled by the past.

Solanus' Huntington letters reveal many insights about his spirituality. Even more, some letters written in the latter part of this first
year there offer a unique insight into his own reflections on the way
God's healing power was extending itself to others through his ministry.
These letters which he wrote about suffering were all written within a
few months of each other. They offer the clearest expression of Solanus' own understanding of what was happening to others as a result of
his healing ministry.

Solanus had a unique approach to the problem of suffering. He con-
fessed that "I don't understand why children have to suffer."[7] Even

though he was not familiar with the contemporary theology of suffering that makes it part of the human condition called original sin, Solanus somehow sensed God wanted to heal. From his perspective—these healings had nothing to do with himself: God was merely continuing to "heal sickness and diseases of every kind" (cf. Mt 1:34) as had been promised to those who had the simplest of faith (Mk 16:17–18).

On one day, December 14, 1946, he wrote two letters to different people. These are among the best on the subject of healing extant thus far. In one he reflected on prayer for healings that were "successful." Such healings came, in part, he noted, because of people's generosity to God shown through their support for the missions. In the other letter he reflected on prayer for healings that were "not successful." These had to be understood in light of God's greater designs which demanded equal generosity from God's people. For Solanus both cases demanded confidence and generous thanks.

In Solanus' mind, the healings worked through him occurred because the people requesting the cure promised to do three things: (1) believe, (2) pray with faith, and (3) make a promise.[8] This promise to do something would manifest the people's efforts to respond to the divine concern that all come to a deeper knowledge of God and God's ways. It did not matter whether the people needing the healing were Catholic, Protestants or Jew. Since God worked in the world of Jesus of Nazareth to heal "all", so now in the world of Solanus of Prescott, God's same Spirit wanted to work to heal broken people.

In the 1940s and 1950s before Jonas Salk invented his vaccine, polio was a plague that struck every summer. People lived in fear that it would attack their families. One family that had not been freed from its crippling effects was the Abraham Trabulsys in Detroit. In writing them a letter, Solanus reflected on a "remarkable case" which manifested God's healing power toward a Jew who enrolled his son in the Seraphic Mass Association. He recalled the story, it seems, to try to involve the Trabulsys in the Capuchin missionary activity as well:

A friend of your daughter Jenny, Miss Rose Faris, writes me that Jenny is very low with polio and asks for prayers

that, if it be God's holy will, she might recover. I am
enrolling Jenny in what we call the Seraphic Mass Association for prayers of hundreds of people.

The members of this association are asked to pray for our
foreign missionaries and their work and for one another.
Those members who can, pray. All those who can afford to
do so are asked to help with an offering of some kind
besides prayers and Masses. I am confident that this will
help your Jenny. This will happen especially if you and
yours do your part.

You will get an idea of what I mean by telling you of a
remarkable case in Detroit about four years ago. I made
note of it at the time. It is about as follows:

January 9th. Judge Healy called this evening:
". . . There is a certain Dr. Kleitzer in my office whose
only child is very low with spinal meningitis. The doctors
give him very little hope of recovery. He is not a Catholic or
a Christian. He is a Jew, a good, God-fearing fellow. I wish
you would enroll the boy in the Mass Association and pray
for him."

"I'll be glad to do that," I answered. "Tell the parents
I'd like to see them."

"I'll bring them over tomorrow," he answered.

"Next day (Saturday), I saw them—the Judge and the
Doctor, waiting over in the corner. It was about 1:15 P.M.
As I was introduced to the Doctor I asked, "How is the
boy?"

"Well, he slept last night (the first time in a week)," the
Doctor responded.

"Now, Doctor, I have a proposition I want you to make
to the Good God yourself. I understand you are a Jew."

"Yes," he replied.

"That is okay, Doctor. After all, if religion can be de-
fined as a science, and I claim it is unquestionably the
greatest science of all times—in fact it is nothing less than
THE SCIENCE OF OUR HAPPY RELATIONSHIP WITH
GOD AND OUR NEIGHBORS, then, there *can be but one*

religion, though there may be a thousand different systems of religion.''

The Doctor seemed pleased but said nothing. They left.

Twenty-five minutes later the Judge phoned: ''I thought you would be pleased to hear what happened. I brought the Doctor right back to the Children's Hospital and in the vestibule we met the mother of the boy. The Doctor's wife was smiling.

She said, ''At 1:30 he opened his eyes and smiled at me.'' (This was the time the Judge and the Doctor were talking about the boy with Solanus.)

''A week later (Sunday) he was brought home in perfect health.''

Hoping that the above may not have been too boring for anyone and that if it be God's holy will, your Jenny may give the doctors and all concerned a favorable surprise of some kind, I remain. . .[9]

Ultimately life and death and sickness and health are impacted because of God's will. Solanus believed that God willed to heal; thus his approach to healing manifested a faith toward God that assumed there would be such healing.

But what about those times when prayers for healing, good works toward those in need (such as contributions to the Soup Kitchen or enrollments in the SMA), or reading to know more about God and God's plan for the world, did not bring about the desired healings? How would these disappointments be reflected upon?

The same day Solanus wrote the above letter assuming that there would be a ''favorable surprise of some kind'' for all concerned, he wrote to another Detroiter trying to explain why not all prayers are answered in the way people would hope. Manifesting the same trust in God and for the persons to whom he was writing, Solanus noted:

I was pleased to receive your kind favor of the 9th even though it was not as bright, as of course, we all would like to see it. However, God knows best, and, while we'll still

> hope for a favorable surprise, we can hardly do better than
> not only being resigned to whatever God permits, but even
> beforehand to thank him for his mercifully loving
> designs.[10]

When people were not cured as they themselves desired, Solanus believed this too was part of God's overall and mysterious plan that could only evolve for peoples' ultimate good. "I recall one day at St. Felix, I was in the outside with some of the novices," Capuchin Ambrose de Groot recalls. "He told the story about the time he was talking to a group of people sitting in a car in front of St. Bonaventure's in Detroit. One of the occupants of the car was a woman who had been crippled and unable to walk for thirty years. Solanus wanted to sympathize with her and said: 'My, but thirty years is an awful long time to be suffering this way.' But she replied, 'Yes, Father, but eternity is worth it.' "

The more he reflected on this story and the more he recalled that Solanus would say at various times, "Religious are people who have the leisure time to suffer," Ambrose de Groot came to believe such reflections on suffering by Solanus revealed a unique approach to this mystery. "I think such statements say an awful lot about his theology of suffering," Father Ambrose noted:

> He saw it as having redemptive value in the life of the
> Mystical Body—that certain people are chosen by God to
> suffer as an apostolate. It recalls St. Paul's statement: 'I
> rejoice now in the sufferings I bear for your sake; and what
> is lacking of the sufferings of Christ I fill up in my flesh for
> his body which is the church' (Col 1:24). It's the church's
> doctrine of vicarious or redemptive suffering. I really think
> he understood this well and was the reason why he made
> such statements; and it was the reason why he never obtained cures for his own brethren.[11]

Above all, Solanus believed, whether one would receive a desired cure or not, one should always give thanks to that God who, as creator of heaven and earth, can do all things. Give thanks ahead of time—for healing or continued suffering—should characterize true believers. Giving thanks beforehand reflects a deep trust in God's power always at work in us. "This is the way we can foster confidence in God," he wrote in his letter to the Detroiter explaining why not all prayers are answered in the way people might hope:

> This confidence is the very soul of prayer, and conse-quently heightens our hopes for supernatural intervention. Not only this, but in fostering this confidence we greatly eliminate the danger of sadness, want of resignation and impatience. While these are not necessarily sinful in them-selves, nevertheless, they sadly frustrate God's merciful designs. Hence the little verse: "God condescends to use our powers if we don't spoil his plans by ours. . . ."[12]

Confidence in the God who can heal was at the heart of Solanus' theology of healing. As early as his novitiate, he had recalled in his notes the words of Jesus: "Ask and you shall receive." He would ask God for healing for his brother and sister, because he was confident in God's promise to heal. *Because* of Solanus' confidence in that God, people, in turn, were heightened in their confidence in God's healing. People believed because Solanus believed. Because Solanus believed in God, people believed in Solanus.

The unique element of Solanus' approach to God's healing revolved around confident thanks shown in good deeds. This was part of the "proposition" people would use to show God their faith. Whether it was before or after the healing, as St. Paul said, in all things people were to "Give thanks to God the Father always and for everything in the name of our Lord Jesus Christ" (Eph 5:20). Again, Paul said, "Rejoice always, never cease praying, render constant thanks; such is God's will for you in Christ Jesus" (I Thes 5:18). Solanus made Paul's advice his own.

Those seeking healing for themselves and their loved ones were to view all healing as part of God's will; thus thanks had to be given ahead of time because of that will of God which can heal. Furthermore, thanks had to be accompanied by comparable generosity—before and after healing—as a confident recognition that all healing comes because of God's generosity to us.

Solanus did not worry about those things that lie beyond the power of humans, like healing. Instead he simply urged people to go beyond their limited power to God. They were advised to manifest their thanks to the God who heals by gratefully doing something both before and after the healing.

Writing to a couple whose little daughter had eye trouble, Solanus articulated one of the best of his "give thanks before-and-after" approaches that is available. This letter too was written from Huntington during the same few months as the others excerpted here:

> . . . shake off the excessive worry and instead exercise a little confidence in God's merciful providence by first promising something—even a little sacrifice of some kind in thanksgiving if things go favorable. Then to show your confidence in his goodness, start and thank him whenever you think of it. Give him thanks for whatever he may see best to do for the little one and for her loving friend.[13]

The acts of confident thanks that Solanus asked of people were varied. Most often they would be asked to support the foreign missions through an enrollment in the SMA. Other times he urged them to give something to the poor. Sometimes non-Catholics would be asked to investigate "the claims of the Catholic Church." For others, both Catholics and non-Catholics, their part of the "proposition" with God might be to read more about the ways of God and religion. As usual one of the vehicles Solanus used to deepen peoples' understanding of the mind of Christ and the ways of religion was to have them read the works of Mary of Agreda, especially her *The Mystical City of God*.

On February 8, 1947, Solanus wrote a man in Brighton, Michigan. In the letter, which was Solanus' response to his request for healing prayers, Solanus commented about the time he asked the wife of a

Methodist to read the works of the Spanish mystic and how the woman did not deliver on her part of the proposition to do so—as her sign to God that she was doing her part in bringing healing to her husband:

I have been down here in St. Felix since last April. So for the present am no more at St. Bonaventure's in Detroit. I was up in Detroit all last week, as the little postcard may at least intimate. You might do well, nevertheless, to visit the Monastery there on Mt. Elliott (#1740). They can enroll you in the Seraphic Mass Association as well as I can, and that is a big feature in the "secret" of the many notable favors reported there as well as in our other friaries. Thanks be to God.

At all events, dear Mr. Taylor, I am going to tell you of just one of the said notable examples that you may draw your own conclusion. I sincerely hope that you might draw from them a happily profitable lesson. The case was noted close to four years ago in my own hand and runs substantially as follows:

March 26, 1943. Andrew Wheeler, a Methodist of 686 Manistique Ave., Detroit, had a "brain-tumor" removed four weeks ago (Feb. 23). At first the operations seemed to have been successful. But two weeks later infection started. On March 12th there was a second operation.

Last Tuesday, March 23, Mrs. Wheeler accompanied by a Catholic neighbor came weeping and lamenting: "They have just operated on my husband the third time in a month and they give me very little hope of his recovery. . . ."

"Now Mrs. Wheeler," I pleaded, "do not take it so hard. We will pray for your husband and enroll him in the Association and try to induce our dear Lord to take over the case himself." So I recorded his name, etc.

Then I said, "Now Mrs. Wheeler, I have a little proposition for you to make yourself to the good God in your own honest way."

"I'll do anything to please the good God," she interposed, 'if he will only spare my poor, dear husband!"

"Well this is the proposition or promise I want you to make, if you choose this rather than something else, whereby to please God. It is more a suggestion, therefore, that you promise or earnestly resolve in your own mind to look into the claims of that Mother Church divinely planned and proclaimed infallible, and the claims of any other denomination or system of religion. Or I might say that you look into the connection between them."

Mr. Wheeler came home the next day, the day before yesterday. He came here with his wife and neighbor today. A patch of about three inches square was taped around his right temple. While I was noting the surprise (in the healing), he remarked to the party who had given him his place (in line): "It is great to feel normal again, although I feel a little weak. The doctors in Ann Arbor, Peet and Wood call it miraculous . . . that a patient should talk intelligently inside of twenty-four hours after such an operation."

"Thanks be to God!"

I had not heard from them for over a year and a half, when Mrs. Wheeler came to lament that her husband was not very well of late. I asked her if she had kept her promise as I had suggested and if she had read the book I lent her, *The Mystical City of God*. She humbly admitted that she had not. She had come without him, as she said, because she wanted to tell me about him first.

I told her without hesitation, "The whole trouble is in your failure to keep your promise, or your proposition, whatever it was."

She promised to return next night with her husband and in the meantime to do something to show her good will. It was a very stormy evening, the next night, so she phoned her inability to come as promised but that they would come the following evening. Following is the note that I made under the original:

October 18, 1944: Thank God they are both here today. He has started to read the wonderful life of the Blessed Virgin, *The Mystical City of God* and is quite enthused about it.

Among other things in praise of the wonderful work, *The Mystical City of God . . .* he remarked: "I find so much in it that I have often wondered about."

I hope, dear Mr. Taylor, that I have not bored you over-much with the above. If I were an experienced typist I would do the whole letter over. Under my circumstances, however, that is out of the question. I am enrolling yourself and Mrs. Taylor in our emergency list and will hope for a favorable surprise of some kind—and a favorable report.[14]

If cures were given, Solanus (like Christ who asked why only one leper returned to report the healing) asked for a "report" as well. That report, like the request for the healing, he "duly noted" in the books he kept at the request of the provincial.

In his letter to the Taylors he added a postscript which made it clear that, as far as he was concerned, God's healing could come to people of all faiths as long as they truly professed and acted on their belief:

P.S.: Incidentally, I think it is slightly an error for one who is a Christian (as I presume you are), or who believe in Jesus our Redeemer, to intimate that he does not belong to the same faith as another who, though believing in Jesus Christ and professing Christianity, happens to differ with him in some details, possibly not even essential. Because I claim that there is really but one Christianity, as scientifically there can be but one religion, though there be a thousand different systems of that "Greatest science of all times and all generations—THE SCIENCE OF OUR HAPPY RELATIONSHIP WITH GOD AND OUR NEIGHBORS."
"Thus says the Lord: Let not the wise man glory in his wisdom and let not the strong man glory in his strength, and let not the rich man glory in his riches. But let him that glories, glory in this, that he understands and loves me, for I am the Lord that exercises mercy and judgment, and justice in the earth. For these things please me, says the Lord" (Jer 9:22–23).[15]

As the quote from Jeremiah made clear, Solanus wanted to make it clear that there were more important things about God than specific religious expressions or institutions. The main thing was that God be glorified and confidently thanked through lives of mercy and justice on the earth. These were the virtues the Lord wanted to be found on earth and which would be the basis of God's final judgment and healing.

Solanus had begun the above letter noting that ''for the present'' he was ''no longer at St. Bonaventure's.'' The reason why he couched his letter in such a way was that, given his need for doctoring as well as the desire of the people in Detroit for this return, there was some discussion about transferring him back to Detroit. While others might have agitated for a transfer to Detroit, for his part, Solanus had reached a point in his spirituality that it did not matter where he was as long as he remained with the good God to whom he could give thanks any place, anytime. Commenting on the rumor that he might go back to Detroit, Solanus wrote his brother Edward:

> There is a possibility that I might be sent back to Detroit or elsewhere, though I hardly think it is at all probable. I have not the least worry about whether I remain here or be transferred. It is after all, essentially quite the same. It is such a surprising privilege to know definitely that one is doing God's will by keeping the rule and obeying. Sorry to say, if we can use the word, it is so little for any one of us to possibly appreciate such privileges.
>
> Indeed, just herein seems to me to be humanity's great weakness—WANT OF APPRECIATION. But again, how fortunate for us that God's mercy is above his works—and his patience is essentially one with his mercy.
>
> Blessed and praised be his holy Name![16]

Again gratitude to God in the form of appreciation was Solanus' approach. Whether it be for healings or transfers, he believed that appreciation should characterize everyone's relationship to God.

The outpouring of love for Solanus which had been shown by Detroiters at his Golden Jubilee of religious vows on Sunday, January 26,

1947, had made the superiors wonder if he should come back. The people of Detroit had not been told where Solanus was. Consequently, until then comparatively few had been in touch with him. However, when *The Detroit News* ran a story about his jubilee in its Saturday, January 25, 1946, edition, thousands came to celebrate with him—and to share with him their problems and requests for prayers.

Solanus had been asked to write a message on the back of a "holy card" which could be given the people as a memento of the occasion. Realizing that people would be looking for a message which summarized his awareness of God's work in his life and his love for God, Solanus wrote and rewrote his thoughts until they finally expressed what he was trying to manifest in his spirituality:

> PAX ET BONUM
> IN MEMORY OF MY
> GOLDEN JUBILEE IN RELIGION
> St. Bonaventure's Monastery
> Detroit, Michigan
> Thanks be to God for uncountable
> mercies—for every blessing!
> Thanks be to my neighbor for his
> charitable patience.
> Fifty years in the Order—almost unnoticed—have slipped
> away from me into eternity. Thither I hope to follow before
> half another fifty: trusting in the merciful goodness of God!
>> Fr. Solanus, O.F.M. Cap.
> DEO GRATIAS

If the superiors had had any second thoughts about not keeping Solanus at Huntington, the large number of people converging upon him at his jubilee in Detroit made them realize they had made a good decision to send him to the novitiate. Staying at St. Felix would be for his welfare. The rhythm of life there was more relaxed. It would be wrong to move him again.

Solanus returned to Huntington a week later laden with gifts, money, a chalice, vestments, an alb and altar linens. Once back at Huntington he wrote many "Thank Yous." High on the list was one to Fr. Simon Hesse, the Spiritual Director of the Third Order of St. Francis Fraternity (Secular Franciscans) at St. Bonaventure's. He and the Fraternity had hosted the celebration. True to the flowery and expansive way he loved to write, Solanus wrote his confrere:

> My Dear Confrere Simon: More than simply to say, "A thousand times many thanks" for your practical help in the elaborate preparations and actual celebration of the golden jubilee at dear St. Bonaventure's a few weeks back, I want to congratulate you and your dear tertiaries . . . and the members of the privileged Eucharistic Mission Band, on their beautiful, artistic generosity. One could hardly feel other than convinced without a second thought that they must all have worked in real Franciscan harmony. They masterly "put over" a fraternal, loyal display. May our dear Lord bless all and each who helped along.
>
> I am sure that, even aside from the solemn holy Mass it-self—whose very ceremonies, etc. I am assured brought tears to many a non-Catholic eye—was the mutually frater-nal simplicity of the whole proposition. It was a source of much happy edification. Writing later on, when the tension of excitement had gone (if there had been such), a certain Jew who attended and understood the beautiful prayers with the epistle and Gospel, assured me that he could not restrain his tears.[15]

Detroit, with its celebration and busy activity, was good to experi-ence again. But it was better to be back in the more reflective atmo-sphere of Huntington. Here Solanus could fit into the regular schedule of the novitiate community and be able to continue responding to peo-ple's needs in a less hectic, more measured manner.

Solanus developed a regular pattern at St. Felix. He arose before the community heard the 4:55 a.m. wood "clappers" that beat out their "sur-gi-te, fra-tres" rhythmically calling: "get up, brothers." He liked to spend that time in prayer before the others came to chapel. Most times he would be there when the rest of the community arrived for morning prayers at 5:15. While the community Mass would be celebrated at 6:15, Solanus would either participate in that or celebrate Mass "privately" at a side altar. After Mass he would join the community for breakfast (always in silence). At the breakfast table he continued his habit of mixing all the breakfast ingredients (from orange juice to cereal) together in his coffee bowl. At 8:00 he attended the Mass celebrated for the novices. Often he remained long afterward, absorbed in prayer. By the time the mail arrived at 9:30 he was ready to get to work answering letters.

Because of the increased correspondence and the difficulty he had in writing, Solanus was now given a secretary to keep track of the letters and requests coming to him.

Another reason why the superiors wanted someone to act as Solanus' secretary was that they had discovered that many letters containing money for various request had not been filed in the correct places. Some had not been answered. In following up people's requests as to what had happened, the superiors found money all over Solanus' room. He had simply taken it and not noted what it was for. There was need for better accountability.

One of the first secretaries was the newly ordained Fr. Blase Gitzen. As a boy he had served Mass for Solanus in Detroit. According to him:

> Generally, Fr. Solanus received from 30 to 40 letters a day. Since most of the letters contained money, it was my duty to open all his mail, find out what the money was for (Masses, Seraphic Mass Association, alms) and record these. Naturally, in looking through these letters I came across four or five in each mailing that were particularly pitiful cases. In my heart, I prayed that Fr. Solanus would answer these himself, and almost invariably, those were the letters he chose to answer personally. The rest I would acknowledge with a short note. In the course of the day, I would receive the answers he had crashed out on an old

battered typewriter. They were typed, mostly, on three by five cards. The spelling was bad, pure fifth-grade stuff, but the contents simply amazed me. With a few words he was able to come to the heart of the problem. His understanding of people, his sympathetic response, his grasp of theology just astounded me. He may not have passed his examinations, but his wisdom was far beyond mine.[18]

Many times Solanus would be interrupted in his room with telephone calls from people in need. Invariably after such telephone calls, he would go to the choir where he would kneel down and become very prayerful. Fr. Blase remembers that "at times he was so absorbed in prayer that it seemed he was in some sort of mystical state. At such times one could not get his attention by motioning or calling to him; he had to be shaken."[19]

Not only the needs of the people had to be brought to God; the problems of society did as well. Society's problems also caused Solanus to be concerned. In evidencing this concern, Solanus revealed a characteristic of an authentic mystic. Experiencing God's presence in his depths, Solanus could not only be sensitive to those realities, or shadows within himself that were obstacles to the divine experience; he had to be equally aware of the "sin of the world." It stood as illusion in face of God's truth which he had come to know in his depths. Thus his concern for the world, not only in Huntington, but beyond.

Although the Second World War ended while he was in Brooklyn, the arms race had begun. For him the invention of the atomic bomb seemed to be saying that somehow God was permitting "men without faith to be preparing the fearfully poisoned lightening fires, with which he will arm his angels of wrath on an adulterous, defiant, atheistic generation."[20] As he looked at the United States, Solanus believed that the nation was becoming increasingly consumeristic and materialistic. These attitudes evidenced the fact that "unbelievers" of every generation will run after such things (cf. Mt 6:31). Thus he wrote:

> What I'd like to stress is the very insanity of trying to reckon on anything material these days as amounting to

anything of importance aside from its use in promoting the glory of God and charity toward lifting humanity—and the necessarily very short time such material things hold their value.[21]

Rather than condemn society for its materialism and militarism, he dreamed of a world where people would use the world's resources to better humanity, especially those in need. This would be the way that the reign of God could be sought in the midst of a generation which ran "after these things." In contrast to the ideology of materialism, Solanus stressed the value of being concerned about its victims, the poor.

The poor were not very evident at Huntington except for the occasional "Knight of the Road." However when beggars did come, they would be met by Solanus and taken to a special room for food that they might eat in dignity. This was his way of fulfilling the scriptural command to be mindful of the poor (Gal 2:10). Solanus wrote around this time: "What a marvelously different society we would have here and what an ideal world we would have to live in if we all would keep in mind the assurance of Jesus, "What you have done to the least of my brethren, you have done to me."[22]

Around the time Solanus wrote this reflection, events made him keenly aware of the meaning of these words both in his own life and on the societal level of international relations.

On January 12, 1949, the Huntington house chronicle notes, "Fr. Solanus received the sad news that his priest brother Fr. Maurice Joachim passed away this morning."[23] The "least of" Solanus' brothers had suffered almost continually throughout his life because of nerves, unrealized dreams and misunderstandings. Now he had returned to hear Christ say "Come, blessed of my Father, inherit the reign prepared for you from the creation of the world." The fact that he could go to Maurice Joachim's funeral, reinforced by this conviction, brought Solanus much peace.

While he believed that his brother now was at peace, Solanus was deeply troubled by societal events that were making it clear from his perspective that there were sheep and goats in the world who did good and evil. The evil, in particular, had been personified in the trial of Cardinal Mindzenty in Hungary for alleged espionage during the early days of what is now known as the Cold War of the late 1940s and 1950s.

In his reflections on events surrounding the trial of the Hungarian Primate, Solanus showed the same indignation at perceived injustice against the innocent which he had shown twenty-five years earlier in his letter about the alleged British injustices against the Irish.

During the time after the Second World War the Soviet Union had brought under rapid control what were to become the satellite nations of Eastern Europe. This created a note of strong anti-atheistic, anti-communistic sentiment throughout the United States. Reinforced by the ideology of the Catholic press and the received theology about the church militant which must fight for truth and justice, especially when its rights were being maligned, Solanus believed his times called for continual fidelity and resistence.

The trial of Cardinal Mindzenty was front page copy for papers around the world. Writing at this time, Solanus offered a wider perspective to the events. In the midst of scandal and division, the wider perspective would come from the followers of Jesus in the forming of confidence:

> I hope this finds you well, which means of course hopeful too. This latter is something that is sadly overlooked (these days) to the great detriment of spiritual progress as well as physical.

> Probably the all-outstanding example of proof of this is the historical scandal that some of the disciples took at Jesus' choice of the CROSS AND CALVARY. There he establishes his Reign of Love rather than any other. This "scandal" drew from St. Peter himself, "Master, far be it from thee. . . !" This drew the alarming response: "Get behind me, satan. . . . You are not serving God."

> It is well to remember that such scandal was never intended to be confined to the Apostolic Age. Hence, S. Bernard, the

outstanding Doctor of the Middle Ages wisely reminds (us): "Since the scandal of the Cross, it is never reasonable to take scandal." Another occasion of the first disciples taking scandal is the detailed insistence of his giving us himself for our own life of soul: "I am the bread of life. Your fathers did eat manna in the desert and are dead. This is the bread which comes down from heaven; that if any man eat of it he may not die." (Jn 4:48)

Of course it is only natural for honest, upright people to resent falsehood and injustice as was St. Peter in striking off the brutal Malchus' ear. The same can be said of the wave of international indignation that the damnable hypocrisy manifest these days in the sacrilegious treatment of Cardinal Josef Mindzenty.[24]

Solanus' own resentment at society's lies and injustices was real. He said it was "natural for moral integrity to resent falsehood and injustice."[25] Despite his anger at the lack of truth around him, Solanus tried to keep his confidence in the more hopeful words of Jesus, "Fear not, I have overcome the world."

For Solanus, the trial of Cardinal Mindzenty revealed the diametric opposition to that reality upon which he founded his whole life—the existence, power and love of God. Since this God was so real for him, he could not imagine how any other reality except insanity or evil incarnate could believe in or promote atheism.

Around this time, Solanus had written a reflection called "THINK OVER" which developed his thoughts about knowing God and atheism. He had written:

If the primary purpose of my creation is to know my Creator, so that I may be happy in his loving service, and if no one but a fool can say in his heart, "There is no God," then the conclusion would seem to be that God's existence must be manifest, one way or other, to everyone that is not a fool, that every normal person able to think can and ought to recognize his Creator. . . .[26]

Solanus did not realize it then, but there are different ways of know-ing God. For him, religion itself was the *science* of our knowing and relating to God. However, trained by his Thomistic background to believe that all experience is rational, Solanus merely concluded that all experience of God had to be equally rational. Not realizing he was equating experience with rationality, Solanus betrayed his own *mystical* experience and, therefore, his mystical understanding of God. Since his experience of God was so real to him, it had to be rational. Thus, for him, only a true fool, who had no rationality, could say there was no God.

Religion cannot be reduced to the simply rational. At the same time, religion is not irrational. There is a realm of experience which cannot be probed or explained in terms of the intellect. It is, F. C. Happold notes, the "realm of the mystical."[27] Solanus had come to know God so intimately and mystically that he simply believed it had to be rational.

For Solanus, there were two ways of knowing God. The first form of knowing could only be reserved for the Beatific Vision. The other form was based on the first and greatest commandment—to know, love, and serve God; this could bring a taste of that Beatific experience to every-one. To *know* this God was the essence of life. To know God in this way is also the essence of mysticism.

It is very natural, then, that Solanus believed that, what we would call knowledge of God in the mystical life, had to be available to all:

> Self-understood there can be no thought of our knowing God in our present state directly and as he is known in heaven. Our privilege here is to start such knowledge as can be perfected only in the great, blessed Beyond. Nev-ertheless, if we stop to think as we ought to do, there must be ways and means close at hand whereby, according to the lives of the saints, we may if we try, to ascend to great sanctity and to an astonishing familiarity with God even here as pilgrims to the Beatific Vision.[28]

The "astonishing familiarity with God" which Solanus experienced "even here" was so real for him that he could not possibly believe that anyone but "the fool" could say there was no God. For this reason he decided that, once and for all, he would try to spearhead an effort open to all "atheists" to prove that God did not exist. Such an undertaking was true to this enterprising personality. When he saw an opportunity his determination directed him to take the first steps and work to meet his goals. The way he proposed that atheists could try to prove that God did not exist reflected a deeply creative imagination! He would inaugurate a contest with a million dollars available to whoever could prove the nonexistence of God.

Solanus had shared the dream about his "essay proposition" as he called it, with the provincial as well as his benefactors, including Mrs. Montgomery Ward Thorne. "Without effort" he noted, she "could donate the whole Prize ($1,000,000) and possibly will do as much."[29] People who showed similar interest ranged from other wealthy friends, like the O'Donnells in Chicago, to the former provincial of the Milwaukee Province of the School Sisters of Notre Dame, Mother Mary Fidelis.

Not willing to relinquish his dream when others challenged it, Solanus decided to further discuss his plan with the O'Donnells and Mother Mary Fidelis when he traveled to Milwaukee in April 1949. The specific purpose for the trip was not the essay proposition, however. He went to Milwaukee for the unveiling of the statue over the grave of his friend and co-worker, Fr. Stephen Eckert, O.F.M. Cap.

They had worked together during Solanus' first assignment at Sacred Heart in Yonkers. While the parishioners realized they had two very special Capuchins in their midst, each Capuchin regarded the other, not himself, as the special one. Solanus remembered Stephen as "a really earnest, zealous priest. He was always willing, not only willing, but solicitous, to help whom and where he might, without exception, high or low, rich or poor, learned or ignorant, Catholic or 'Atheist.' "[28]

Stephen Eckert had left Sacred Heart in Yonkers to begin a boarding school, St. Benedict the Moor, for blacks in Milwaukee. Since it was one of the few available in the Mid-West in those days of school segregation, it attracted students from all over the United States (includ-

ing notables such as Lionel Hampton, Red Foxx, and Mayor Harold
Washington of Chicago). Solanus deeply respected Stephen for his
commitment to racial equality; yet he also recalled his friend as a man of
deep prayer and introspection. "In fact, unless he could see an advantage toward doing some thing to benefit others, he was decidedly reti-
cent and preferred to be alone." Solanus recalled, "He was wont to
retire to Jesus in the Tabernacle as often as convenient without being
noticed, even in time of recreation."[29]

Soon after Stephen's death, people began to press for his canonization as "The Apostle of the Colored Race," who had pioneered in
breaking down racial stereotypes and barriers. Solanus himself had been
working to promote Stephen's cause at least since 1935. With the Superior at Detroit, he had easily persuaded the Felician Sisters there to
"mount some relics" from Stephen's habit to a prayer card with a
picture of Stephen.[32]

Part of the official process introduced in Rome was that Stephen
Eckert's body had to be exhumed. This took place in 1948, twenty-five
years after his death and burial in Mt. Calvary Cemetery in Wauwatosa,
Wisconsin (where Capuchins who died in Milwaukee were buried at
that time). Instead of reburying him in his grave, it was decided to place
his remains in a small courtyard on the grounds between Saint Benedict's Church and Saint Anthony's Hospital which had been built by
Stephen's successor because blacks in those days did not have adequate
access to good health care.

Part of the celebration of this next step in the canonization process
was the dedication of a larger-than-life statue of Stephen Eckert. Solanus and many other friars made sure they would be in Milwaukee for
the special dedication in April 1949.

The trip from Huntington was long, a good eight hours. Fr. Ambrose
deGroot recalled it well; for this time he was the driver:

> We arrived in Chicago from Huntington around supper
> time. Fr. Solanus said he knew some people in Chicago
> who would willingly give us something to eat. (They were
> the O'Donnell Family.) . . . It turned out they were

wealthy people who lived in one of the high rise apartments along Lake Shore Drive. We found ourselves ushered into a beautifully furnished apartment overlooking Lake Michigan, many stories from the ground level.

I personally felt embarrassed, calling on these people unannounced, and expecting an invitation to supper. I was rather amazed to see these people brighten up when they saw Fr. Solanus. They felt sincerely honored and just could not do enough for us. They called a caterer and had a beautiful dinner sent to the apartment. It was borrowed glory as far as I and the rest of us were concerned. It was Father Solanus all the way—the wealthy couple just hung on his words and just didn't know how to express themselves concerning the honor that had come to them.

Father Solanus took it all in stride and just did not notice the fuss made over him. To him these were simply good people who had told him that he would always be welcome in their home. And so he accepted the invitation. I imagine St. Francis felt and acted the same way when he visited the wealthy owner of Mt. Alverno and accepted his hospitality. Christ too visited the wealthy and ate with them (e. g., Lazarus, Martha, Mary, and also Zaccheus and others) and accepted their hospitality.[33]

Having shared the hospitality of the O'Donnell's (as well as quite probably his ideas on his "essay project"), the friars left thanking them for the fine ham dinner and kindness that had been shown them.

At Milwaukee the celebration brought hundreds of devotees of Stephen Eckert to the unveiling of the granite statue overlooking State Street. Afterwards all went next door to another ham dinner to continue the festivities. Little did Solanus and about twenty others know—the ham had been contaminated. It was ptomaine poisoning. In very graphic terms Solanus described how the illness hit him as he was visiting Mother Mary Fidelis, explaining his "million dollar essay Contest" at the School Sisters of Notre Dame Motherhouse, a mile from St. Benedict's:

> I mentioned the proposition to Rev. Mother Mary Fidelis, helpless invalid at the time, and afterwards to about fifty of her nuns. . . . Well, Mother Mary Fidelis and her nuns seemed quite interested and promised to pray the good God to bring it to success. I had hardly come to the parlor after blessing them with several relics and a little visit in the Chapel when I urged, "Sister, please get me a vessel quickly. I'll have to vomit. I'll wait right here on the floor."
>
> Luckily nothing came but strenuous wrenching 'til the vessel arrived, and then very little, with quite a relief of very short duration, again and again. Then the ambulance came and took the patient to St. Michael Hospital where he stayed about forty hours.[34]

"The patient" spent two days at St. Michael's Hospital which was next door to St. Francis Friary where Solanus had studied theology. Then he returned to St. Felix.

On the return trip from Milwaukee, some of the friars noticed Solanus rubbing his legs together as if they were itching. Once back at the friary, he walked very deliberately up the stairs to his room. It was a pace very unfamiliar to the man who was known even after seventy-five years to take the stairs at a run. As Solanus walked haltingly to his room, Fr. Blase met him. "I noticed something was wrong with his feet and legs," he recalls:

> After a bit of persuasion he finally let me look at them, and they were as raw as a piece of meat. We bathed the sox off and sent him at once to . . . the hospital in Fort Wayne. There the doctors recognized the seriousness of his condition. Fearing the loss of blood circulation, they prepared an operation room for probable amputation. Every three minutes a nurse checked his circulation.
>
> It was decided by the friars that word of his hospitalization would not be mentioned. We knew he was seriously ill, and we wanted him to get some rest. To my utter surprise, despite a big "DO NOT DISTURB" sign on the door, I

found fifteen people in the room the next day when I visited him. Some had come from as far away as Detroit. How they found him, I'll never know. But here He was, propped up in bed, with a white canopy over his legs, amiably chatting with his visitors. And sure enough, every three minutes, a disapproving nurse came in to check the pulse in his legs.

His attitude toward his illness was one of such lack of concern, that I was curious whether he knew how seriously ill he had been and brought up the subject on the way home from the hospital. Yes, he knew that his legs might have to be amputated, but he had the attitude: 'If they came off, it was alright; if not, that was alright, too.' He showed absolutely no shock, surprise, worry or upset. He knew, and said calmly, that it was caused by his allergy to ham.[35]

For Solanus the entire time at St. Joseph's Hospital seemed quite extended: "two long weeks—16 days"[36] he wrote his brother, Msgr. Edward. However, as he reflected on the experience, Solanus noted that, "according to the way one looks at difficulties and crosses, I was one of the dozens of unfortunate ones, although I would rather say fortunate ones. It was surely to nature a very unpleasant experience. But, thanks be to God, I feel that my soul profited greatly by the experience of about a month in the hospital. . . ."[37] Reflecting on the experience of suffering which St. Francis had endured, as well as those in the military who suffered during the recent World War, he continued:

It was a "bitter pill that turned to sweetness of soul and body," as St. Francis tells us in the Holy Rule, about his personal experiences with the poor, dear lepers of his day, and as many chaplains and soldiers tell of what they went through in the Second World War.[38]

For years Solanus had been having problems with his legs. Some doctors called his disease "weeping eczema"; others called it psoriasis. At any rate, the open sores caused by the disease gave Solanus great pain, especially in the last decade of his life.

On Christmas of 1947 his skin problem was so great that he had to stay in bed most of the day. At other times, the house *Chronicle* simply notes that Solanus "again" was having problems with his legs.

Because of its proximity Solanus usually went to Fort Wayne for doctoring. Once in a while, however, he would go to Detroit for relief. On those occasions he renewed acquaintances with old friends.

Fr. Cefai, from St. Paul Maltese Church in Detroit where Solanus had gone many years for weekend helpouts, recalls that Solanus knew that at St. Paul's he would always get a good meal to begin his return to the Motor City.

> Sometimes he would telephone my sister telling her he was on his way to St. Bonaventure's Monastery in Detroit, having come from Huntington, Indiana. As simply as a child he would ask her if he could have some of her sphaghetti on the way. He liked a glass of wine. He also liked Maltese cheese cakes.[39]

Like Francis of Assisi with the *mostacciolo* cakes of the Lady Jacoba di Settesoli (which he requested even as he was dying)[40], Solanus had his Maltese cheese cake; he knew a good deal when he ate one!

On one of his visits to Detroit, a young man by the name of James Allen Maher sought him out. "The first time I met Fr. Solanus was back in 1950," (he recalls):

> I went to see him at the Monastery on Mt. Elliott, and I told him I was thinking of going into religious life as a Franciscan Brother.[41] I had quite a conversation with him. He asked me where I worked and when I told him I worked for the railroad, he said he always liked the railroad, and then we got off on a conversation about Jessie James and his gang. He said that while he was a prison guard in Minnesota he had met Jim and Cole Younger who had been with Jessie James. He said he befriended Cole Younger, and Cole had given him a chest or clothes trunk for him to keep and he said, "I still have it."

Maher's reflections about Solanus—from his unique insights about James' own vocation to marriage rather than to celibacy, about Solanus' concern for hitchhikers, and about his prayerful presence and sensitivity to others for interpreting the law—are so clearly articulated by the young man, his reflections on spending a few hours with Solanus deserve to be quoted in full:

> I asked him whether he thought I had a vocation to the religious life, and he started asking me questions to see how much I knew about the Bible.
>
> He told me as I was leaving he thought I should wait awhile before I made a final decision to go into the monastery.
>
> I had gone down to see Fr. Solanus with a Franciscan Brother from Duns Scotus College. He wanted to talk to Fr. Solanus about some problems he was having. While he was in talking to him he asked Fr. Solanus if it was true he was going to Huntington, Indiana, the next day. Fr. Solanus said he was. Br. Rumold asked him if he had a ride down there and Fr. Solanus said he had a ride with a couple who said they would be happy to drive him, "but they are Protestants and I would rather go down with some Catholics, because I would like to say some prayers on the way down there, especially the rosary and it would be kind of awkward if I went down with this Protestant couple."
>
> So Brother told him he had a friend who had a car and that we would be happy to drive him down. As it turned out the Brother couldn't go. His superior wouldn't let him take the day off. So I drove him down myself. We left on Wednesday afternoon. I was supposed to pick him up in the morning, but about 10 o'clock in the morning, my car was not working right. The brakes needed fixing. I took it to a service station and had to wait a few hours for it. I called Fr. Solanus and told him. He said, "Get the car fixed and give me a call when it is ready." The car wasn't ready until about 3 o'clock in the afternoon. So I called Father again and he said that he would meet me at the service station.

When he got there he asked me if there was a Catholic Church nearby. I told him we were near the church I went to (Presentation Church on Pembroke and Meyers). So he said, "Let's go there and say some prayers before we leave for Huntington."

We drove over to the church and when we got inside he took out his rosary and said, "Let's say the rosary."

We left the church and started for Huntington about 4 o'clock. Father said he wanted to be there about midnight. So I thought we had better go pretty fast as I figured it would take about eight hours to get there.

On the way we came upon a hitchhiker. We were going so fast that by the time Fr. Solanus told me to stop and pick him up, we had gone quite a distance. Father said, "Well, we missed him. But if we come across any more hitch-hikers, stop and pick them up." We had not gone very far when we came upon another one. I stopped the car.

When the hitchhiker came over to the car, he looked pretty downcast. Father got out of the car and let him get into the back seat. As we started out, Father began asking him questions. He asked the hitchhiker where he was coming from. He said that he had just left Detroit and was on his way to Chicago to look for a job. Father asked him what happened in Detroit. The hitchhiker said, "I lost my job and couldn't seem to find another one. So I am going to Chicago. Maybe I'll have better luck there." Father asked him if he went to church. He said, "Yes, I am a Catholic."

The next town we were coming to was Niles, Michigan. Father said, "We had better stop to get something to eat." I said, "OK." Then Father asked the hitchhiker if he was hungry. He answered, "Yes. I haven't eaten for two days."

We stopped at a restaurant and pulled into the parking lot. Father had a cardboard box and a valise in the back seat of the car, so I locked the car.

We sat down in the restaurant. The hitchhiker ordered a hot beef sandwich. I ordered the same. Father ordered a plate of fish. While we were eating I noticed Father had pushed some fish toward the back of his plate with his knife. He seemed to be taking his time eating the fish that was in front of him.

The hitchhiker ate his hot beef sandwich up in no time at all. In fact, I hadn't eaten more than half of mine by the time he was through.

Father noticed this and asked him if he was still hungry. He said, "Yes, a little bit." So Father said, "I have this fish you can have. Hand your plate over." Father took his knife and put the fish on the hitchhiker's plate.

As we were leaving the restaurant, Father asked the hitchhiker if he had any money. He answered, "No." So Father gave him about $5.00, and I bought him some cigarettes.

Father said to the hitchhiker, "We are going to Huntington, Indiana, and you are going to Chicago, so we will have to separate here." The hitchhiker said, "Well, I sure appreciate your helping me. I wish I could repay you for what you've done." Father answered, "Well, we are happy to do it. But there is one thing that you can do for us. When you get to Chicago, will you go to the nearest Catholic church and say a prayer for poor sinners." The hitchhiker responded, "Yes, I'll do that!" We then went to the car.

When we got to the car I took the keys out of my pocket to open the door. Father reached in front of me and opened the locked door. I stood there thinking I must be going crazy. I said, to Father, "that's odd, I thought I locked the door" and he said, "Oh?" I dropped the subject, but still was puzzled and wondered about it for years. . . .

When we got to Huntington it was about 12:30 A.M. Thursday morning. We first went to chapel. Father wanted to thank God for being with us on the trip. After praying, Father bent down and kissed the floor in front of the altar. I might add that we also said the rosary about three times on the way down.

After we left the chapel, he asked me if I was hungry. "Yes," I said. "But it is after 12:00 o'clock and I wanted

to go to Mass and Communion in the morning.'' Father
said, ''Oh, that's all right. It's only after 11:00 o'clock
Detroit time and that's the time we are going by.''

Father cut some homemade bread for me and gave me
some milk and honey for the bread. After eating he showed
me where I was to sleep for the night.

Thursday morning I was awakened by one of the brothers
and I went to Mass at 6:30 A.M. in the chapel. Father was
celebrating Mass at a side altar. He was like he was in
another world.

I had a nice visit with Father afterward. I had asked him a
lot of questions on the trip, such as, ''Why is it some people
have told me you have powers to cure people?'' He said, ''I
don't cure anyone, God does it.'' I said, ''Well, people say
you bless them and they are cured of different ailments.''
Solanus answered, ''I have a relic of the true cross and the
apostles which I bless people with. If God wishes to cure
them, they will be cured if they have the faith.''

Father gave me this definition of an atheist and an agnostic. He said, ''An atheist is a person who knows there is
a God, but denies it, as he wants to live life his own way.
He continually tells himself there is no God and finally
convinces himself there isn't, and eventually gets to the
point in life where he has completely convinced himself
there is no God.'' He said that this is a form of insanity.

''An agnostic is a person who is looking for God and
can't see him nor can he establish any reasoning to prove
there is one. But eventually this person will find proof there
is a God. It may take him some time but he will eventually
find the proof there is a God.''

I left Fr. Solanus after he gave me those definitions. I got
back to Detroit that afternoon just in time to go to work.[42]

Just the fact that a young man like James Maher would happily
volunteer to take Solanus to Huntington from Detroit (a good four-hour
trip in those days) and immediately return for another four-hour trip
attests to the kind of aura and veneration people had for him. Whether

they were young or old, black or white, rich or poor, Protestant, Jew, or Catholic, people jumped at the chance to be with this man.

While people continued to come to Solanus about their sicknesses, their marriage problems, or like James Allen Maher, about vocational choices, Solanus' skin ailments gave him no relief. On June 16, 1950, he was taken again to St. Joseph Hospital in Fort Wayne because of the sores on his legs; he stayed two weeks. Far from being depressed by the lack of healing in his own body, he felt comfort believing "whoever is dear to me I—chastise" (Rev 3:19).

Given his ability to bring a contemplative approach to life, Solanus not only recognized God's hands in his sickness, he was able to use his recuperation—which often took him out-of-doors—to deepen his confidence in God and contemplation of nature. Soon after his return to the novitiate he wrote that his reflections on nature reminded him of earlier, happier days:

> I was in St. Joseph Hospital, Fort Wayne, a couple of weeks myself recently. Thanks be to God for the same and thank him doubly I am back at St. Felix since last Friday. It is quiet here just about a mile from town. With other birds that entertain, I am listening to the simple call of the turtle dove and the quail, so familiar more than seventy-five years back. Their old "bob white" call is musical now. Perhaps because, like an old-time song, it brings back memories of innocent days, maybe, happier dreaming. Deo gratias.[43]

Solanus' union with God, the Creator, brought him into a deep union with all of God's creation. An evening sunset could bring words of profound delight from him. The beauties of nature could hold him wrapped in thanks for long periods of time. Of all creatures bees especially were his love. Often on his strolls through the orchards and vineyards of St. Felix, he would stop near the beehives. There he would sit, reflecting on the beauty of those creatures.

Now and then bees would alight on his hand. As he would watch them move around his hand and around his fingers, Solanus would be utterly fascinated by their intricate construction and operations. He would often say some words of praise, such as: "My dear God, how could you have created such a marvelous thing!" Because he was so relaxed with the bees, Solanus was asked to become the assistant beekeeper. Each class of novices seemed to have its own story about the credulous soul who would come upon Solanus talking to a bee as he held it in his room or in the friary corridor. He then would be asked by Solanus to take the bees outside. Inevitably, the stories noted, the novice would be bitten.

Now and then Solanus himself would get stung. While the stings never really upset him, it was different with Fr. Elmer Stoffel, the novice-master. He also helped to take care of the bees. Fr. Elmer remembers how Solanus "was in the habit of soothing them by playing his harmonica." One day, around 1950, he was stung by three bees. He fell to the ground in great pain. Seeing his co-worker in such agony, Solanus gestured a simple blessing toward him. Immediately, Fr. Elmer recalls, the pain left; he had no ill effects whatever.[44]

Although Solanus had much more time to enjoy nature and to use it for contemplative reflection, the people's growing discovery that he was at Huntington brought more and more to the friary door. Often, they arrived by the busload. Soon the friars got used to the hundreds who called or came regularly. The August 13, 1950, house chronicle notes matter-of-factly: "Brother Gabriel, a Conventual Franciscan from Chicago came to visit Fr. Solanus. As there were so many people to visit Fr. Solanus today, Brother Gabriel remained overnight so that he could visit with Fr. Solanus Monday morning."[45]

To all the people who wanted to talk with him, Solanus was equally gracious, open and kind. He might initially show frustration when someone like Br. Pius Cotter would come to his room telling him of a phone call or a front office visitor. But such a look revealed an initial emotional reaction, the kind that comes when one is interrupted in thought or other preoccupations. Within a second or two, Solanus' face would move from a frown to his broad Irish smile. He then would get up and go to talk to the person in need.[46]

Although more people came to visit Solanus, the numbers never reached the peak days of Detroit. While the numbers of people did not increase, however, the volume of mail did. This growth demanded additional help from secretaries. One of his first secretaries was Fr. Blase Gitzen. He had a good working relationship with Solanus. However, their personal relationship was not really friendly, partly because "close friendships were looked on askance in those days."[47] "I reverenced him, but did not stand in awe of him," Blase recalled:

> He was genuine, kind and understanding, but I hardly ever had a heart-to-heart conversation with him. In some ways he offended my Prussian regularity and orderliness. He had money on him (which he just stuffed into his habit pockets) and money all over his room (which he stuffed into the cubby holes of his desk, or used as page markers). And he didn't know to which account that money was to be credited.
>
> So one day, with the blessing of the superior, I went through his room and collected $153. He never said anything, but I got the impression that he wasn't very pleased that I cleaned up his room. Not that he cared about the money. He never took care of it because he just couldn't care less. But I lost his place in many a book![48]

It was Solanus' character not to let his feelings be known. Similarily, he did not let his strong opinions or inner convictions get in the way of relationships, especially if fraternal charity might be upset. While he had very definite opinions about issues and would make them known—especially when issues of truth and justice were at stake—he usually tended to keep his feelings to himself. However, in some cases sensitive friars in the community could pick up his feelings. Especially in matters of justice and the defense of the rights of others (not his own), they could sense when Solanus had strong feelings about this world event or that friary incident.

One such case dealt with the decision to construct a swimming pool in the backyard. In order to build it, some of the apple trees had to be cut down. This decision created problems for Solanus for both poverty and aesthetic reasons. He judged the pool to be unnecessary and un-Franciscan. However, when it was explained that the novices (who never were allowed out) might get a little release for their pent-up emotions, and that the novices themselves would be building the pool, Solanus actually came to see merit in the idea. He made a point of being one of the building "inspectors" at the construction site each afternoon during his "jog" outdoors.

Besides his jogging (really a fast walk), there were other rituals Solanus regularly performed during his afternoons. At noon he would eat with the community. Then he went to the "Priests' Recreation Room" (in those days the Brothers and Novices each had their own recreation rooms). Sometimes he would tell tales about his family and childhood (often repetitious) or listen to stories from the others. Other times he would play billiards. Fr. Blase recalls, "He was no hot shot, but he joined me often in playing billiards. He didn't make it obvious, but he was trying to make me feel at home, especially since none of the other priests were interested in billiards."[49]

At 1:30 he would take a "siesta" until 2:00 or 2:30. If he had finished his mail, he would often walk outside, watch the construction of the swimming pool, do some pruning in the orchard, or hoe weeds from the garden or ground paths. Often he would walk up and down the paths around the friary, many times praying the "Little Office of the Blessed Virgin." He would say the Office with the community at 5:00. At 6:00 he would join the community for supper, followed by a short recreation and night prayers at 7:15. His evenings were usually spent in his room, reading and praying (from books that no longer could be marked with the dollar bills but with "holy cards").

If he had had no exercise during the day, he would run around the paths of the friary and orchard, "to keep in trim," he would say. For him jogging was as good for health as was a proper diet. Fr. Blase recalls, "He loved to run, especially up and down stairs. After awhile, we were able to judge the state of his health by the way he managed the stairs. If he ran, he was feeling well; if he walked, something was wrong."[50] Other ways Solanus "kept in trim" were by playing tennis and volleyball even when he was eighty. In everything he did, he enthusiastically played with all his energy. If he'd stumble or fall, he'd pick himself up and continue as intensely and concentrated as ever—a sign of a healthy competitiveness he never abandoned. Such energy and enthusiasm applied not only to sports but to his life in general.

In 1952 the Province of St. Joseph split between its Eastern and Midwestern sections. The New York–New England branch was given the name St. Mary's Province. The Detroit-to-Montana branch kept the name St. Joseph's. Solanus chose to be part of St. Joseph's Province. Thus, after the split, it was decided he would stay at Huntington.

With fewer novices, it was decided that the novitiate for the priest-candidates would return to Detroit. St. Felix in Huntington would be the college. Thus any friar who was a cleric-novice from 1946 until 1952 would have experienced Solanus at Huntington. Many of the recollections of the young Capuchins at that time have helped balance the image of Solanus from one who never showed negative human emotions to a person who could get periodically agitated at typical novitiate pranks, critical over little things that he thought were important (such as his concern in a Midnight Mass sermon to the novices that some friars were trimming their beards), to his insistence that Mass start on time—not because of personal hardship to himself, but because the people "who made a great sacrifice to come in the first place, might not be further inconvenienced."

There were other times when his deep emotions were not always kept under his usual control, although with age and wisdom, emotional flareups seldom if ever occurred. When he did show anger, it arose not from selfish reasons but in reference to a cause for justice or in reference to faith and confidence in God. When some might question whether God would really forgive sins or answer prayers for needs, there were times that Solanus' eyes would either flash in momentary anger or well up in tears. Then he would ask, his voice a tone or so higher, "Aren't we going to let the Lord do anything?"

Various other secretaries succeeded Fr. Blase. In June 1953 Br.
Booker Ashe took over as Solanus' secretary. When Booker had come
to Huntington as a postulant in 1951, he made such a positive impression on Solanus that he had written to his friend, Br. Leo, "Thank God
we have a very promising bouquet of brother-candidates, including a
very carefree, happy darky."[51]

Even in those days, for black people, the term "darky" was insulting
and derogatory. However, when uninformed white people, such as
Solanus, used the terms "carefree" and "darky" they were used,
subjectively in a positive way, even if they were paternalistic. With
Booker's profession as a Capuchin Franciscan and his assignment to
ultimately act as Solanus' secretary, the two struck up a deep relationship of mutual trust. Booker recalls that Solanus' effect on him was
profound as well as prophetic:

> In those days the young brothers were sort of lost at
> Huntington, and we did not receive much instruction. I
> personally went through a great deal of trepidation and inde-
> cision within my own self. I think it was through his encour-
> agement that I was able to persevere. He told me that I
> would make solemn profession, that I would see my twenty-
> fifth jubilee, and that I would help to bring about a lot of
> changes in the Province. Now I think that many of those
> things have really come to pass. He even told me that I
> would do things that no brother had ever done.[52]

Solanus' prophecies about Booker proved true in all cases. After
various other assignments around the Province, Booker helped found
and direct "The House of Peace" in Milwaukee, a large direct-ministry
and service program for the inner city poor. His visibility in Milwaukee
brought many civic leaders to his small office for consultation. He
served on many government commissions. He became the first brother
in the history of the modern Capuchin Franciscan Order to become a
provincial councilor, serving for two terms. He was president of the
Clergy group of the National Office of Black Catholics and represented

the North American Capuchins at the plenary council of the Capuchin Order which dealt with the theme of "Prayer" at Taize, France. The awards he won and the testimonies to his service and creative talents (he directed various high-school plays for years, receiving awards for outstanding performances) are myriad. Certainly he proved Solanus' prophecy true that he would "do things that no brother has ever done."

According to Br. Booker, Solanus' way of communicating with people seeking help was somehow continued through him. Often Booker experienced a power within him that was able to say just the right thing in the right way at the right time. The good Solanus did for others was able to be continued through Booker:

> I was quite concerned at first. I wanted to know if he was going to dictate all the letters, but then I quickly discovered that, no, he didn't have to dictate them. Everyday, I opened his mail, read it and informed him as to what people were writing about and he usually had a word or so to say to people and somehow I was able to get them out. I think it was sort of a miracle in itself, because I certainly was never experienced in that. The letters just came off. And, they were, I must admit, rather beautiful. I'm not an experienced typist but I used to sometimes get out a hundred or two letters a day. And around the various holidays like Christmas, Thanksgiving, Feast of St. Francis, his name day and other days like that, mail would just double or triple.
>
> If I asked him a direct question that someone wrote, he usually would tell me what to write back. Otherwise he would tell me just a word or two to write. He would sometimes say, "Well, you tell Mrs. so and so that she doesn't have to worry about that. She doesn't have to see the doctor again, or, when she sees him again, he will discover there was nothing wrong. But she really doesn't have to because it may be a waste of money since she had to pay a price to see him."
>
> Sometimes people would write back in reply to those kinds of prophecies. At one time, I kept a separate file of

such replies. What happened to them after I left, I don't know. But I would say that during the time I worked for Fr. Solanus, there must have been five or six hundred such letters from people who were helped through his words of encouragement, through his prayers, and so on.

It made me very humble, too, because people would write back and thank him for the beautiful letters and words of encouragement. It was what they really needed to resolve the problems they wrote about. Even though I typed it, I looked upon it, certainly, as Fr. Solanus' words.

Usually we put his rubber stamp on the letters because at that time it would have taken him several minutes just to sign one letter. He was a very popular person in that sense, that so many people wrote to him for his prayers and his help.[53]

Besides answering letters for Solanus and taking care of hospitality for the many guests who came to see him, Br. Booker also acted as Solanus' driver. He recalls:

Whenever I had to drive him anyplace, we always said the rosary. Then we always talked about Christ "in Francis." He very seldom ever talked about Francis without Christ. Christ was always there. Whenever he would relate something to Francis, it was always turned to Christ. And he sort of impressed that upon you, and always so beautifully done. It was always important to Fr. Solanus to get Christ in everything.[54]

Besides centering his life around Christ, Solanus continued to develop his own devotion to the Blessed Virgin and to promote Marian devotion in others. Besides the rosary, he always tried to pray the Little Office of the Blessed Mother. Often he would go to the infirmary where his classmate, Fr. Damasus, lived in blindness. He would pray the Little Office of the Blessed Virgin with him.

The 1950 proclamation of the Dogma of the Assumption of Mary had special significance for Solanus. It seemed to strengthen him in his commitment to spread to others the writings about the Blessed Virgin contained in Mary of Agreda's *The Mystical City of God*. Around the time of the proclamation he wrote that the proclamation, as well as the "unprecedented progress in the blooming and ripening these later decades and generations in 'Devotion to Mary,' "[55] demanded some kind of narrative of the Blessed Virgin's life. For him, such a biography of Mary could be found in the writings of the Spanish mystic.

While Solanus loved to joke and had a quick wit, if jokes were directed to or about matters of piety, especially about the Blessed Virgin or the Saints, he did not hesitate to correct those who did so. Someone who experienced his fraternal correction was his own local superior, Fr. Francis (then Thomas Aquinas) Heidenreich. He recalls:

> One time we were in the recreation room. I jokingly referred to "Mary O'Grady!" He said, "We should never speak disparagingly of people, especially holy persons. Mary of Agreda has been recognized by the Church as a holy person."[59]

In a special way, Solanus considered devotion to Mary very important as a stem to the perceived increase in atheism. Like many in the 1950s, Solanus saw atheistic communism all over. The fifties were the era of Joe McCarthy from Appleton, Wisconsin. He had many avid supporters among the Capuchins at that time. The fact that he was from Appleton and often worshipped at St. Joseph's where Solanus celebrated his First Mass made his words and anticommunism all the more convincing to someone like Solanus. As he had supported the anticommunism of Rev. Charles Coughlin in the thirties, that loyalty was easily transferred to McCarthy. Joe McCarthy was said to have found a communist in every movie studio and in the very halls of Congress. For his part, the gullibility of Solanus Casey was able to be exploited with stories about communists in religious orders and seminaries. Solanus was not reluctant to share such stories with others. Writing to a Grand Rapids Dominican Sister during the height of McCarthyism, it was clear that, while Solanus might have intuitions about matters of the Lord, they were not always paralleled in his social analysis:

There is such a thing as "red communism" stealing into convents and monasteries. Very clever young men have been known to offer themselves as candidates for the Order who have turned out after months, sometimes after years, to have been nothing more than secret promoters of unrest and red communism. Such candidates, I have heard of and in one case at least have known to show themselves very clever and experienced and naturally older than real promising candidates. They are in their late 20's or even middle 30's and, of course, are not too fervent at all, even though they keep the rule fairly to the letter.

Of course, to suspect anyone deliberately without a con-science [sic] observance and prayer, is a rather dangerous course. Nevertheless, self-preservation and "charity begins at home" where right order and charity always must begin. Superiors especially are expected to be on the alert concerning any subject who persists in refusing to speak to, or associate with any other member of the religious family.[57]

It would be wrong to single out Solanus Casey as unique in his anticommunism; it was simply all-pervasive in the early and mid-1950s.

Possibly Solanus' bias and closed-mindedness regarding the "communist threat" were founded; perhaps they were not. Only a history not-yet written will reveal the truth. Possibly because he was in so much pain himself, Solanus' inner frustration was able to be projected onto these "unknown" communists who were seen infiltrating their way into American life and institutions.

As for his physical pains, Solanus continued to receive doctoring in Fort Wayne and Detroit. Throughout 1951, he spent much time in Fort Wayne getting relief. In 1952 he was in Grace Hospital in Detroit. There he made a great impression on those who tried to help him. The fact that he didn't want anyone to make his bed, but would make it himself, contributed to make him so popular that, when he left the hospital, "doctors, nurses, patients and visitors all formed two lines from his room to the entrance door all seeking his blessing."[58] In 1953 he referred to himself as a "poor, clodding, stupid brother—just at the present a stumbling, three-fourths invalid."[59] In May 1954 blisters broke out all over his body when a doctor gave him the wrong medicine to combat an infection.

Despite his failing health and "semiretirement," Solanus continued to actively promote the missionary activity of the Capuchins through the Seraphic Mass Association. After almost fifty years of encouraging people to join in this effort, word of his activity reached Fr. Benignus, the head of the Capuchin-Franciscans in Rome. He wrote a letter of commendation for Solanus' untiring effort on behalf of the worldwide Capuchin mission:

> Dear Father Solanus,
> We have heard, through Our Secretary General for the Missions, Very Rev. Fr. Tiziano of Verona, of your magnificent work for the Seraphic Mass Association. Fr. Tiziano was very eloquent in your praise; and when We Ourselves examined the details of your work We realized the justness of his words. Further, knowing that you are no longer young in years We could not but marvel at your tremendous zeal and energy, both of which reveal a heart and will still youthful.
> . . . If your marked success in that work gives Us a paternal joy and pride, must it not be for you, in the inner recesses of your heart, a source of great consolation.
> We feel that you, dear Father, will deplore even this little publicity, making your own the counsel of Our Lord: "when you have done all these things, say we are unprofitable servants." Yet, whilst respecting that sentiment, We wish to thank you very sincerely for your grand work, and We pray the Lord of the harvest to grant you many more fruitful years.[60]

Solanus never answered the letter; yet it brought him much encouragement. It was a great support to receive in the face of declining health and abilities.

Even though he was not well, it did not deter him from preparing for the Fiftieth Jubilee celebration to the priesthood at the end of July 1954.

During the middle of July, *The Detroit Times* ran a feature story about the upcoming celebration of his ordination. It noted that the jubilarian, Fr. Solanus:

> . . . at 83 stands amazingly erect, although his tall frame is gaunt in its brown homespun habit from many decades of fasting and self-denial.
>
> But his most striking characteristics are his eyes and his voice. The eyes . . . are the eyes of a man 50 years younger. At times they are shrewd and penetrating, but when he speaks of his faith they shine like the eyes of a child.
>
> His voice is low and warm and somehow it can make his simplest remark sound like a benediction.[61]

Offering his own personal reflections as to why God had been so powerful in others' lives through his fifty years of ministry, Solanus merely stressed the need to come to know God and God's power and to translate that into active concern for others: "One need not be a priest to be an instrument in God's hands. If a man lives as he should, he will be given the knowledge to aid people. And if we are interested in saving souls we must have an interest in others,"[62] he concluded.

On the day of the jubilee celebration, Solanus was feted along with the house superior, Thomas Aquinas (Francis) Heidenreich and Cuthbert Gumbinger (who later became Archbishop of Smyrna, Turkey). The latter two celebrated their silver jubilee of ordination. Fr. Clement Neubauer, who was at Huntington between terms as Minister General of the worldwide Capuchin Franciscans, preached the sermon. He based his words on the Magnificat. He compared the joy of the jubilarians to that of the Blessed Virgin Mary at the time of her visit to her cousin Elizabeth.

By this time, Solanus no longer seemed to need the attention and respect of others as he had in his earlier years. He no longer even desired to be recognized. However, the large turnout of people showed how recognized he had become.

Due to the large crowd, the Mass was celebrated at St. Mary's in

Huntington. The dinner was held a couple of blocks away at Saints Peter and Paul. The meal began at noon and did not conclude until 3:00 "due mainly to the number and length of the after-dinner-speeches." The house chronicle noted: "It was a terribly hot day and not too conducive to sitting in one place for a long time."[63] Solanus concluded the day with a thank-you talk, stressing as usual his main theme: the need to show gratitude and thanks to God. He recognized that a great deal had been given to others in his life; yet Solanus secretly wondered if he had been as successful as the people made him out to be. At any rate, God should get the glory.

Solanus was firmly committed to the life he had chosen. In fact, by his jubilee, Solanus' concern and interest and intensity in matters of God and religion was as strong as ever. He had never stopped his inward journey, searching ever deeper into himself and his calling that he might be more faithful.

The day after his jubilee, Solanus and Br. Pius Cotter were talking. In that conversation Solanus let slip an underlying motive for his seeming bravado in making sure that people would "thank God ahead of time" for favors-to-be-received. When Pius asked Solanus why he always urged people to "thank God in advance for the grace you are about to receive," Solanus said: "It's like putting God on the spot." After all, didn't Jesus say, "Ask and you will receive" (Mt 7:7). Solanus, in his simple, direct faith, was not at all ashamed to take Jesus at his word. In this way, by Jesus' promise, people could always "put God on the spot" and assume that God would be faithful.[64]

Some months after the jubilee celebration, under the inspiration of Mr. and Mrs. Daniel Ryan of Detroit, a "purse" was raised and presented to Solanus totalling $6,000. As Solanus read the list of hundreds of donors—who had given donations from 25¢ to $100, tears of thanks glistened in his eyes. Nothing like this, he managed to say, had ever happened to him before. Repeating his oft-used phrase in thanking God and the people who had been so generous, he said, "The first sign of intelligence is gratitude to God." The money was used to redecorate the chapel at St. Felix.

People might expect that someone whose official assignment was "retirement," who had just celebrated fifty years in the priesthood, and who also happened to be eighty-five years old would now slacken his efforts a bit. While Solanus' legs definitely slowed him down, his pace with counseling people in person and by letter did not let up. In all his dealings with the people he maintained his deep sensitivity. He continually urged them to get involved in resolving their problems by showing some deepening of their relationship with God or by doing something good for others. These efforts, he was convinced, were one reason why results did come. It was important that these "extra" acts manifest confident faith, he wrote his sister Margaret Therese in October 1954:

> Last Palm Sunday we had quite the cause for celebration here. It came from Wyandotte, Michigan. A certain Mrs. Magolan called from that suburb of Detroit, saying, "Father, we were figuring on coming down to Huntington next Sunday. But my husband had like a stroke this morning and we don't know where we're at. He is not himself."
>
> That was Thursday, about 9:00 A.M. This family for several years had been bringing at least one bus load of people down to the Corpus Christi celebration. They have wonderful faith.
>
> "Oh, Mrs. Magolan!" I answered. "Where is your faith? I'll tell you. Get your friends to start a triduum of Holy Communions for the glory of God on that day and at the same time in thanksgiving for his answer to our prayers. We will all be helping tomorrow, Saturday and Sunday."
>
> "Oh!" she exclaimed. "That is grand."
>
> I could almost see the tears in her voice. I said nothing to anyone further about it. But in the meantime I was appointed for the High Mass at 8:00. . .
>
> Mr. Magolan was the first to receive Holy Communion. He had driven himself about half way, 175 miles. Deo gratias. I'd never seen him before look so well. He's been 100 percent himself ever since.[65]

With stories like this being circulated around the Midwest, New York and the West Coast, where Margaret lived, more and more strangers were seeking Solanus' advice and prayers, to say nothing of the regular callers and writers who had known of Solanus for many years. One of these "strangers" who sought Solanus' help and who ended up experiencing a very helpful and human person was Frank J. Brady, the president of Frank J. Brady Company of Huntington Woods, Michigan. He noted:

> My wife, Katherine M. Brady, was seriously ill approximately in 1955 or 1956. She was in traction in the hospital waiting surgery on a calcified disc in her neck between the fifth and sixth vertebrae. She was in constant pain and could not sleep nights because of it. Her condition had developed into degenerative arthritis due to a whiplash injury incurred when she was a young girl and was in an accident in which her head had gone through the windshield. She had been to a neurosurgeon. The operation had been decided upon as a last resort. Because the operation was so close to the brain, chances of survival were slim.
>
> I had heard of Fr. Solanus for years, but I had never met him. He was then stationed at St. Felix Friary, Huntington, Indiana. A friend of mine, Clarence C. Wetzel, suggested a telephone call to Fr. Solanus. I talked to Fr. Solanus and told him my wife was in the hospital and was going to have the operation. We had four children. He listened for a minute and then said, "Oh, no, she won't have the operation. She'll be all right. She'll be out in a few days. She'll be back with those children. Now, tell me how the Tigers are doing."[66]

It was as uncomplicated as that. Mrs. Brady would be healed. The next item of business was to find out the latest score for the Detroit Tiger's baseball team and where they ranked in the standings. Healing and baseball could all be made part of God's glory. While Solanus might have been pressured in the face of trying to meet the needs of others, he never lost his human touch. He could never abandon the baseball roots. He was a real fan of the Tigers.

Mrs. Brady came home without the operation and gradually improved. "As far as I am concerned," Frank Brady noted, "It was miraculous."[67]

However, just as he had heard of Fr. Solanus from others and sought his help in time of trouble, so Mr. Brady became one more fan of Fr. Solanus. Frank Brady too would tell others about the power God was manifesting to many through the Capuchin at St. Felix. One of the people to whom Brady told his story was a nurse whose mother was seriously ill:

> I suggested that the nurse call Fr. Solanus. She did telephone him in Huntington. Fr. Solanus said, "Your mother is quite old. God wants her." The mother died two days later. The daughter, being prepared by Fr. Solanus, was reconciled to her mother's death."[68]

Where did Solanus get this prophetic gift to make such utterances? Certainly a thorough analysis of his personality, or even his handwriting at that time, would show that he had virtually no natural intuitive abilities. His gift could have only come from another source beyond himself. Living in union with the Spirit, he was able to draw on the charism of prophecy from that same Spirit and use it to build up the members of the Body of Christ (cf. Rom 12; 1 Cor 12).

Although his own body might be failing, he was being inwardly renewed by this Spirit of Christ who continued to work through him, not only manifesting God's power in signs and wonders, but doing so in a way of Capuchin joy. The house *chronicle* noted on July 21, 1955, that:

> Fr. Solanus, although 85, is still as busy as ever, consoling all the people that come to him. Despite the fact that he receives many calls every day, he is a model to all in his faithfulness to religious exercises. His favorite pastime is

killing the weeds on the lawn and of course he is never without his gracious smile.[69]

Solanus' gracious smile covered tremendous suffering. His pain was both physical and emotional. At times the agony from his "weeping eczema" and varicose veins was almost unbearable; in unguarded moments, an attentive friar could see Solanus wincing in pain.

His physical suffering was compounded by his concerns about the troubles in the world. While no cause of his own pain could be diagnosed, he consistently diagnosed society's problems arising from materialism and atheism. Even though he felt strongly about these "sins of the world," he was able to sublimate this strong aversion to them and was able to give the impression of wholesome peace and joy; a real sign of his union with God.

By early January 1956, Solanus' pain was becoming so great that it was quite difficult to hide. Since no further relief could be found in Huntington or Fort Wayne, it was decided that he should be driven to Detroit by the brother infirmarian, Br. Gabriel Badalamenti. They left on January 12 amid wishes that things would go well with the doctors, so that, as it had happened many times in the past, Solanus would return to Huntington quickly.

This time, events would not let those wishes be fulfilled.

CHAPTER EIGHT
The Last Year
January 12, 1956–July 31, 1957

Within a week of his arrival in Detroit, part of Solanus' health problems was diagnosed as skin cancer. The resulting operation was successful, and it was concluded that Solanus' overall condition was not that serious. For a man with his skin problems and his age, he was in quite good shape. However, it was decided that he should stay longer in Detroit for recuperation and doctoring.

On February 15, 1956, Solanus received the news that his brother Patrick had died in Seattle. Just a few months before another brother, Owen, had died in Seattle as well. The combined loss of two more brothers was difficult for Solanus. When his brother, Msgr. Edward came to visit him in late February, the two of them realized more fully that now only they, Margaret (LeDoux), and Genevieve (McCluskey) were left of the sixteen children of Bernard and Ellen Casey. Their days too were numbered.

Although Solanus' days might be numbered, he was not willing to sit around counting them. His energy was as vibrant as ever. In fact his love for people now seemed almost boundless. He was ready to continue his counseling in the front office of St. Bonaventure's as he had done for so many years before. However, the local superior and doctor had other thoughts.

Even though Solanus wasn't ready to slow down, to their mind Solanus was just too weak to bear the burden of the continual stream of people who would be coming once they knew their friend and helper

225

was back in Detroit. It was decided that the friars were not to talk about Solanus' presence at St. Bonaventure's. Solanus too was asked by the superior, Fr. Bernard Burke, not to let people know he was in Detroit. Despite all efforts, however, the word did leak out. This made it more necessary than ever to be insistent that Solanus' visits be curtailed. Solanus accepted the restrictions without complaint. By now the frustrations he had in his earlier years had passed, as had his temper and argumentativeness. Even though inwardly his Irish defiance made him want to be with those in more difficulty than himself, he respected the wishes of his superior. This made a deep impression on Fr. Bernard. For him Solanus' obedience

> showed up during the final two years of his life when I was his superior. We had to limit his acceptance of phone calls and visits to the monastery office because of his feebleness. He was asked not to go to the phone or the front office without special permission in order to save his strength. To my knowledge, he complied with my wishes in this regard.[1]

Complying with such orders for Solanus was never easy. At this time in his life his will power and determination seemed strengthened anew. Why couldn't he be with the people? Acceding to this request was doubly difficult, yet he did so willingly. Solanus not only had deep pastoral concern to meet the people's needs (which he placed before his own health needs); his natural dispositon was to be very independent. He loved his freedom and mobility. Again, his natural tendency was to debate the wisdom of his superiors. Such restriction on his availability was not easy, from an emotional consideration, to accept. "Why won't they let me see the people?" Solanus asked Br. Ignatius one day.[2] His question was not so much an undermining of his superior's decision but a frustration that he could not be about his ministry as his spirit led him. However, even though he might chaff under the obedience, his will power was stronger. He wanted his will to be submissive to that of his superiors as a manifestation of his vow of obedience. Besides, he real-

The Last Year   227

ized, his superior was asking for this restriction for his own health and
longevity.

The assistant superior of St. Bonaventure's was Fr. Lawrence Merton. Reflecting on Solanus' obedience, he noted that a few months after
he had arrived in Detroit for his doctoring and recuperation, that:

> some people came to the monastery and were very insistent
> on seeing Fr. Solanus. Because of his physical weakness,
> the Superior wanted to protect Fr. Solanus from fatigue and
> had forbidden visits to him. Sometimes, however, the Supe-
> rior had granted permission for limited visits. In the absence
> of the Superior, I was the Vicar. Once when an insistent
> visitor continued to ask to see Fr. Solanus, I followed the
> precedent set by the Superior and granted permission for Fr.
> Solanus to visit for thirty minutes.
>
> Now the people were always inclined to overstay the
> allotted time and Fr. Solanus paid no attention to time. He
> just wanted to help people. So I went in at the end of thirty
> minutes and concluded the visit. Although it was hard for
> Fr. Solanus to say goodbye, as his natural inclination would
> be to spend a longer time, he nevertheless very readily
> acceded. There were never any arguments. His attitude to-
> ward authority was always marvelous.[3]

While the friars were able to curtail some of the demands of the
people, they were not able to control Solanus' health. His friend and
Provincial, Fr. Gerald Walker, had felt for months that Solanus should
stay in Detroit. Despite all efforts, Solanus just was not improving. In
fact, his health was a source of deep inner and outer pain to Solanus.
Even though he didn't let on, his superiors knew the pain. They decided, after consultation with his doctors, that Solanus should not return to
Huntington. On May 10, 1956, he was officially transferred from St.
Felix to St. Bonaventure's.

With Solanus' visits curtailed, he was able to spend more time in
prayer and reflection. At this time in his life, he didn't need to talk

much; he desired to listen—not only to God in prayer, but to his fellow friars in community. Being more available to the members of the community had its benefits; it also had its drawbacks, in at least one case.

It happened that Fr. Elmer Stoffel—whom Solanus had blessed when he got the bee stings at Huntington—had come to Detroit in 1952 at the time of the split into two provinces. Again St. Bonaventure's became the novitiate as it had been when Solanus joined the Capuchins. Now Elmer was in Detroit in his capacity as novice master.

In those days, all seating in the dining room, in the choir and for all other formal functions was arranged according to rank and seniority. Because of this rule Elmer always sat next to Solanus. Because Elmer was in charge of the novices and because novices had come to Solanus for advice at various times, Elmer had sincerely concluded that Solanus was giving bad advice. At that time he also felt that, at least to a degree, Solanus was glorying in the prestige he had been receiving. On those days when talking was allowed at table, Elmer would let Solanus know some of his feelings. At times they would be expressed in the form of kidding; at other times they would come out as barbs. It was clear that Solanus did not measure up to Elmer's expectations.

When he would see Solanus picking at his food or not eating very much, he would ask, "Are you trying to be a saint?" At other times, in referring to the many people coming to see his tablemate, he would say, "You're trying to work miracles and taking the honor for them while the Seraphic Mass Association is doing the work."[4]

Since Fr. Lawrence sat on the other side of Solanus at meals, he heard Elmer making these comments. As he recalls:

> These accusatory remarks got a little strong at times, but Fr. Solanus just looked down and continued eating. He would never in any way be grieved or get mad. He took it. Sometimes he laughed, and other times you could see it hurt a little. Other friars kidded him a lot about many things, even mispronouncing a word. Some would say that he was bluffing the people, but they couldn't get him angry.[5]

In his earlier days, a keen observer of Solanus would be able to sense that he was quite sensitive to such criticism. With the years, Solanus had been able to integrate gradually such critical comments within his own self-acceptance and awareness of God's acceptance of him. The accusations and barbs no doubt had stung, and stung deeply. But by now it was quite clear that Solanus Casey was beyond the criticism of others. In his last years, which probably brought him the greatest conflicts and criticism, he had come to be concerned only about the one critique that mattered—the one from his own God whom he was experiencing in prayer and preparing to meet in judgment.

In Fr. Elmer's own defense, it must be added that subsequent years changed the novice-master's opinion of his tablemate. While he did think at that time that Solanus was imprudent in his advice or was trying to "steal the show," later events made him change his mind. He, too, became convinced of Solanus' sincerity as well as his genuine holiness.

If Solanus had to contend with someone like Fr. Elmer, there was another friar at St. Bonaventure's who treated him exactly the opposite. Fr. Gerald Walker, the Provincial, was headquartered at St. Bonaventure's. He had revered Solanus ever since he was a little child in Detroit in the 1920s. Now, as Provincial he was one of Solanus' greatest supporters. In part, it was through Gerald Walker's efforts that Solanus had returned to Detroit.

If Elmer questioned the motivation for Solanus' ministry, Gerald could find only manifestations of deep faith. Time after time Solanus had demonstrated to Gerald his religious depth and sincerity. "When I was Provincial, I had a beautiful experience of this total faith of Fr. Solanus," he recalls. One time, he had noted,

> Faced with what seemed to me would be a tragedy, I asked him to pray that God would spare me from it. He promised that he would. A week passed by. The situation seemed more threatening. I went to see him again to ask if he was praying, as he had promised. He assured me that he was. I went back to my room.

Soon there was a knock on the door, and there was Fr.
Solanus, the tears pouring down his cheeks. Evidently hurting very much, he said, "Gerald, I am so disappointed in
you."

Paining to hear that from him, I asked, "Why?"

He said, "Because I thought you had more faith than
that!" Then, referring to Jesus' words in the Gospel, he
said, "Remember that Jesus said, if you ask, you shall
receive."

It was a lesson in faith I needed.

By the way, I then received what I asked for.[6]

Solanus' faith was based in his conviction that God *is*. He loved to go
to chapel just to be present with his God. The novices hearing about
Solanus' holiness and deep prayer life, subjected him to little "jests" to
make sure that his prayer was "authentic contemplation." Identifying
mystical prayer with freedom from distraction, the novices' jests always
found Solanus getting passing grades. According to Capuchin Dan
Crosby,

How well we all remember his exact place in the friary
chapel. There he would be so completely absorbed in the
Lord that the novices would frequently decide to test out the
depth of his absorption. On their way to their place in
chapel a novice would deliberately detour to walk directly
in front of Fr. Solanus. Other novices would have previously been alerted to the test being conducted. Kneeling
in their place they would watch to see if Solanus' eyes
would open or at least flutter because of the distraction. To
their amazement no change was ever registered. Solanus
always passed the test.[7]

Solanus used the additional time on his hands not only to pray but to
keep abreast of world events. With the Korean War just ended and with
the continual news about atheism and the nuclear threat, Solanus became keenly aware of the need for global peace. In a letter to Miss

Loretta Mary Gibson, he described the times as both unsettled and glorious—for people of good will. To those of good will, peace could come. Never one to lack a vision, Solanus believed that such peace could come through justice and prayer.

To do his part in promoting peace, he decided to enclose a copy of a "Prayer for Peace" in his letter to Miss Gibson. He mentioned to her that as he prayed it, he sensed that it had been written by someone with a saddened heart. He noted that "My own heart filled up, at my first official praying thereof."[8] As with all genuine mystics who experience rest and peace in their experience of God, Solanus reflected on his world in light of that experience; thus his concern that the world experience the peace he had come to know "beyond all understanding." The Prayer for Peace which he had typed and which had come to mean so much to him in his last days in Detroit read:

> Almighty and Eternal Father, God of Wisdom and Mercy whose power exceeds all force of arms and whose protection is the strong defense of all who trust in Thee; enlighten and direct, we beseech Thee, those who bear the heavy responsibility of government throughout the world these days of stress and trial. Grant them the strength to stand firm for what is right and the skill to dispel the fear of discord. Inspire them to be mindful of the horrors of atomic war for victor and vanquished alike, to seek conciliation in truth and patience. Grant the strength to see in every man a brother—that the people of nations may, in this our last day, enjoy the blessings of a just and lasting peace. Conscious of our own unworthiness, we implore thy mercy on a sinful world in the Name of Thy Divine Son, the Prince of Peace and through the intercession of his Blessed Mother and all the Saints. Queen of all Saints, pray for us. Queen of Peace, pray for us.[9]

While Solanus was very concerned that nations come to new ways of establishing just relations and peace with each other, he spread the same message to husbands and wives, religious in communities, and indi-

viduals with their God. At peace with himself and his God, he was able
to communicate that same peace to others. As Fr. Lawrence (who at
times would take people to Solanus' room when it would be too difficult
for him to come to the front office) remembers:

> Sometimes those with troubles were told that this was the
> first requisite to gain God's help—to make their peace with
> God. Oftentimes he enrolled people in the Seraphic Mass
> Association so that they might benefit from the Holy Sacri-
> fice of the Mass. Then with the spiritual uplift and the faith
> inspired by Fr. Solanus, things did go much better. And at
> times God did grant extraordinary favors. He was so under-
> standing of human hearts and minds, yet he could not un-
> derstand how it was possible for anyone not to believe in
> God. . . .[10]

For someone experiencing God so intimately and mystically, it was
increasingly becoming unfathomable for Solanus to believe that anyone
in their right mind could declare that there was no God. One day, Father
Lawrence recalled:

> A professed atheist was brought to him. The latter with a
> bold and flippant front said, "Father, what would you say
> to a man who does not believe in God?"
> Solanus' immediate response was, "I would say that
> such a man is a fool. The height of insanity is not to believe
> in God, for only the fool says in his heart that there is no
> God when the heavens and the earth proclaim his glory."
> Fr. Solanus discovered God in all the beautiful things he
> had made, in the grass on which he trod, the flowers he
> admired. He found God in his own soul. He found him in
> Divine Providence. "God is so good!" he often said. Even
> sufferings helped him to unite himself to God. He could say
> "Thanks be to God" even for pain.[11]

Possibly because he experienced so much pain, Solanus empathized
with those in pain themselves. He often described their details about

their problems as "pathetic." The word "pathetic" is based on the Greek word "pathos" or sympathy.

God's very revelation, according to the Jewish theologian, Abraham Heschel, is identified in God's *pathos*.[12] It results from God's awareness of need and pain. Since Solanus increasingly was experiencing God in prayer he increased in empathy because of his identification with God. Because he was now living so closely in union with God, God's pathos was being revealed in the world as Solanus' own. Like the God of Exodus, Solanus too was able to say, "I have seen the afflictions of my people; I have heard their cry of complaint; therefore I will deliver them" (Ex 3:7).

On December 2, 1956, all efforts that had been made to shelter Solanus from the people of Detroit were shattered. A feature article on the 100th anniversary of the Capuchins' establishment in the United States ran in *The Detroit Sunday News*. The article highlighted the various Capuchin activities which had taken place in the Midwest Province since its foundation in 1856. However, the house chronicler noted, "Fr. Solanus was spread all over the front cover of the Rotogravure section."[13] The article might have been about the Capuchins, but the real story was about Solanus Casey being back in Detroit.

The only quote featured in the article was that from Solanus. It was a response to a question of how a Capuchin felt about the Franciscan life of prayer, study, and work: "Fr. Solanus Casey, who is 86 and in his 60th year in the order, said, 'It's like starting heaven here on earth.'"[14]

With the publication of this article many for the first time realized that Solanus had returned to Detroit. It brought a deluge of calls on Monday morning. The house chronicle noted that "The Brothers at the front door office desk were suffering a headache from answering the avalanche of telephone calls from the people who wanted to know whether Fr. Solanus was available for consultation and blessings.[15]

Again, seeking to shield him from anything that might be a further drain on him, the answer to the people's requests was a gentle, but firm, "No, he is not able to see anyone because of his delicate health." Generally, the people accepted this explanation. They merely asked to be remembered to Solanus. They were aware that Solanus was growing weaker. When Christmas came in 1956 some wondered if it would be Solanus' last. One Capuchin who recalled Solanus' celebration of Christmas that year was Fr. Dan Crosby. He recalled:

> Fr. Solanus' last Christmas on earth happened to be my first Christmas in the Order—at St. Bonaventure's in 1956. Christmas evening I was on my way to community recreation and stopped in the friary chapel for a visit to the Blessed Sacrament. While kneeling there I heard a familiar squeaky noise coming from the larger church, which I immediately knew was Fr. Solanus playing his violin. I wanted to see the sight, however, and so opened the door from the friary chapel to the main church. There I saw Fr. Solanus alone in the choir-loft playing Christmas carols on his violin and singing them to the Christ Child.[16]

On the morning of January 14, 1957, Solanus celebrated the sixtieth anniversary of his investiture in the habit of St. Francis and his entrance into the gospel way of life as expressed in the Capuchin Franciscans. The fact that the sixty years of trying to live in a way that would "start heaven on earth," became very evident at that point in the liturgy when it came time for Solanus to renew his vows. The further he prayed the vow formulary, the more choked-up he became. The realization of all the good that God had done for, in, and through him was too much to bear. By the time he came to the part where he would rededicate his life to "live in obedience, without property, and in chastity," the overpowering realization of God's goodness enveloped him. With tears in his eyes and his throat too choked-up, he could not continue. Father Giles Soyka had to finish the renewal of vows for Solanus.

The place where Solanus had renewed his vows was only a short distance from the place where, in 1897, he had knelt as a novice to receive the habit, committing himself to begin living the Capuchin Franciscan way of life.

In describing the 1957 ceremony to his brother Msgr. Edward, Solanus wrote:

I would hardly know how it could have been more beautiful, under the simple circumstances. . . . I had come to the holy novitiate Christmas eve. It was six months ahead of the seven other students who joined me the following July. They are all gone to Heaven now, we hope, with the senior of them all, Fr. Damasus, in his 90th year. Had he waited five months longer, he and I would have had our golden jubilee together. He was patient and joyful to the last. May he be privileged to await in the peace of the saints, the inconceivable glory of the general resurrection.

Please pardon the digression. Today, Deo Gratias, it is sixty years and sixty days since I was invested.[17]

Even though his life in the Capuchin Franciscans had been lived without the faculties to formally preach or hear confessions he had lived it in a way that probably reached more people than had any other friar in the 100 plus years of the Capuchin presence in the United States. Even though he had been a "simplex" priest, fifty years of priesthood had made it evident that the decision of his superiors to keep him from hearing confessions had been accepted then as well as later in a spirit of equanimity. This was made clear from the recollection of Fr. Michael Dalton, a priest of the London, Ontario Diocese who came to St. Bonaventure's during Lent of 1957:

I said Mass in the monastery chapel and a very elderly friar served my Mass. I did not know then that he was a priest. I was quite impressed when I saw him kneel and kiss the floor when he passed in front of the tabernacle. I thought it very devout and humble.

After Mass he took me in for breakfast. Taking me down a long monastery hall, he went into a room with the name "Fr. Solanus" over the door. When I saw who he was I asked him to hear my confession. He is the only priest in seventy-five years who refused absolution saying, "I'm only a simplex priest—no faculties to absolve."

He told me, however, that his work in the office, meeting

troubled humanity, was similar to confession. He talked at breakfast of being a streetcar operator in his youth.

At eight-six years he was my oldest altar boy.[18]

The fact that Solanus was able to serve Fr. Dalton at the celebration of the liturgy, as well as to kiss the floor in reverence to the Blessed Sacrament (which was a Capuchin custom in those days, following the suggestion of St. Francis), attests to the fact that by late winter and early spring, Solanus had experienced some respite and actually regained strength from his various ailments.

With some relief for himself, Solanus was able to be more available to others in pain. Often, as he spent time with the people and as he had done with Fr. Dalton, Solanus would reminisce about his childhood and the happy memories he recalled about his family. In the case of Earl and Adeline Striewski and their son Tommy, such recollections spanned a two-hour visit. Fr. Solanus seemed very glad to talk to them; he said he loved to visit. He brought up many things about his boyhood and life on the farm. He spoke about his brothers and sisters—all fifteen of them— whom he said were all "bright." "But," he said, "I was not very bright; all the others were more brilliant than I." Mentioning the difficulties he had in school, he added, "But God was good to me."[19]

The realization of how good God had been to him brought Solanus a rare moment of candor. He began to reflect with the Striewski family about the many miracles or favors people had experienced. He said several times, "Oh, God is so good," as tears of thanks and joy rolled down his cheeks. He spoke about people who had come to him and the trials and troubles they brought and how so many times people's suffering had been relieved. He just seemed to want to talk. Mrs. Striewski recalls that they couldn't get him to leave. Even though the dinner bell rang, Fr. Solanus seemed to want to stay and talk about God's goodness and power to heal.

Another person who was able to talk with Solanus—not in person— but on the telephone, was Mrs. Edward Klimczak. In March, 1957 she called St. Bonaventure's asking to speak to Fr. Solanus. In a unique account of the long dialog that followed she recalls that Solanus made it clear that, if her request would be answered, she would have to make an extra step by seeking to know more about Christ. In her case this would be achieved by examining the mysteries of Mary and her Son, as contained in the writings of Mary of Agreda. Even in Detroit Solanus never stopped promoting *The Mystical City of God:*

> When I called, I asked to speak to Father. The priest who answered the phone told me Father Solanus was too ill to come to the phone. I asked Father if I could tell him what I wanted and then he could ask Fr. Solanus to pray for this intention.
>
> After telling Father my problem, he said, "Just a minute."
>
> After a short wait I had the joy of hearing the words, "Fr. Solanus speaking." Fr. Solanus then asked me to tell him my problem. I have often thought since that time that only God and those very close to him knew what it had cost him to answer that phone call, being as ill as he then must have been.
>
> His voice sounded weak but one of the things I remember most about it was the sound of joy in his voice and his fervent and joyous phrases praising God.
>
> I asked Fr. Solanus' help for my mother, a good practicing Catholic, who after many years of hardship and an extremely distressing trial was at the point of despair. After speaking with Fr. Solanus, I sat down immediately and wrote down our conversation while it was still fresh in my mind. The only thing I have added to the notes was to put in (Mrs. Klimczak) and (Fr. Solanus) at the beginning of each quotation. I recopied the notes as the original copy is quite faded and battered. . . .

Mrs. Klimczak: "Fr. Solanus, did Father tell you what I had just told him?"

Fr. Solanus: "No, I was just finishing my prayers."

I repeated what I had said to the priest that answered the phone ending with, "I thought you would tell us what to do, Father."

> Fr. Solanus: "Have you heard of *The City of God,* the volumes written by Mother Mary Agreda?"

> Mrs. Klimczak: "Yes."

> Fr. Solanus: "It was dictated by the Holy Mother herself, written at her command. Do you know what I mean?"

> Mrs. Klimczak: "Yes, Father, it's a book, isn't it?"

> Fr. Solanus: "Yes, it is four volumes. You need not get all of them at once, just the first volume."

> Mrs. Klimczak: "Yes, I know right where I can send for it."

> Fr. Solanus: "Yes. Well get the first volume and begin reading it, all the family together and promise the Blessed Mother that if she will take all into her hands, you will read this book. I am sure if you read this first volume you will want to read the rest. You will be amazed at the wonderful change that will take place in your family. I am sure everything will turn out all right. God be praised. It will all work out for the greater honor and glory of God. Glory be to God!"

Fr. Solanus asked about my family and I told him a little about my husband, our children, and my mother, two brothers and sister with whom we were living. He then asked:

> Fr. Solanus: "Do you receive Holy Communion regularly?"

Mrs. Klimczak: "Yes, Father, every Sunday."

Fr. Solanus: "Try to go more often. Where are you?"

Mrs. Klimczak: "I'm calling from Alpena, Michigan."

Fr. Solanus: "That's hm-m-m."

Mrs. Klimczak: "It's 250 miles from Detroit, North."

Fr. Solanus: "Yes, I want you (all) to come to see me. I would like to see you."

Mrs. Klimczak: "Oh, yes, Father, we would like very much to see you. Maybe I could bring my father."

Fr. Solanus: "Yes, come to see me. I have received many great favors. On the 8th of this month I received a call from Oakland, California, from my niece, my oldest sister's daughter. She said her mother's plate had been bothering her and she went to her dentist and found she had cancer. Her husband is an invalid, the result of a heart attack. She has had a hard time to get along. Just last week a lady came to see me, very distressed and at the point of committing suicide. I told her about my sister and asked her to pray for her (Father's sister). She said, "Why don't you call your sister now. I'll pay for the call." I did. The thought of suicide passed in a moment like a shadow. God is never outdone in generosity. He will always take care of you. All will be well again. Don't delay. Do your part right away. Don't wait. It may be too late. Begin right away. If you do your part the Blessed Mother will take care of everything. Don't worry. Ev-

erything will be all right. Don't worry any-
more. What is your name?''

Mrs. Klimczak: "Mrs. Ed. Klimczak, Mary.''

Fr. Solanus: "Mrs. Klimczak, (here he paused and then
said) God bless you. (Then added) As sure
as the sun is now rising, things will change
today. Come to see me. Promise you will
come.''

Mrs. Klimczak: "Yes, Father, we will come.''

We did not visit Fr. Solanus while he was still alive, but I
did not forget my promise to come and see him. So when
we were able to go to Detroit, my husband, my sister and I
visited Father's grave. It was a completely overcast day. As
we knelt at Father's grave the sun broke through the clouds
briefly almost as though Father was letting us know he
knew we were keeping my promise to visit him.

Yes, I did get the books *The City of God*. I sent out an
order for them that day explaining that I needed my books
right away to fulfill the request Fr. Solanus made. I enclosed all the money I could spare, $7.00. They wrote back
saying that I would have to buy the set of books (4) and that
since my situation was unusual, they would accept pay-
ments, whatever I could send, until the books were paid
for—something they just did not do normally. In the meantime so as not to lose anytime in beginning to keep our
promise to do our part if the Blessed Mother would take all
in her hands, I asked the Sister at our parish convent if they
had a copy of the first volume of *The City of God* that I
could borrow until our books arrived. They had the
abridged copy and lent it to us. And we, as a family, mother, brothers, young sister, husband and son read the book
each evening.

Fr. Solanus had said that we need only read the first
volume of *The City of God,* but he was sure that once we
began reading it we would want to read the others as well.
And of course we did.

Mother was able to take courage and go on after I told her everything Fr. Solanus had said. We did all that Fr. Solanus told us to do, beginning that same day. Our prayers were answered. My Father, who was living a sinful life was given the grace to turn away and begin the long road back to Jesus.''[20]

Solanus' respite from serious pain was very brief. In early May, skin eruptions appeared again on his body. As the condition worsened, the doctors diagnosed the lesions as severe erysipelas. When the condition became even more serious, on May 15, it was decided an ambulance should take him to St. John's Hospital. Once there his condition worsened; it appeared he was close to death. He was anointed, and an oxygen tent was placed over him to help him breathe.

Once the oxygen was administered, he seemed to rally. Now out of danger, one of the first things he did was to begin singing a hymn of thanks to the Blessed Virgin. Br. Gabriel, assigned to care for Solanus, had to urge him to stop singing lest he use up the little strength he had left. Even though Solanus thought Gabriel's overprotection of his health was somewhat officious, he immediately stopped; after all, he had been told to obey this Third Order Brother.

As the days wore on, his strength returned; so did his humor. When one of the nurses, Sr. Arthur Ann, came into his room, she said, "Father, throughout the years I have so often heard people speak of you."

"Yes," he replied, "people often speak of Jessie James too."

"But these people, Father, spoke of wonderful things that occurred through your prayers for them."

"Ah," he conceded, "many wonderful things have happened—but the people had faith."

Another day Sr. Arthur Ann came into his room and asked, "How about a blessing, Father?"

"All right," he smiled, "I'll take one!"

After sharing a good laugh he blessed her. Then they talked about the concern that had been the source of many of his reflections toward the end of his life—the rise in materialism and consumerism. He said, "So often people hope to find happiness in money or the things money buys. If only they would stop running around, acquiring this and that, instead of seeking happiness only where it can be found—in love of God. They are so foolish."

Solanus began to improve. As he got better he liked to be taken in his wheelchair to chapel where various people would read to him from *The Mystical City of God*. Others would pray the rosary with him. When he was strong enough, he would celebrate the liturgy. Whenever he was on his way to or was in chapel the word quickly spread.

People would come into the corridors asking for a blessing, or would quietly come to the chapel to participate in his celebration of the liturgy. When the liturgy was finished, they would ask to be blessed or to have Solanus pray for their intentions. Always he would be gentle and generous in his response, even though he did not like the personal attention that he was receiving. Rather than say anything about it, he deferred to their wishes. Such was the case with Sr. Arthur Ann. Solanus asked her to recite the rosary with him. Taking her own rosary, she said, "Father, will you use my rosary. Then I can regard it as a keepsake associated with you."

Rather than protesting, he extended his hand graciously and said, although reluctantly, "All right, give it to me."

Because of the excellent treatment Solanus received at St. John's, he was able to return to St. Bonaventure's. However, he had to return on June 14. After more treatments, he was able to return to St. Bonaventure's again, but, on July 2 he was forced to go back. He would remain at St. John's until his death.

Even though the erysipelas was creating severe discomfort, Solanus never lost his sense of humor; it reflected an inner peace and joy. One of the sisters who was assigned to nurse him, Sr. M. Margretta, recalled that he radiated Christ-like holiness.

> A Sister companion and I often read to him—always from *The Mystical City of God*. Always, too, he would precede the reading by asking us to recite with him a prayer to the Holy Spirit. As we read, he would close his eyes, and

seem to doze. But let the word be misread, and he would open his eyes, and we'd note a twinkle in them as he corrected us. Or some passage would strike him, and he would exclaim—"Glory to God."

He told us that he had "prayed" the four volumes of *The Mystical City of God* through three times, kneeling.

His sickness brought excruciating suffering. He developed a skin reaction that enveloped his entire body. This alone caused intense pain. Tubes, needles, examinations— these added to his discomfort.

Yet there was never a complaint from him, and he was rational at intervals even on the morning of his death.

In his presence it was impossible not to feel his Christlikeness, his genuine simplicity and humility, his great love for mankind, his selflessness. Even in his pain, he wanted to continue working to bring more people closer to God. "I can't die," we overheard him say, "until everyone loves him."

. . . He frequently spoke of God's mercy with such childlike tenderness that tears came into his eyes. "God is so good," he would say, and then repeat slowly and quietly, "Glory be to God. Glory be to God."

The Sisters realized that he was suffering intense pain, and sought to alleviate it. "Where do you hurt, Father?" one compassionately asked.

"Oh, I hurt all over—thanks be to God," he responded.

Because of poor nutrition and continuous intravenous feedings, his hands had become red and raw. "Your poor hands," said Sister Arthur Ann, as she prepared to remove a needle. "I hate having to remove the adhesive tape."

"Well, Sister, don't feel badly about it," he comforted her. "Look at our Lord's hands."

Sr. Carmella, one of those who read to him, noted that one would go in and out of the room, and he wouldn't know it. His mind was elsewhere. He seemed to be thinking continuously of the love of God. "The love of God," he would say, "is everything." As he said this, his face would shine with an inner light.[21]

It was John of the Cross, the author of *The Inner Light,* who wrote that "In the evening of our life we will be judged on love." Now, in the evening of his life, the constant preoccupation of Solanus was how he might still extend the love and desire for unity in the world for which Christ prayed at the Last Supper. Solanus always had been a man with a vision. Now at this time his vision was expressed as an obsession for unity.

When the Provincial, Fr. Gerald Walker, (who was also his closest confidant in Detroit), came to see him he asked, "Where do you hurt, Father?"

"My whole body hurts. Thanks be to God. Thanks be to God," he immediately responded. Then he added: "I am offering my sufferings that all might be one. Oh, if I could only live to see the conversion of the whole world."[22]

When Br. Ignatius Milne came to visit him, he walked into the room as Solanus was scratching himself. "Gee, Father, you must be hurting quite a bit," he said. Without hesitation Solanus replied, "Would to God it was 10,000 times worse."[23]

At another time, as he lay quite close to his last hours on earth, Fr. Gerald recalls how Solanus said to him:

> "I looked on my whole life as giving, and I want to give until there is nothing left of me to give. So, I prayed that, when I come to die, I might be perfectly conscious, so that with a deliberate act I can give my last breath to God." I looked at him there on his deathbed, clothed only in a little hospital gown, a rosary in one hand and a little relic in the other, and felt like crying out, "My God, there is scarcely anything left of him to give."[24]

Before he left, Solanus said to Gerald, "Tomorrow will be a beautiful day." The two of these had become very close; they both understood what Solanus meant..

Realizing Solanus had little time to live Msgr. Edward had come to be with his brother, as had his sister-in-law, Martha, the recently widowed wife of Owen. She arrived on the feast of St. Martha; and Solanus was alert enough to note the link. Martha Casey proved to be especially good at keeping visitors away, having learned to do this so tactfully in her role as administrator of a nursing home in Seattle.

On Wednesday morning, July 31, Msgr. Edward celebrated an early Mass, especially remembering his brother. Then he went to Solanus' room about 8:00. Solanus seemed his old self; better than any time Edward had observed the last few days. Even though Monsignor tried to keep him from talking, Solanus seemed compelled to talk about only one subject. It had come to obsess him the day before his death in the same way as St. John says it had for Jesus—the need for the world's conversion and his desire to do all that he could to bring the world to unity in the love of God.

Relieved, feeling that Solanus seemed so much better, Edward went to his room in the hospital to write the relatives that things were looking better. Solanus seemed much improved.

Around eleven o'clock, a nurse came to bathe Solanus, taking the rosary and relic from him and slipping the hospital gown from around his frail and wiry body. As she gently bathed him, she heard Solanus whispering, although his voice was too weak for her to catch the words. Suddenly, his eyes opened wide and, as she held him, Solanus Casey stretched out his arms and said very clearly: "I give my soul to Jesus Christ." He fell back, offering to God his last breath. Solanus' desire had been fulfilled; he was able to consciously and deliberately offer his last breath to that God whom he had experienced as lover and friend, that God, whom, in turn, he had loved so deeply and fully.[25]

It was 11:00 A.M., July 31, 1957. Fifty-three years before, to the hour, Solanus Casey had begun the celebration of his First Solemn Mass. Now his own sacrifice of praise was complete. He had given his body for the life of the world and its unity. It had been accepted by God the Almighty, Creator of heaven and earth.

Because it had been decided that it would be better to have the wake for Fr. Solanus at a regular funeral home than in the friary chapel, his body was taken to Van Lerberghe Funeral Home. This was announced over the radio and television with the report that people could come to the mortuary at 10:00 the next morning. At 6:30 A. M. the people began to gather. As people filed by the coffin they touched his body and touched religious articles to it. People came with infants; teenagers approached the coffin with the deepest respect and awe. There were many priests and religious.

People would come up to the various Capuchins, Fr. Gerald recalls, and say:

"... meet my son. Fifteen years ago he was dying of polio, Fr. Solanus blessed him, and today he is in the best of health." Someone else would introduce an elderly lady, saying: "Father, met my mother. She was dying of cancer and Father blessed her, and she is here tonight." Others would tell us that they themselves were here because he (allegedly) had cured them of some serious illness when they were doomed to die . . . One lady began to cry and pointed to him saying, "He was the best friend I had in the world. Some years ago I was in utter despair and just want-ed to die. I spoke to him and began to live again."[26]

By the end of the day, the people who came in droves to show their thanks to and respect for their friend, confidant and helper numbered some five thousand.

One of the thousands who came was Bernadette Nowak. After her first child she had lost three babies by miscarriage and had been desper-ate to have a second child. Because her blood was RH Negative, the doctors were skeptical as to the possibility of having a live baby. When she began to suspect that she might be pregnant in December 1956, seven months before Solanus' death, she immediately wrote a letter to the man who had helped her at another time fifteen years before. In her words:

I addressed it to the Monastery with a note attached saying that if Father was too ill, not to bother him with my prob-lems. In the letter I asked him to pray that I could have a living, normal baby. I also explained my previous medical history. Shortly after, I received a reply saying Fr. Solanus had been very happy to have the letter and would indeed pray for such a good intention. He urged me to name my child *now* after two of God's saints, enroll the intention in the Seraphic Mass Association along with enrolling the Poor Souls. I did so. I also promised God to call my child, if a boy, Anthony Joseph. I cannot remember the girl's name I chose, but I think it was Mary Anne. My pregnancy progressed uneventfully and the baby grew. Fr. Solanus died a month before the baby was due. I went to Van Lerberghe Funeral Home to view his body. The baby had lain so quietly within me the past few days, and when I approached the casket, the baby seemed to leap inside. I could see my dress moving and I was embarrassed. I felt sad because I wanted to tell the good news to Fr. Solanus and now I could not do so. . . . During the labor I, indeed, felt a comforting presence although I was in the "preparation room" all alone the entire time except for an occasional visit by a doctor or nurse. It was a swift, easy, uncomplicated delivery. Joseph was born with the cord around his neck, twice, and it had a knot in it. Despite all these things, the baby was fine and I never felt better. I was up and around and at home in three days.[27]

Somehow the man of God who had ministered to her in his life was now assuring her that he could be counted on to minister to her in his own passover to his God.

The next day, Friday, at 10:00 the body of Fr. Solanus was brought to St. Bonaventure's chapel. People were already lined up to pay their last respects. From the beginning a steady stream of people began to move to the casket. After short prayers, many would go aside to tell others of their stories of Solanus and his goodness to them. For twelve hours, until the doors closed at 10:30, the lines continued to file past the coffin where the thin old man laid in his rough brown habit, a rosary in his hands, a stole around his neck, and the Rule and Constitutions beside him. At least ten thousand filed by that day.

On Saturday after the regular 8:00 a.m. Mass, the crowds were asked
to leave the chapel that it might be prepared for the funeral liturgy. After
this the chapel was again opened and the huge crowd began again to fill
the pews. Rapidly, all available places were filled. Loud speakers were
set up to share the service with the people who now lined the sidewalks
of both sides of Mt. Elliott Avenue. They were kept in order by a squad
of police who had been sent to make sure no disruptions would take
place from eager enthusiasts looking for a remembrance of the man
whom people were now calling a saint.

So many thousands had come to St. Bonaventure's that Fr. Bernard
Burke recalls saying that he would truly believe in the greatness of
Solanus Casey if the morning could take place without any unsettling
disturbance. "I was present for his funeral," he recalled. "The calm
and the order that pervaded the crowd, to my mind, was a miracle itself.
Even the police officers were surprised at the calmness of such a large
crowd."[28]

Msgr. Edward Casey, now the only surviving brother of the Casey
brothers family, celebrated the Mass. Bishop Henry E. Donnelly paid a
final tribute on behalf of the clergy and people of the Detroit Archdiocese. Fr. Gerald Walker preached the funeral sermon.

Gerald spoke not so much as the provincial superior of Solanus, but
as the spiritual son of a saintly man. "Fr. Solanus was a man I loved
dearly," he began. As he continued, he often had to stop, choking back
his tears. The tears came as a combined response to his close friend's
passing from this life as well as from a profound realization of all the
good that had been done to others through the confident faith of this one
man. In concluding he said of the man who often declared, "I have two
loves. The sick and the poor":

> His was a life of service and love for people like me and
> you. When he was not himself sick, he nevertheless suf-
> fered with and for you that were sick. When he was not
> physically hungry, he hungered with people like you. He
> had a Divine love for people. He loved people for what he
> could do for them—and for God, through them."[29]

After the funeral liturgy, the friars carried the body of their brother to be laid to rest in the small cemetery next to St. Bonaventure's Friary. On many other days Solanus had gone there to think of the Brothers with whom he had shared his life as a Capuchin Franciscan and to pray for them. Now he would be with them sharing in their eternal reward. As he never tried to be different from his brothers in life, so in death, his grave marker would be the same as all the rest:

REV.
Francis Solanus Casey
O.F.M. Cap.
Born Nov. 25, 1870
Ordained July 24, 1904
Died July 31, 1957
Age 86   Religious 60
RIP

Overlooking his small gravestone as well as the others stands a large granite slab covered with a bas-relief of St. Francis. He is represented proclaiming the words he used from the Canticle of the Sun at his own death: "Praised be the Lord for Our Sister Bodily Death." Toward the bottom of the monument are the words of the Capuchin Franciscan motto which Solanus Casey spent 87 years trying to experience in his life and express in his living:

"MY GOD and MY ALL!"

CHAPTER NINE
The Spirituality of Solanus Casey

On April 26, 1946, Solanus Casey began his official retirement. At least that is written on the "Personal Record" of his assignments filed in the archives of the Capuchin Province of St. Joseph. How he experienced his "retirement" is clear from one of the many letters he wrote during that time:

> Since my transfer, my personal callers have been by no means as heavy; though my letters—possibly because I have to take care of them myself—seem as heavy as ever. You can imagine how I appreciate it to have someone like one of the Brothers or Fathers in Detroit continue their generous assistance in the work that, even with such help, often keeps me busy—with others duties—from 5:00 A.M. to 11:00 P.M.[1]

Solanus wrote this letter while he as assigned to St. Felix Friary in Huntington, Indiana. The letters he wrote during his decade there were more numerous than any comparable period. These letters also have served greatly in summarizing his approach to God, people and creation.From them we can generally characterize Solanus Casey's spirituality as that of a "Mystic in Action."

Upon first reading, some might be surprised to hear Solanus Casey called a *mystic*. Their recollection of him conjures up images of healing and wonder-workings, combined with a deep concern for the poor.

Others, while accepting the fact that Solanus may have been a mystic will react against his being called a "mystic *in action.*" For them, the concepts "mysticism" and "action" are contradictions in terms. Yet, in authentic spirituality religious experience can never be divorced from ministerial involvement. According to F. C. Happold:

> The true mystic is not like a cat basking in the sun, but like a mountaineer. At the end of his quest he finds not the enervating isle of the Lotus Eaters, but the sharp, pure air of the Mount of Transfiguration. The greatest contemplatives, transfigured on this holy mountain, have felt themselves called upon to "descend below themselves," to take the humility of Christ, who "took upon Him the form of a servant," and, coming down to the plain, to become centres of creative energy and power in the world. In whatever field of active life they may engage, because they have become completely detached, because the selfhood has been entirely subdued in them, because they partake of the Divine Life and are united with that Ultimate Reality we call God, the world can no longer touch them. Hidden in God, inflamed with the Divine Love, serene and confident, they possess a creative strength and power, which ordinary men, tossed hither and thither by the passions of primitive self, do not possess. [2]

The twentieth century in which Solanus lived called for mysticism in action. Solanus had come to Huntington not long after the atomic bombing of Hiroshima and Nagasaki and the beginning of "The Cold War." The confrontation between East and West affected his outlook, especially when he considered the potential impact of nuclear weapons from the perspective of faith. "And just these days of atomic invention," he wrote, "it would seem that God might be permitting men without faith to be preparing the fearfully poisoned lightning fires with which he will arm his angels of wrath on an adulterous, defiant, atheistic generation." [3]

Many people who reflect on today's atomic age despair of the reality they view. Yet, when the mystic interprets reality, that critique is based on a worldview which holds that the observable world and individual consciousness are only parts of a total reality to be considered. Both manifest a further reality—one's relationship to the Divine Ground of God which contains all partial realities.

Many who cannot place life in this wider context will despair or become atheists. Solanus considered the very tensions and conflicts of his time to be linked to what he called "atheism." The only solution Solanus Casey could offer to address this global alienation was the answer he experienced within his heart. This is what he called "religion."

In his way of thinking, religion was part of one's psyche. To deny religion was to deny one's self. Once he wrote to an Irish police officer whom he had helped take "the pledge" (to abstain from alcohol) and who later on declared himself an "atheist":

> Many a time, however, I have wondered if "big W. Mack" ever tried to realize in any way what he has been missing in refusing to believe in RELIGION. . . . Of course, the very fact that I respect you as I do, ought to be proof sufficient that I am confident that you cannot be a true atheist, except possibly such a one as have been heard to thank God for their atheism![4]

In all his writings, no single topic received more attention from Solanus than the notion of religion. By understanding what he meant by "religion" we can grasp why his spirituality reflected mysticism in action.

Spirituality is the experience and expression of the nature and activity of a Supreme Reality. Spirituality encompasses how that experience and expression are communicated to others. The "science" or study of that spirituality for Solanus was religion. Throughout his letters and statements, he continually returned to his definition of *religion:* "The science of our happy relationship with and our providential dependence on God and our neighbor.''

Given the theology of that time, especially since he was trained in that era's brand of Thomistic theology, it is not surprising that Solanus considered religion a *science*. After all, was not theology faith seeking understanding? And doesn't understanding relate to reason and rationality? Are not reason, rationality and observability the realm of science? For Solanus, what could be more rational and observable than God? ''There is nothing more rational in reason than to love God,'' he wrote. ''By stifling reason and gratitude, sin begets atheism—atheism, the unqualified climax of intellectual insanity, of moral degeneracy, of diabolical blasphemy.''[5] Atheism, for Solanus, was the stifling of reason and knowledge itself.

There are five possible ways people come to ''know'' reality, including God. The first deals with the material world outside ourselves which we acknowledge through our senses. The second arises from the reflections we have about the sensed world. The third form of ''knowing'' deals with the application of reason to the sensate world and our reflections about it. The fourth level adds intuition to the rational element; intuition and rationality combined reveal a highly developed mind. The fifth level of ''knowing'' goes beyond the other four to the level of mystical experience. At this level, mystics have a direct and highly personalized experience of that which simply *is*. Given this experience, they become convinced of the complete certitude of this experience; to them it is very experiential and very knowledgeable even if it is beyond the purely rational. Thus Solanus (because he did not distinguish the rational or demonstrable levels of knowing God from his mystical experience of that God) could not possibly fathom how anyone could say there was no God. Truly, only the fool—an irrational being—could say there is no God.

For Solanus, knowledge of God demanded a threefold response: appreciation, love, and service. ''To know and appreciate is to advance in the one science necessary—sanctity,'' he wrote.[6] Furthermore, ''man's purpose as a rational creature, is to recognize and to know his Creator, so as to be able, intelligently to love him, confidently to hope in him, and gratefully to serve him."[7]

Years before, St. Teresa of Avila had linked appreciation and gratefulness with knowledge and service of God when she noted in her Seventh Soliloquy:

> Be joyful, my soul, for there is someone who loves your God as he deserves. Be joyful, for there is someone who knows his goodness and value. Give thanks to him, for he has given us on earth someone who thus knows him, as his only Son. Under this protection you can approach and petition him, for then his Majesty takes delight in you. Don't let any earthly thing be enough to separate you from your delight, and rejoice in the grandeur of God; in how he deserves to be loved and praised; that he helps you to play some small role in the blessing of his name; and that you can truthfully say: *My soul magnifies and praises the Lord.*[8]

Capuchin Dan Crosby recalled how, like Teresa, Solanus also linked appreciation and gratitude:

> The word I heard more often than any other on Solanus' lips was "appreciate." To me it sums up his whole spirituality, so much akin to that of St. Francis who was constantly filled with praise and gratitude to God for his blessings. Frequently he would say, "If only we would appreciate our faith" or "If only we would appreciate what it means to be a Capuchin." The word "appreciate" came from his lips like honey, in the same way that Celano describes St. Francis' saying the word "Bethlehem."
>
> A humorous incident reinforced this for me and brought out as well his deep contemplative attitude. One Sunday morning in 1956 the novices gathered in the choir loft at St. Bonaventure's in Detroit for the 9:00 o'clock High Mass. Fr. Solanus sat directly in front of me. I was a novice. Fr. Cuthbert Gumbinger celebrated the Mass. In his sermon he

told a story about a farmer and his donkey, except that he
used the term "ass." Hearing this unaccostumed word the
novices broke into laughter. My laugh was more of a loud
snort and so Solanus turned around to say to me: "The
trouble with us is that we don't appreciate what he is trying
to tell us. If we did appreciate it, we wouldn't think it was
so funny." At this I only laughed the louder, but I have
come to appreciate his meaning of appreciation.[9]

The truly religious person is the most aware of all reality. Thus,
through knowledge, love, appreciation, and service, Solanus saw his
definition of religion being fulfilled: *The science of our happy relationship with and our providential dependence on God and our
neighbor.*

At the time Solanus referred to religion as a science, to consider
religion and religious experience (much less mystical experience) as
part of science was unthinkable in academic circles. Yet, times have
changed; there is much more openness to make such a link now. As
John Macquarrie has written:

In venturing to speak of the Holy or God, mysticism does
supply that lost dimension in the experience of a secular
age; but in speaking of the Holy or God in a modest, undog-
matic way, frankly recognizing the ineffability of the Holy
and the inadequacy of our highest symbols, mysticism
chimes in with the cautious mood of modern philosophy.

Here we must touch more directly on the relations of
mystical religion to contemporary science. Just as the mystic acknowledges the inadequate and therefore meta-
phorical nature of his language about God, so physics after
Einstein and Planck has come to acknowledge the symbolic
character of its language. While that language articulates an
understanding of the physical world, it does not claim to
give a literal description. In this regard, the twentieth-cen-
tury picture is far more open to the possibility of a religious
interpretation of the universe than was the nineteenth-century picture.[10]

(Left) Solanus at the Farm of Mr. & Mrs. Ed Bishop, near Detroit, 1935.

(Right) Solanus at his desk in the front office, St. Bonaventure's, Detroit, about 1939.

(Left) Solanus helping at the Soup Kitchen, about 1939.

(Right) Solanus reading the Scriptures in the front office. Note the prayerful reflections he penned on this picture he gave to Edward and Selina Wollenweber, 1943:

"Only in heaven can we be satisfied as being fully and really converted. Therefore—including the above poor Fr. Solanus—pray for the conversion of sinners—and that God send laborers into His harvest."

(Left) Solanus Casey at his Fiftieth Jubilee as a Capuchin, Third Order Hall, Detroit 1947. Behind Solanus is his sister, Grace Brady and his brother, Owen Casey. Monsignor Edward is at Solanus' left.

(Left) Solanus in the front of St. Felix Monastery, Huntington, after a blessing, about 1950.

(Below) Solanus at his favorite pastime, 1952 at Huntington, Indiana. One of his favorite pieces was "Mother Machree."

The Golden Priestly Jubilee of Solanus Casey. The Silver Jubilee of Thomas Aquinas (Francis), Heidenreich (left) and Cuthbert Gumbinger (right). At far left is Cyprian Abler, the Provincial. At far right is Clement Neubauer, former Minister General of the Order who preached. Monsignor Edward Casey is with Solanus outside St. Mary's Church, Huntington, IN, 1954.

Solanus about to give priestly blessing in the choir chapel, St. Bonaventure's, 1956. (*Detroit News*)

(Left) Solanus praying the Little Office of the Blessed Virgin in the garden, St. Bonaventure Monastery, 1956. (*Detroit News*)

(Right) Last photo of Solanus, 1957, Cloister Garden, St. Bonaventure's.

Funeral procession from the chapel to the friary cemetery, St. Bonaventure's, August 3, 1957.

IHS
REV.
FRANCIS SOLANUS CASEY
O. F. M. CAP.
BORN NOV. 25, 1870
ORDAINED JULY 24, 1904
DIED JULY 31, 1957
AGE 86   RELIGIOUS 60
R. I. P.

Gravestone, Solanus Casey, St. Bonaventure's,
Detroit.

Solanus Casey's understanding of religion thus offers a powerful message for this age wherein many people believe we will either be mystics or atheists. His definition of religion contains two equally important elements. First, it is the science of our happy relationship with God and our neighbor. Second, religion reveals our providential dependence on God and our neighbor. How these elements of religion were articulated in Solanus' own spirituality (his words and deeds), as well as by the testimonies of those who knew him, will constitute the main thrust of the rest of this chapter.

1. *Religion is the science of our happy relationship with God and our neighbor.*

When we consider human existence as it is expressed in day-to-day living, we discover that it entails an encounter or relationship with ourselves, with God, and with others, as well as with creation itself. Since the basic encounter of the person is with God, in God, one comes to be in union with all other reality including creation. For Solanus religion was never a purely individualistic experience. As early as the novitiate he realized that religion deals with *our* relationship or encounter with God and others. Thus his novitiate jottings contain a brief entry into his notebook after the phrase Pater Noster, stressing the *"noster."* He saw in the "our" the *"totius ecclesiae,"* the whole church.

Every person is a child of God. Each of us is called to have a happy relationship with God and each other, because, as images of God we are social beings. "We should be grateful for and love the vocation to which God has called us," Solanus wrote. "This applies to every vocation, because after all, what a privilege it is to serve God—even in the least capacity."[11] At a time when people arranged and ranked various callings according to a predetermined hierarchical order, Solanus saw his vocation no greater or lesser than any other Christian's. Like all members of the Church he was merely called to be faithful to *his* call. Often he would rejoice in his specific call to live the Capuchin expression of the Gospels: "How can we ever be grateful as we ought to be for such a vocation in the Order of the Poverello of Assisi?''[12] he once wrote.

Religion was the science of *our* happy relationship with God and our neighbor. All happy relationships begin with acceptance of oneself. Solanus Casey had a positive relationship with himself. He was genuinely integrated and at peace. The positive sense he had of himself was based in an awareness and sense of call and purpose that got expressed through his outgoing personality. He did not seek popularity or fame. Neither did he depend on the acceptance of others, yet he loved to be with them.

Though few people realized the depths of his feelings, Solanus Casey was a highly emotional person throughout his life. Highly emotional individuals like Solanus tend to be people-oriented. They have the ability to relate to others and to appeal to them. In turn, people are attracted to them and can more easily place faith and trust in them.

Solanus' honesty and sincerity seemed to empower others to quickly respond to God in confidence. People had confidence in God because Solanus' honesty and sincerity made them trust in him. If Solanus believed in God, the people believed in Solanus' belief in his words about God (cf. Jn 17:20). In his early years, having suffered the loss of his greatest dream—to become a priest, able to function fully—Bernard Casey and later the early Francis Solanus Casey did not have a great amount of trust in himself. He was quite unsure of the direction he was to take. His fluctuating goals and mobility reflected this uncertainty and confusion. Nevertheless, he never lost sight of the overriding goal he had set for himself—to live in faithful union with God in the Capuchin Franciscan Order, complete with its rules, regulations, and rituals which he believed were his calling to express the gospel way of life.

Being faithful to the challenge of such a goal demanded a personality that integrated intelligence and drive. That Solanus had the intelligence is now clear. Unfortunately, Solanus was a good student in studies but tended to slack off. This tendency was never challenged by his superiors who just believed Solanus was not intellectually equipped to comprehend the Latin and German. That he also had the drive to achieve the goal is equally evident.

To achieve such a high and long-range goal one must have two important traits to keep the drive alive: enthusiasm and strong willpower. Solanus' enthusiasm was always evident in abundance. Fr. Solanus certainly was not wanting in willpower but he was hardly a self-starter except in rare instances such as his Essay Contest on Atheism. He compensated for his any lack of strong will by almost boundless energy, decisiveness, and determination. With whatever he set out to do, he would follow through in a clear and well-organized way. These traits are marks of a definite leader. Never coveting political leadership among the Capuchin brothers, Solanus remained humble and a man of the people. He used his leadership capabilities to inspire others to draw closer to God and their neighbor.

His humility is evident in his consistent feeling throughout his life that he was not as good as others believed. Though he was personally quite integrated and came off quite sincere, he never was absolutely confident in himself. Others were not aware of this side of him; in fact his appearance of confidence is what gave them hope. They saw him as being very sure of himself, confident, self-assured, but he was not this way inside. His inside self was deeply affected by an inner humility that only added to his charm.

Such charm, combined with Irish wit, made him very likable and open to others who found him to be very approachable, never causing fear or alienation. Because his philosophy was broad and quite expansive, others found him to be very open. He was receptive to those whose philosophies of life might not have agreed with his own. He was not religiously restrictive, but interested and concerned for others. He learned from them just as they learned from him.

Because people revered him as a holy man for years before his death, they rarely, if ever, could find weaknesses in him. Yet weaknesses were there, even if they were minor. Throughout his life he had to battle with those emotions that could easily get expressed in anger, intolerance, and excessive concern over little things. He determined to overcome these failings with enthusiasm; he knew his conversion from their control would draw him closer to God. Although his was a continual struggle to overcome these weaknesses, Solanus always seemed able to call on some reserve strength at the precise time to enable him to succeed in coping with them. This was the grace of God dwelling within him.

Given his strong emotions, Solanus' approach to himself, others, and the world reflected a consistency and integration that was uniquely unshaken by doubt, anxiety or fear. Toward the end of his life, for a person who remained as emotional and outgoing toward others as he was, he was remarkably uninfluenced by fears. By the end of his life, his fears had become minimal or nonexistent.

Certain values governed his actions. He was able to deal with personal weakness in a way that his pity did not become self-pity, his natural desire for affirmation did not become self-aggrandizement, his resentment at injustice was not simply a release of pent-up anger.

In viewing Solanus one received an overriding impression of integrity and freedom. The distinctive thing about Solanus was the way he articulated the quality of his love of God and others without denying his own positive self-esteem. He was able to "bear all things, believe all things, hope (in) all things, and endure all things" (1 Cor 13:7). Consequently, the relationship Solanus had with himself was a happy integration of his surface self and drives with his real self. This integration ultimately found him in control of himself; and this control directed him to a fuller and greater freedom.

Besides having a genuinely positive or happy relationship with himself, Solanus had a happy relationship with God which was especially manifest in his spirit of gratitude and thanksgiving. He did not experience God "out there" or beyond himself, but deeply within himself. God was the very ground of his being, the source of his power. He referred to this relationship—of his being with God—as a kind of "blending" of his existence with God's.[13] Through God's goodness, Solanus experienced the power of God's graceful presence at work in him. Because he was "blended" with God he was empowered to continue God's work of creation which began in Genesis and continued in Jesus of Nazareth. Now, in the twentieth century the God "in heaven" was to come on earth in the person and experience of Solanus of Prescott, Wisconsin. What God expected Jesus to do in Capernaum and

Jerusalem, Solanus was expected by God to do in Detroit and New York.

Solanus could have no excuse not to become involved in the world, nor could anyone else. The power of God had been given every person to continue creation on earth according to God's plan. "In his divine economy," Solanus wrote, "God has honored his creatures—most especially rational ones—by giving them each according to his ability, a part of his own work to do—by participation in his own divine activity."[14] "We are continually immersed in God's merciful grace like the air that permeates us," he wrote, indicating his deep faith in the abiding presence of God.[15] The only way that rational people could evidence their faith in this reality was by cooperating with God's grace: "Were we only to correspond to God's graces, continually being showered down on everyone of us, we would be able to pass from being great sinners one day to be great saints the next."[16] God's grace enabling each person to experience the divine, is the basis of faith.

God's life of grace in each person is cultivated through deep, abiding and conscious faith. Faith reveals the heart of religion: "Our Faith—Religion, is the science of our happy dependence upon God and our neighbor—of our living in his grace and dying in his love,"[17] he wrote.

As Solanus looked at his times and the depressing way so many people dealt with their problems, he sensed a deep lack of faith. He discovered much unhappiness, worry, and anxiety. For him, such alienation spelt the absence of sufficient faith. "Humanity's sad weakness," he wrote, is "lack of faith and, consequently, want of confidence in God."[18] Solanus connected lack of faith and lack of confidence in God to peoples' worry and sadness. Thus he continually urged people to nourish their faith and confidence in this God whom he experienced as so totally personal and real: "In fostering confidence," he noted, "we greatly eliminate the danger of sadness that frustrates God's merciful designs."[19]

No worry was worth the erosion of that confidence in God which anxiety represents. In fact, the only worry Solanus might allow in others was to be directed at "the little progress we make in conversion and perfection.''[20] No friar ever recalls Solanus' manifesting excessive worry, anxiety or depression. The only worry that Solanus ever did express came in those momentary expressions of frustrations that evidence emotions. Often these came after he talked with some people who shared serious problems with him. But such worry is not based in anxiety. It flows from deep, human concern about responding to those problems; much like the groaning of Jesus in the face of human pain (cf. Jn ll:33ff).

How did Solanus believe this confident, happy relationship with God could be cultivated? By prayer (personal and communal), celebration of the sacraments, devotions to the saints, especially the Blessed Virgin, the practice of discipline through bearing crosses, and the practice of charity.

First of all, prayer was to be at the heart of one's relationship with God. The greater the relationship the greater one's confidence in God. Authentic prayer generated confidence, and confidence gave rise to gratitude and thanks. Because these attitudes of gratitude and thanks characterized his own personal and confident relationship with God, Solanus naturally felt impelled to lead others to deeper faith and prayer that would give rise to these attitudes as well. In a remarkable letter he wrote to a woman experiencing anxiety and a deep sense of failure:

> . . . Why do we have discouragement as long as we have a spark of faith left? What a different view we get by exercising and by fostering the "triune virtues of FAITH, HOPE, CHARITY!" In the first place "life" here in this world is so short—comparatively so momentary—that in regard to its success or failure one is inclined to think: ". . . After all, what is the difference"—"Life" so short, that worldlings are so inclined to worship as the only LIFE—as worth everything .
>
> How is it possible that man can be so shallow-minded and still be considered "rational"?
>
> Your failure, yes, is an indication of weakness of some kind somewhere. But if "the weak things of this world hath God chosen to confound the strong. . ." as St. Paul so

wonderfully assures us—and the history of religion abounds in examples and all creation says Amen—then why ever be discouraged: unless it be that our faith, more or less, weakens?

Why dear sister, you ought rather thank God for having given you such an opportunity to humble yourself and such a wonderful chance to foster humility—and by thanking him ahead of time for whatever crosses he may deign to caress you with, CONFIDENCE in his wisdom. Confidence in God—the very soul of prayer—hardly comes to any poor sinner like we all are, without trials and humiliations, and your failure, though simple and possibly single, has no doubt been quite a little cross, at least for a "little soul" to carry. There is a little verse I am sure will profit you to keep in mind and ought to help you foster confidence in God: *God condescends to use our powers, if we don't spoil his plans by ours.* God's plans are always for the best: always wonderful. But most especially for the patient and the humble who trust in him are his plans unfathomably holy and sublime.

Let us therefore, not weaken. Let us hope when darkness seems to surround us. Let us thank him at all times and under whatever circumstances. Thank him for our creation and our existence, thank him for everything—for his plans in the past that by our sins and our want of appreciation and patience have so often been frustrated and that he so often found necessary to change. Let us thank him for all his plans for the future—for trials and humiliations for as well as great joy and consolations; for sickness and whatever death he may deign to plan; and with the inspired Psalmist let us call all the creatures of the universe to help us praise and adore him who is the Divine Beginning and the everlasting Good—the Alpha and the Omega.[21]

Solanus' counsel to others about confidence being at the heart of prayer did not arise from reading books on spirituality. It flowed from his experience; he grew in confidence in himself and God because of the many hours he spent in prayer.

From observation it would seem that Solanus had the gift of infused contemplation, or mystical prayer. During the last decades of his life spiritual writers made much ado about distinctions between *acquired* and *infused* contemplation. They said that acquired contemplation could be achieved by one's own efforts—through simple words and phrases repeated, or by the quiet prayer of the heart. Infused contemplation, the equivalent to mystical prayer, they insisted, came only to those specially called.

Solanus did not bother with such distinctions. He just knew he was experiencing God and God's abiding presence. That experience enabled him to know God personally, intimately, and thankfully.

Today's theologians approach contemplation differently than during Solanus' time. Because of our grace-filled sacramental encounter with God they say that mystical prayer and the mystical life that flows from this kind of prayer should be available not only to a few specially graced persons, but to all. "Mysticism . . . occurs within the framework of normal graces and within the experience of faith," Karl Rahner has written. "To this extent, those who insist that mystical experience is not specifically different from the ordinary life of grace (as such) are right."[22] Solanus Casey agreed. At the time of Solanus, theologians distinguished between the phenomena of *mysticism* and the *charismatic phenomena*. The mystical dimension of prayer was authenticated in the fruit of the Spirit—inner peace, joy, and charity. These gifts were evident in Solanus' day-to-day living. Thus, not only because of his abiding sense of God's presence in his life, but also because of his peace, joy and charity it can be assumed that Solanus Casey experienced the phenomena of mysticism to a high degree.

Solanus Casey also expressed his experience of God in charismatic phenomena. However, because he lived at a time when the *charismatic phenomena* were discounted as "Protestant," his contemporaries in the Catholic Church were not able to explain the nature of the charismatic phenomena expressed in the life of this priest-porter. People just accepted his gifts of healing and prophecy as uniquely from God; they never identified these gifts with charismatic phenomena available to all.

It is a given today that Solanus was highly gifted with at least some of the charismatic gifts. Certainly, healing was a gift he used to give glory to God. He also had deep insights into others, especially in his later years when he hardly used his natural intuitive abilities. While such a prophetic characteristic generated a certain wariness when Protestants exercised these gifts, none seemed to question these same manifestations in Solanus; prophecy was accepted as "normal" in him. Other gifts of the Spirit were expressed in some of Solanus' various modes of praying. His continued "Deo Gratias" was equivalent to today's "Praise the Lord."

Many found Solanus late at night in chapel lying on the floor. Today this would be called the manifestation of his being "slain in the Spirit," or "resting in the Spirit." If it was not that, it was certainly an intense form of adoration and obeisance before the presence of God.

We will probably never know about other expressions of prayer connected with the charismatic phenomena such as trances, revelations, and ecstasies. However, a contemporary spiritual writer, Benedict Joseph Groeschel, is convinced that he witnessed Solanus in a form of prayer that revealed a deep ecstatic experience. As noted in the previous chapter novices of each class were intrigued by Solanus' prayer life and experience of God at prayer. Thus Benedict writes:

> When I arrived at the Capuchin novitiate in Huntington, Indiana, in 1950, Fr. Solanus was there and obviously was a person of very profound spiritual dimensions. He spent his days in prayer receiving an endless procession of people who came to ask for his counsel and prayers and even for healing. Although he had never preached a sermon or heard a confession, he did celebrate the Eucharist in a very recollected, yet unostentatious way. In fact the only example of exceptional behavior I observed in the year I lived with him is as follows:
>
> It was a very hot night and I was unable to sleep. About three o'clock in the morning I decided to walk around the

cloister a few times and came to the side door leading into the friars' chapel. After a few moments kneeling in the dark I became aware that someone else was in the chapel quite close to me. Slightly startled, I reached over and put on the spotlight which flooded the sanctuary with bright lights. About ten feet in front of me, kneeling on the top step of the altar with his arms extended in an attitude of profound prayer was Fr. Solanus. He appeared to be totally unaware that the lights had gone on although his eyes were partly opened and he was gazing in the most intense way at the tabernacle on the altar. I am sure that he did not know that I was there because it would have been totally uncharacteristic of him to remain in this extraordinary posture if he knew he was being observed. I watched this scene for three to four minutes. He never moved at all and seemed to be scarcely breathing. After thirty years, I recall the profound sense of presence I observed in his fixed stare at the tabernacle. I do not recall ever seeing anyone in such fixed attention, although I had observed something remotely similar at a great moment in a musical presentation or as an effective preacher reached the high point of a sermon. I have never seen a human being more absorbed in anything in my life. After a few minutes, I felt that I was intruding on an event so private and intimate that I should not have been there. I put out the light and left. I later learned that it was not uncommon for the first brothers down in the morning to find Father Solanus already in the chapel either praying or sometimes asleep curled up at the foot of the altar.

Although Fr. Solanus' life was filled with the unusual, and with people coming for help who often were healed or assisted, he was a very sane man. He was quiet and self-effacing. He had a good sense of humor and interest in other people and was always courteous and deferential. Although extremely ascetic, he took care of his health and in his late seventies was the first jogger I had ever known. Despite his reputation for holiness he loved to entertain the novices with

his fiddle and was fond of playing "Pop Goes the Weasel"
and "Mother McCree."[23]

Besides his personal and mystical prayer and the regular communal
prayer which was part of Capuchin Franciscan living, Solanus cultivated his confident, happy relationship with God through the celebration of the sacraments. For him these signs of faith flowed to and from
the heart of religion. They could not be taken for granted, just as faith
could not be taken for granted. "How little we appreciate our incalcula-
ble privileges—the blessings of our holy Faith,"[24] he noted. Because
he considered life "the vestibule of heaven," the sacraments were the
steppingstones that would get us there: "When we were baptized, we
became candidates for heaven," he wrote, "and every time we receive
the sacraments of Mother Church, we take another step forward. How
wonderful and legion are our privileged opportunities!"[26] This is the
underlying reason why (reflecting the contemporary stress of that time
which often placed a value on Holy Communion independent of the
Mass), he would stress frequent Communions. Communion not only
deepened one's happy relationship with God, it promoted one's relationship with others: "Frequent Communion brings peace into a family
and into the soul. It also fosters faith in God and heavenly relationships
with all God's dear ones in heaven."[26]

Solanus' understanding of the doctrine of the "communion of
saints" reached its peak in the Eucharistic banquet. There he was at one
not only with God but all his "dear ones." He could call on these dear
ones in heaven as much as he had called on them when they were on
earth. Among "God's dear ones," he said, were our parents, relatives,
friends. Also remembered were the special people the Church called
"saints." Now that Therese of Lisieux, Conrad of Parzham, and Francis of Assisi were in heaven, they could help him and all others on their
heaven-bent journey as well. This was especially true of the Blessed
Virgin. "Learn to know Mary," he wrote, "that you may love Heaven
and heavenly things."[27]

To Solanus, the saints were those special models who could not only inspire us to follow Christ more closely; they were our special intercessors and friends in heaven. Of course, Mary was the most important friend and model. By discovering more about her, people could better discover how they could live, even with their difficulties. "How little we realize what a benefit it is that we taste sorrow now and then. Get acquainted," he urged, "with the Queen of Martyrs—God's Mother suffering— and you will learn something of how we ought to love sorrow and pains in this life."[28] Mary was not only seen as heroine. Solanus viewed Mary as the co-parent of redemption. Following the Bonaventurian theology of the Church's being born from the side of Christ on the cross, he wrote: "Mary gave birth to Christ in a manger at Bethlehem, and to the rest of us thirty-three years later, under the cross at Calvary."[29] Mary was the Mother of the Church, the body of Christ.

In addition to his theological training that influenced his Mariology, Solanus came to know more about Mary through his regular reading of the four volumes of The Mystical City of God by the Spanish mystic, Mary of Agreda. Mary of Jesus (of Agreda [1602–1665]) was the foundress and first abbess of the Franciscan Recollects at Agreda. She was known for her virtue and for her prolific writing. Among the latter The Mystical City of God has proved to be the most important[30] and most controversial.

While she said that anyone who did not believe its contents committed a sin, various Roman authorities thought otherwise. It was first condemned, in 1681, especially because of some farfetched statements. Despite her holiness, the Franciscan Pope, Clement xIV, stopped her beatification process (March 12, 1771) because of the book. In no way did he discount her sanctity or her extraordinary union with God, Poulein implies, only her revelation.[31]

Despite such negative influence, Solanus believed an equal number of Church experts, popes, and bishops fully endorsed the work. His own endorsement of The Mystical City of God reflects the strong faith in private revelation that was part of Catholic spirituality before Vatican II. Solanus, in his tendency to take people at their word, accepted Mary of Jesus' contention that her writings were almost word-for-word given by the Blessed Virgin.

If there is any part of Solanus' life that created confusion for others and indicates his possible gullibility, naiveté and excessive faith in the goodness of others, it is evidenced in his deeply held conviction that Mary had dictated the words contained in *The Mystical City of God* to Mary of Agreda. Solanus deeply believed that the four volumes reflected Mary's deepest thoughts about redemption and salvation. Given this conviction it was very natural that Solanus would want to share these reflections with others that they might draw closer to Christ, the Redeemer and Savior and, ultimately, to God.

While all things led ultimately to God, Solanus believed it was God's will that Mary be given special honor. "There is no one else on earth or in heaven, that God himself loves as he loves his ever Virgin, Immaculate Mother, and wishes her to be known and loved."[32] Probably the hardest self-denial he had to endure was the demand by his superiors not to associate directly with Ray Garland, the man who had helped him promote the four volumes. To the superiors Garland was an opportunist, gaining a reputation through Solanus. To Solanus, Ray was a trusted and dedicated co-worker, equally devoted to a devotional aid which he sincerely believed would draw people closer to God. Given his strong streak of rebellion and independence, submitting to their demand was emotionally difficult to Solanus. It did violence to his intense convictions. Yet he believed that this denial of his emotional-self would bring his true self into deeper union with God who would exonerate Mary of Agreda and her writings if that was God's will.

Self-denial was an important way Solanus tried to cultivate his happy relationship with God. The discipline of self-denial was part of his approach to God. He had joined the Capuchin Franciscan Order when, in comparison with other religious orders, it was known to be very austere. Furthermore, among the U.S. Capuchin Provinces, the St. Joseph Province was noted for a special austerity.

Through prayer, fasting, and the traditional forms of ascetical discipline practiced in the Province, Solanus developed an approach to people and things that facilitated his relationship with God. If anything or anyone got in the way of that relationship, he would try to avoid it not because it might not be good, but because of that God whom he wanted to experience more deeply. "Oh, if we would only learn to keep an eye on ourselves, e.g., on our inordinate inclinations to pamper our own whims and desires," he wrote, "so that we might be like Jesus, catering and adjusting himself to the will—not only of his Father, but to the meanest of men . . . even to death on the Cross!"[33]

Solanus Casey believed that the easiest way to imitate Jesus on the cross was by faithfully and happily "taking up our crosses." Crosses were "the best school wherein to learn appreciation for the love of Jesus Crucified."[34] Somehow, like the Resurrection flowing from Jesus' acceptance of the cross, daily sufferings could lead people more closely to a deep relationship with God. "If we only try to show the dear Lord a good will and ask him for resignation to the crosses he sends or permits to come our way," he wrote, "we may be sure that sooner or later they will turn out to have been just so many blessings in disguise."[35] In light of his experience of that God who "blended" with his life, Solanus was able to place human suffering in a salvific context.

He suffered much throughout his life from chronic ailments and a painful skin disease. One he wrote that the pain was "excruciating. Though I tried to thank God for it," he admitted, "my principal prayer was: 'God help me.' "[36] This suffering of his own led him back to the experience of God: "If we were to get a glimpse into the infinite depths of eternity and the glory reserved there for those who suffer patiently; or at least resignedly, the momentary joys and sorrows of time would seem like nothing."[37] In fact, viewing suffering contemplatively, he realized that it provided the opportunity to experience final resurrection even now: "How merciful is the good God in letting us now and then run up against a snag of some kind, halts us for at least a moment of reflection on the real purpose of our existence as rational creatures: ETERNITY IN GOD."[38]

On the one hand, Solanus viewed suffering as redemptive in the way it could lead to closer union with God. "In the crosses of life that come to us, Jesus offers us opportunities to help him redeem the world. Let us profit by his generosity,"[39] he would say. Or again, "We do well to remember how very short after all, it is till our suffering and our time of merit too, will be over. Let us offer everything, therefore to the divine Spouse of our souls, that he may accept it as helping him to save immortal souls, our own included."[40]

On the other hand, while such redemptive suffering could bring eternal happiness to one's neighbor, most people identify Solanus Casey with bringing temporal happiness to many of his "neighbors"—of every race, religion, and economic background—through his extraordinary faith that resulted in these people's healing. This brings us to the last way Solanus' spirituality fulfilled his own definition of religion: *our happy relationship with our neighbor*.

Empowered by his faith, Solanus was able to be an instrument of healing in others' lives and relationships. Solanus' faith in God was based on a conviction that God's power was without limit. He was not about to set limits on what God could do for others, whether those "others" lived at the time of Jesus or in the twentieth century. Setting limits was a sign of weak faith. From his religious experience of God, Solanus was convinced that God wanted to be powerful in the world—now through humans made in the image of that God. "We are so weak in faith," he would say, "setting limits to God's power and goodness."[41] Since God's power was and is manifest in God's care and solicitude, humans should simply believe that God does care about those things that cause us concern, especially suffering. "Let us turn to God," he therefore urged, that God "whose solicitude for our welfare—temporal and as well as spiritual—puts all created solicitude out of the picture."[42]

The solicitude and care of God became Solanus' solicitude and care for others. Like Jesus whose "heart was moved with pity at the sight of the crowd," Solanus was "moved with pity" at the sight of various needs and suffering of those who flocked to him from all over this continent. Jesus' *pity* at the sight of the crowds was Solanus' concern about people's "pathetic" condition. Solanus used the word "pitiable" more frequently than any other word when he referred to people's descriptions of their various pains. Full of pity, God was able to use Solanus of Prescott as Jesus of Nazareth was used by God to "heal sickness and diseases of every kind" (cf. Mt 4:23, 9:35–36). Somehow, in Solanus' presence, even when healing did not happen as people might have hoped, invariably a deeper healing in the form of calm and acceptance was received.

Not everyone was healed in the way they had originally hoped; yet they were touched by other dimensions of healing that "went forth from the man." Probably the most moving tribute about this gift of healing given Solanus came from the Chancellor of the Archdiocese of Detroit, Msgr. Edward J. Hickey:

> He heard more of the ills, of the sufferings, of the worries and fears of people of our city, perhaps more than all the priests in any one parish or more than two or three parishes combined. From morning to night he would be listening to persons with worries and cares and disturbances and with all the humility and all the patience in the world he would give them fatherly advice and often enkindle their courage and hopes and reassure them in a brief time their troubles would be finished or counsel them to be resigned to suffer with Christ. "Tomorrow at 9 o'clock," "in two days at 3 o'clock," or "within a short time" if you have faith these troubles will disappear.
>
> It is my conviction that after reading his biography and the records of cures which seemed to have resulted from his prayers, perhaps there were more cures reported in these notes, which he kept by order of his superior, than were reported in the Gospels, than were reported perhaps at Lourdes, at St. Anne de Beaupré or at Fatima, in the same length of time.
>
> Now that would be a very surprising record if the dear Lord was working more supernatural cures through the prayers and faith inspired by Fr. Solanus here in our city on

Mt. Elliott Avenue than in all the notable shrines of Christendom combined.[43]

Besides the gift of healing which brought happiness to many, Solanus also used his gift of prophecy to encourage, challenge, and to bring back hope to others. Usually his "prophecies" took the form of dealing with the future and what would happen to people. Yet somehow, as early as his years in Yonkers, people felt he could "tell the future." The Sisters of St. Agnes at Sacred Heart, his first assignment, had a saying: "If, in June when you go back to the Motherhouse in Wisconsin, Fr. Solanus says, 'See you in September,' you will be coming back; if he just says, 'Good-bye,' you will be transferred." Such insights could hardly have been based on intuitions alone; how much was based on the actual prophetic gifts described by Paul (cf. Rom 12 and 1 Cor. 12) will never be known.

Even when his prophecies spelled continued suffering or even death, people received the strength to approach their pain with greater peace. One of these people was Mrs. Eva Dugall. She lived in Windsor, Ontario, and suffered from tuberculosis. She was in her late thirties and had two children. She had been on the verge of dying for many months, but struggled to live because of her children. Someone drove Solanus across the river from Detroit to visit her.

When he entered the house, the first things she said was, "Oh, you look just like Jesus Christ, himself." His dark beard and his tall, lean frame in the brown habit, combined with his gentle blue eyes and peaceful composure had often brought such a response. Solanus had learned to take such comments in stride.

"Well, I'm taking his place," Solanus replied. "I was sent here by him. I came here because the Lord has a crown waiting for you. Why don't you resign yourself to go to heaven and forget about your children? The Lord has a lot of good mothers, especially the Blessed Virgin, and she will take care of your children."

"Oh, I feel so different now," the woman responded, sensing a calm which so many others seemed to receive in Solanus' presence and words. "Well, if you do," Solanus said, "let's all pray for you and you pray with us."

Everyone knelt down and Solanus led a decade of the rosary. There was not a dry eye in the room. When he finished, Solanus said, "I promise you the Lord will help you today."

By eleven o'clock that same night the woman was dead, relieved from her pain.[44]

At other times, Solanus had ways to imply that people would receive healing. He used terms such as, "the doctor will be surprised," "have the doctor look again," or "I don't think there is a need for that." Such responses would often be made after people approached him for prayers and his blessing. He would often look away as though he was thinking deeply, or close his eyes for ten or fifteen seconds. Then he would say something like, "She'll be better in seven days."

Solanus' gifts of healing and prophecy were united more deeply in the gift of discerning wisdom. Somehow Solanus knew what was best to say or not to say in all sorts of situations. To some people who were not Catholics, he would say nothing about becoming a Catholic; he just urged them to grow in fidelity to their own religious practice, whether they were Jews or Christians. However, to others, he seemed to sense an openness to Catholicism. When he sensed such receptivity, he requested them, as part of their response to what the good God was already doing in and for them, to "at least investigate the claims of the Catholic Church."

Despite the many who sensed genuine wisdom in Solanus, others felt he was imprudent in the way he offered advice to people who, in turn, would misinterpret his comments. Such imprudence and naiveté, they felt, evidenced a certain lack of wisdom. Fr. Elmer Stoffel, the novice-master, was one of them. He was happy that the Constitutions forbade the novices to speak to the professed because he thought Solanus gave bad advice. Msgr. Hickey, the Chancellor of the Archdiocese of Detroit was another. At times he became unsettled because many people would take every word Solanus said and accept it as gospel, sometimes at great inconvenience to themselves. In a special way this applied to those people who would immediately purchase all four volumes of Mary of Agreda's *Mystical City of God,* even though they could ill-afford it.

Not everything Solanus said was always accurate; this could be said especially of those situations wherein he was not exercising his role as counselor to people in need. Solanus was not perfect; he did make mistakes; he did try to be *made* perfect (cf Mt 5:48) by God's power at work in him; yet, he was human, and all humans err. Misunderstandings did arise, yet even Solanus' critics will agree, for the most part, much confusion and disappointment happened because people naturally interpreted Solanus' words literally or through their own "filters" to support positions from which they refused to budge and which they wanted to be endorsed by Solanus' authority.

Incidents such as the ones just described indicate, at the least, lack of wisdom on the part of others, if not on the part of Solanus. Yet there are many more situations that have been recounted that indicate he possessed a deep gift of wisdom.

To a certain Capuchin friar who had his share of illness—but who also had more than his share of hypochondria—Solanus' wisdom, understanding and counsel are clearly evident in a letter of deep brotherly sensitivity:

April 28, '45
Pax Domini!

My Dear Frater Sebastian!
    God bless you and yours.
May 11th
    You see I made very little progress two weeks ago on the card Br. Leo gave me and suggested I write to you. However, while I would like to write you more of a real letter, which in fact I proposed to do, I found it not easy to get anywhere. However, I am sending you herewith a letter written to a priest who at times was in Yonkers, N.Y., and quite inclined to worry about one thing or another; nearly always about imaginary things, i.e., about something that turns out to have been more or less just a temptation.

Of course we are all naturally inclined that way. From our dear Lord's "Sermon on the Mount," you can see how the Apostles themselves are no exceptions. Just read the 5th, 6th, and 7th chapters of St. Matthew and see how our dear Lord almost scolded them for their want of faith.

No one blames you, self-understood, for trying to be healthy. That's only a part of the first law of nature. But to be over anxious about it is not good; or to think that the good God should work a miracle for us. Because we ought to know that he is the only one who can work a miracle. We can try of course, to induce him—through the intercession of the saints and our Blessed Mother, Mary Queen of all.

When Fr. Ex-Provincial Theodosius (Foley) was a cleric, it was generally feared he'd never be ordained. So keep up your courage dear Frater—just one day at a time and leave the morrow and yesterday to the Good God. And please pray for this poor sinner.[45]

Insights such as those expressed in the above letter might be attributed to natural wisdom. Yet the fact that Solanus spent much time prayerfully seeking the wisdom of God before and even as he would talk to people or write such letters, reinforces the belief that he brought healing, prophecy, and wisdom together in his ministry toward others from a source beyond the purely natural. In this light, the thoughts of William Johnston in his contemporary work on the mystical life bear recalling:

> . . . Let us never underestimate the wisdom of the desert. For the fact is that the person who has spent long periods in authentic prayer and meditation knows about the sufferings of the world because he has experienced it all within himself. How often a repentant sinner, filled with remorse for his iniquities and failures, has gone to the solitary monk to confess his crimes—and, lo and behold, he has found someone who understands the whole story. For the monk has experienced it all within himself—in another way. He

has met the devil and seen his own awful weakness and potentiality for evil. It does not shock him to hear about murder and rape and violence—and he is filled with compassion for the weakness of a human race to which he himself belongs. Moreover, like (the Buddhist god/goddess Bodhisattval) Kannon who with that exquisite smile of compassion for the cries of the poor, the mystic also has in his own way heard the cries of the underprivileged, the downtrodden, the victims of violence and deceit and exploitation—just as Jesus knew it all in Gethsemane. Of course, it will do him no harm to read *Time* and *Newsweek* also. And if he does, he will find there things which the authors of the articles did not realize.[46]

Solanus was able to find in the human condition many things that touched his heart, evoking God's pathos in him. As a result, he had compassion on the crowd. Events took place that seemed truly marvelous "in the sight of the people." Far from appropriating these marvelous and miraculous powers to himself, Solanus simply believed they should be expected as normative in our age as much as in the former age in which Jesus said, "These Scriptures are being fulfilled even as you listen" (Lk 4:18). "To doubt the truth of miracles in any age of history," he noted, "would be nothing less than to fall in line with the ideas of the unbelieving world—deaf, dumb, and spiritually blind."[47]

While the gifts of healing, prophecy, and wisdom were extraordinary in his life, "the greatest of all these gifts" (cf. 1 Cor 13) in Solanus' 87 years was charity. Charity not only characterized his happy relationship with God, it overflowed in the warm, caring, fraternal and even humorous way he related to his neighbor. "Charity is always good; always to be commended and fostered," he wrote. "But after all, rightly ordered charity begins at home. To my mind, that means it should begin right in one's own heart—to be practical, in my own soul."[48]

Building on a positive love for self, Solanus manifested his charity in positive relationships with others. He viewed charity as the fountain of happiness. He let it bubble up in the many different ways he worked to bring joy to others. In many ways, whether it was in the ways he ministered to his own fellow Capuchins (like the gentle ways he tried to help his classmate, Fr. Damasus, in his blindness and old age) or his nonthreatening demeanor which seemed to quiet even noisy babies when he touched them, charity was the hallmark of his life. This characteristic, even more than his purported healings and mystical phenomena, witnesses to the heroism of his virtue.

Just as "charity, properly ordered," begins at home toward others so did judgment of one's neighbor. He referred to himself as "this poor sinner . . . who more than anyone else gives me the most trouble." Then he would add, "I consider it a mercy that we need examine one conscience only!"[49] However, when it came to judging others, his understanding of charity demanded that we "be as blind to the faults of your neighbor as possible, trying at least to attribute a good intention to their actions."[50] Given his strong convictions, Solanus had a natural tendency to be critical. He learned how to harness it in generosity in interpreting others and their motives. Solanus lived out his words about examining only his own conscience, even when his judgment of a situation might be considered superficial or when it created conflict as it did with his "blindness" to the faults and virtue of someone like his coworker, Ray Garland.

Those who lived and worked with him, including his own confreres (who could be very critical of him) cannot remember a time when Solanus spoke negatively of another human being. Somehow, it seemed, he tried to act on his belief that each person was a spark of God's goodness and, in response to that goodness, he could only be grateful. This brings us to the conclusion of the first part of Solanus' definition—the idea of gratitude.

Gratitude was the unique way Solanus manifested the "happy' part of his relationship with God and neighbor. Because "gratitude is the first sign of a thinking, rational creature,"[51] ingratitude, whether it be toward God or neighbor had to be "poor humanity's sorrow, or unhappiness."[52] "Be sure," he warned, "if the enemy of our souls is pleased at anything in us, it is ingratitude of whatever kind. Why? Ingratitude leads to so many breaks with God and neighbor."[53] Because any break with God or neighbor reflects a break in charity, gratitude would be the way to preserve not only a happy relationship with God and neighbor, but union with both as well.

2. *Religion is the science of our providential dependence on God and our neighbor.*

The second part of Solanus' definition of religion builds on his thoughts related to gratitude. It also contextualizes them in his understanding of God's plan or design. "How wonderful are all God's designs for all who confide in him. How fortunate! How humbly grateful we ought to be!"[54]

Solanus' various elaborations on the second part of his definition of religion indicates that he viewed "our providential dependence on God" as having two elements. The first element implies *passive* abandonment or trust in God's will to do good for us at all times. "Trust in God," he would write: "his providence governs all things sweetly, even though we cannot see it immediately. This is where we must have faith and confidence."[55] The second element involves *active* abandonment or the willingness to be co-creators with God in history. This second part, active abandonment, will be discussed a bit later.

The heart of Solanus' spirituality flowed from his confidence in God's providence. This was his passive abandonment. Solanus' faith convinced him that there was a God. Such a faith-conviction was built on his personality which was goal-oriented and single-minded (others might say it reflected his hard-headed Irish convictions!). Solanus reasoned that if he had a happy relationship with God, it was because he experienced this God as one who wills to bring order from disorder, healing from pain, fulfillment from poverty and loving union from sinful alienation.

The only things that could place obstacles to the power of God at work in the world were doubt and fear. Thus his conclusion that "one of humanity's greatest weaknesses is setting a limit on God's power and goodness.''[56] Solanus' experience of God freed him from the control of doubt and fear. It created a pure-hearted confidence that assured him God wanted to work in him on others' behalf.

Consequently almost unshakeable confidence earmarked his whole approach to God. In ''fostering confidence, we greatly eliminate the danger of sadness that frustrates God's merciful designs,''[57] he wrote. Solanus' stress on confidence was faithful to the spirituality of his era which was highly influenced by the work of the eighteenth-century Jesuit, Pierre de Causade, *Abandonment to Divine Providence*. De Causade's theory was that the height of perfection can be achieved by lovingly and confidently fulfilling the simplest of common duties. Probably the most well-known interpreter of that insight was Therese Martin of Lisieux, France.

''The Little Flower''had died when Solanus was twenty-six. When her *Autobiography* was released it had touched something deep in the spirit of Solanus. Her simple way of trustful confidence in God's providence resonated with him. ''She makes sanctity really attractive and so beautifully simple,''[58] he wrote to his sister in 1915 (little aware that his own confidence was already at that time beginning to help people in their path to God).

An experience Solanus had several years before was likely instrumental in developing his spirituality around confident trust in a way that was similar to the Little Flower's. One time (in 1909 while he was in Yonkers), he confided to a former Capuchin novice:

> I had completely lost the hearing in my left ear and the same condition was rapidly threatening the other side. I had returned a certain Thursday evening from the specialist with a throbbing earache after a very painful treatment and very delicate and dangerous proposition. Five years before that, I had read the life of Sr. Therese Martin, till then seemingly unknown, and had greatly profited thereby; happy in the communion of saints as I felt, on having another heavenly friend. I had felt from the first reading that she would be canonized. Well, in my anxiety that night I made a ''mental

proposition'' to her that if she would help to save my hearing I'd read her life again. I was even then confident that
she could help me and that being already in heaven, she
would.[59]

His ear was healed.

Already then (around the time of his ordination) Solanus' spirituality
was beginning to reflect a childlike trust in God's loving providence.
Because God's care for us is deeper than the greatest of our cares for
ourselves, Solanus reasoned that we should abandon ourselves to that
greater care, confident that all things will work out for the good. Like
Jesus in the Sermon on the Mount (Mt 7:31ff) Solanus urged people to
"Shake off excessive worry and exercise a little confidence in God's
providence."[60] His experience of God's loving providence assured him
that no faithful follower of Jesus would ever be asked to do more or bear
more than can be borne. "How merciful the good God is," he once said
with his Irish wit, "always fitting 'the back to the burden,' if not vice-
versa, as often is the case!"[61]

"How wonderful are all God's designs for all who" have confidence, Solanus would say over and over again. He saw God's designs
unfolded both in the manifest and the hidden events of life. With confidence, a hope-filled person should be able to see beyond these manifestations to a God by whose grace we are "fortified to profit by them
all."[62]

In his mind the chief obstacle to living providentially dependent on
God was grounded in worry. Just as Jesus said, "Do not worry,"
because he knew there was a God whose very nature as parent demanded that our needs would be met, so Solanus advised others to think
about that same God-parent, rather than being controlled by fear and
anxiety. "Why worry? Rather foster confidence in his divine providence by humbly and in all childlike humility venturing to remind
him—remind him in the person of our Brother Jesus—that we are his
children."[63]

Even though the psychologist in him wisely realized that "worry is a weakness from which very few of us are entirely free," the theologian in him saw that worry could also indicate lack of faith. We should "be on our guard against this most insidious enemy of our peace of soul," he wrote. We maintain our guard when we "foster confidence in God, and thank him ahead of time for whatever he chooses to send us."[64]

One of the amazing things about Solanus Casey was the fact that so many people over such a long period of time were brought to healing through his intercession. Yet he never appropriated their adulation and praise to himself but to God. Perhaps this might be because he remained faithful to a note he wrote while still in his novitiate: "Beware of congratulating thyself on the blessings wrought through thy medium."[65]

Investigating Solanus' responses to people's comments about his "healing power," it seems his radical confidence in God's will to save was linked to his belief in the power and value of the sacraments and sacramentals of the Catholic faith. He believed these latter actually *were* the instruments of healing the theologians and indulgence-givers said they should be. Invariably, he connected healings with various blessings of the True Cross, membership in the Seraphic Mass Association, feeding the hungry or caring for the sick, the blessing of a priest, or some spiritual or corporal work of mercy. Referring to the specific sacraments and sacramentals of the Catholic religion, he noted, "If we could only learn to appreciate the holy Faith and the innumerable blessings flowing from it and the blessings otherwise surrounding us; we should never have time to worry about anything."[66] Solanus just could not appropriate such divine power to himself; he placed the value of healing in the efficacy of prayer and good works.

Such deep-seated humility revealed that wisdom which is gained from deep prayerful encounter with God. By experiencing God through the Spirit of Jesus in prayer, we have all things revealed to us (Mt 11:25–27), especially the fact that we have been given the power of Jesus to deal with events with the mindset of Jesus. For Solanus, anxiety was the only obstacle to appropriating this "mind of Christ." "We worry our heads and hearts about many things," he noted. "As a result people almost totally undervalue the invitation most beautiful of all: 'Learn of me because I am meek and humble of heart.' "[67]

The more we learn about Jesus, the more we grow in wisdom. Thus, we can look back on our lives and our world's history from a new perspective. Where fear and worry might have reigned previously, wisdom generates that peace and gratitude which can become the common-sense attitude toward all events, including those that are most trying: "Shake off anxiety," Solanus wisely urged. "Last year it was something that you now smile about. Tomorrow it's about something that will not be serious if you raise your heart to God and thank him for whatever comes."[68]

Besides gaining wisdom through prayer, another way passive abandonment to God's designs may be cultivated is connected to our intelligence itself. Memory enables us to recall; recollection empowers us to make connections. Both facilitate that knowledge by which rational creatures become aware of God. "What a wonderful gift of God is memory! But what is it compared to hope?" Solanus asked. While they were different, they were far from exclusive. He concluded that "they cooperate together to glorify God, along with the other two triune virtues of faith and charity."[69] Memory also helps develop gratitude.[70] "When we think of past blessings and the merciful providence (not withstanding our sins), whereby God has blessed us," he asked, "why should we not foster confidence by thanking him for the future?"[71]

Although he remembered the past, especially in his later years, it was rarely for nostalgic reasons alone. The past was remembered in the present so that the future might be lived more fully. In considering the future, Solanus came to the conclusion that he was not only dependent on God; God was providentially dependent on him. God depended on all other creatures to create a future that reflected the gradual fulfillment of God's original plan. From this creation-centered theological perspective Solanus Casey's *active* abandonment to divine providence can be best understood.

We not only need God as creator; God needs us as co-creators. "Who can fully appreciate the privilege that God has given us of the possibility of our helping him in the work of redemption," he wondered, "thus saving our own 'destiny for eternal glory.' "[72] In the way humans are present to each other in making history, God's creative work is continued in the world.

Besides being the science of our providential dependence on God, religion thus involves mutual dependence of humans on each other. "How wonderful, in the promotion of mutual and common charity," he wrote, "that next to our happy dependence on God himself, he has made us mutually dependent on one another."[73] In responding to others in their needs, as God has responded to us in our needs, we reveal ourselves as images of God. In the process, we not only reveal God's care or *pathos,* but experience ourselves cared for by God. In doing a favor for our neighbor, Solanus reasoned, the favor is done for God; thus we become favored by God.[74] If more people would only live by this basic principle of the Last Judgment, Solanus believed, the world could be transformed: "What a marvelously different society we would have here, and what an ideal world to live in if we would all keep in mind the assurance of Jesus, 'What you have done to the least of my brethren, you have done to me.' "[75]

Given this conviction of humanity's interdependence, Solanus could not imagine a me-and-God approach to spirituality that was limited to an inner, personalistic dimension. On the contrary, he clearly stated that any spirituality controlled by individualism was incomplete: "If we are interested in saving our souls, we must have an interest in our brothers and sisters."[76] Such a statement places Solanus' spirituality among the best mystics-in-action. According to the Belgian mystic, Jan van Ruysbroeck:

> . . . even in eternal life, happiness would not exist without activity; God himself would not be God, if he did not act, and happiness would have no existence for him.
> . . . Interior consolation is of an inferior order to the act of love which renders service to the poor. Were you rapt in ecstasy like St. Peter or St. Paul, or whomsoever you will, and heard that some poor person was in want of a hot drink,

> or other assistance, I should address you to awake for a moment from your ecstasy to go to prepare the food. Leave God for God; find him, serve him in his members; you will lose nothing by the exchange. What you give up for love of him, God will give you back with abundant interest.
>
> All who are drawn by God produce acts of virtue, living and fruitful, after the likeness of the Blessed Trinity, according to the measure of worth and dignity they have received.[77]

Faithful to the insight of van Ruysbroeck, Solanus' greatest concern was for others in need. Much of this compassion was expressed in his healing ministry. But to many, even more than healing, Solanus' concern about providing "the food" for others, is what made his virtue heroic. Unfortunately too many people have remembered Solanus Casey for the former gift and not the latter; yet he often said, "I have two favorites: the sick and the poor." Not everyone might be so gifted with Solanus' unique healing powers, yet all can imitate him in his concern for the poor. In Solanus' eyes, all baptized people, including all religious, should be concerned about the poor. Among all the baptized this should be the special concern of those who follow Francis of Assisi. "Our lot," he said, referring to the Capuchin Franciscan vocation, "has been cast among the simple lives of the poor."[78]

Barney Casey's parents taught him to be concerned for the poor; his solicitude for them continued throughout his life. From his earliest notebooks as a young Capuchin in formation, Solanus noted that responding to the needs of the poor brings us directly into relationship with God: "The poor stretch forth the hand, but God receives what is offered,"[79] he noted. People—from his first assignment at Sacred Heart in Yonkers to his death at St. Bonaventure's in Detroit—recall his continual care for the poor, the unemployed and the outcasts of society. Anyone in need was to be welcomed as a representative of God.

During the height of the Depression, Solanus Casey was instrumental in establishing the permanent "Capuchin Soup Kitchen" in Detroit, which, along with a host of other services today, feeds close to 1,000 people each work day. Because he believed we are mutually dependent on each other's providence, he was never embarrassed to request aid from those who requested help from him—whether it was a wealthy woman in Grosse Pointe, a farmer with abundant crops, or the Detroit Mayor who had connections to ensure jobs for the unemployed. At times Solanus' solicitude for the needy got him into trouble, as it did with the friary cook who didn't quite agree that the poor had as much right to the food he prepared as did the friars. Yet no one denied that Solanus' love of the poor was grounded in the Gospel and the best in aescetical spirituality.

One person who seems to remember Solanus more for his concern for people in need than for healing, was a person who was on the receiving end of Solanus' care. Andrew Lawrence was not a person in need of daily bread; this priest of the Holy Trinity Mission Congregation was in need of funds that would enable his congregation to survive. Andrew Lawrence first met Solanus in 1930. Desperately in need of monies to continue the fledgling Congregations's ministry among the poor in Southeastern Alabama, he and a companion had come to Detroit trying to raise money.

On the way to visit the Diocesan Director of the Propagation of the Faith, he mentioned the need for housing to a man in the elevator. In his testimony he notes:

> This man said, "Well, if you have need, why don't you go and see Fr. Solanus?"
> We said, "Who's Fr. Solanus?"
> He said, "Oh, he's a very holy and wonderful Capuchin priest. He's very good to the poor and helps so many people."
> The man spoke with such deep conviction that Brother and I found out where the Monastery was located. . . . We found our way out there and this very sweet, kind, wonderful gentleman welcomed us. He was an older man at the time we met him, and had a long beard covering a very ascetic face. We thought he was a lay brother and we asked to speak to Fr. Solanus.

He said, "Well, what can we do for you? Come in."

So, the first thing he did was bring us in and give us some coffee and some bread and some food. He was so very kind. He made us feel very much at home. Then we told him we were Trinity Missionaries and that we were working with the poor in our own country but that we just had no place to stay and no money to go to a hotel.

"Well," he said, "I'm sure that Father Guardian will be happy to have you stay here. We are delighted to welcome those who work with the poor."

He was so fine and friendly. He not only got Father Guardian and pleaded our cause for hospitality, but he took the bags we had and carried them. He wouldn't even let us carry our own bags. He took us upstairs. He was . . . very solicitous about these two beggars who came in unannounced.[80]

Solanus' ministry manifested itself in concern about alleviating the cry of the poor, be it that of a fellow religious like Fr. Andrew, a hitchhiker on the road, or the people in the bread lines.

Faithful to the best in Pauline theology, he also used the defensive weapons of truth, justice and peace in the way he used the word of God (cf. Eph 6:10–17) to meet the needs of the poor and oppressed and address the problems of his world. "Only lovers of justice and truth can possess the kingdom of heaven," he said. "And to be children of God we must be lovers of justice, truth, and peace."[81]

The era at Huntington when Solanus did the majority of his existent letter writing was the post-World War II era. The anticommunism of Joe McCarthy, (a native of Appleton, Wisconsin, where Solanus offered his First Solemn High Mass and earlier worked on the street cars) was rampant. The Korean Conflict was waged during this period. Solanus called the times, "at once so restless and so foreboding. . . ." Yet he also believed, "by the grace of God" working through humans, the world could again become "so colorful and so promising."[82] Since, in times of war and conflicts one of the first victims is often veracity, Solanus placed a great stress on truth among humans, and groups, and institutional leaders.

Solanus had a passion for what he believed to be true. Because he was so convinced that no rational person could not possibly believe in God, he tried to raise one million dollars to give as a prize to anyone who could prove that the existence of God was not true.

His concern for truth overflowed into his concern for justice. Faithful to his continual linkage of religon to rationality, he once wrote, "Disregard for the claims of justice—under whatever pretext—has always been a manifestation of, to say the very least, shallow thinking—or rather a betrayal of real thinking."[83]

Whether it was his concern that truth be told his provincial about a Capuchin confrere whom he believed had suffered injustice at the hands of his local superior in Harlem or the articulations of "the facts" related to the British subjugation of the Irish, he made it very clear to whatever "powers that be" that truth and justice were absolutely necessary for authentic human relationships. At the same time, when he himself would be slighted by others' untruths or injustice, especially by the very few fellow Capuchins who could mock him or slight him, he never, to anyone's memory, tried to justify himself or retaliate (cf. Is 53:7). He accepted corrections patiently, even when accused of mistakes that were not his fault.

While not at all keen on defending his own rights, his concern for the rights of others and for various justice issues at different times might raise some eyebrows today. For instance, faithful to his Irish heritage, he wrote such a stinging reply to the *Catholic News* about an apparently (to Solanus) pro-British article that the paper rejected his "letter to the editor." It was subsequently printed in the *Irish World and Industrial Liberator*. Another indiscretion in justice efforts was shown in his early support of Fr. Charles Coughlin. While Solanus had the gift of prophecy to deal with some situations and people, his reference to Coughlin as "our prophet,"[84] shows it was not necessarily applied to all events!

There were times that he had very harsh words to say against groups of people whom he thought were violating basic principles of truth and justice. Yet, while he spoke out against these situations, such as the history of England's alleged crimes against the Irish, he loved the

British. Similarly, he could condemn atheists as a group; however, he could find only compassion for individuals who said they were atheists.

The St. Thomas Aquinas whom Solanus had studied so diligently as a student wrote that courage is the virtue that is needed in the promotion of justice. Whether it was for this reason or because he linked courage so closely with confidence in God and building God's reign on earth, Solanus made courage one of his major themes. In one's relationship with God, he believed, confidence was the very soul of courage.[85] For him, confidence was merely courage divinely reinforced.[86] With God's power at work in us, we should not be afraid of any possible humiliation or persecution; at the time of misunderstandings and trials, if we have been faithful, we will be given the courage to speak truth, justice and peace.

Courage is the stuff of martyrs. Recalling the victims of oppressive regimes who were suffering persecution for justice' sake, Solanus wrote,

> It is hard to reckon the extent of modern martyrdom the Church has suffered these several decades, and probably less possible to surmise what seems still shortly to follow— the judgment awaiting enemies of truth, as well as the glory reserved for those who will have persevered—suffering for justice and truth.[87]

Because truth is the foundation of justice and justice is the foundation of peace, perhaps the greatest "Pauline weapon" Solanus used in his defense of the Gospel was his inner peace and effort to bring peace to others.

First of all, Solanus possessed the gift of peace personally. From this source of peace Solanus was at rest with God. He thus could communicate a calming effect to others even in the midst of very trying circumstances. "Peace is an outstanding characteristic of charity," he wrote. "They accompany each other and must begin if really genuine, between God and the individual soul."[88] For Solanus, no human could achieve this peace except "in the willing service of his Creator."[89] Remaining true to his definition about religion vis-à-vis God *and* neighbor, Solanus' peace had to extend beyond his own relationship with God into his service of others, with whom he led a mutually dependent life.

By natural disposition (of all the sports he played as a youth, he never took up boxing), Solanus was nonviolent. Though he was competitive and loved to debate issues, he did not give in to his strong emotional bent to be violent toward others. He was able to control his tendency to judge and lash out. He came to terms with his anger; he was able to sublimate and direct it toward faith and justice. By purifying his natural emotion of anger and by sublimating it in his concern for others, Solanus was able to manifest *just anger* or more aptly, the passionate love for justice.

Such discipline demanded continual, on-going conversion. Aware of his tendencies, as well as his real human feelings, Solanus continually asked others to pray for his conversion. He said we should be "praying for one another's conversion, till some day we can sin no more and the good angels will bear us off to eternity, forever really and truly converted."[90]

For Solanus Casey, conversion was not connected just to his baptism or his entrance (and perseverance) into the Capuchins; it was a lifelong process that demanded continued, ongoing and radical transformation. Conversion had to touch all the dimensions of his life so that, in him, Paul's words to the Romans might come true: "Do not conform yourself to this age but be transformed by the renewal of your mind, so that you may judge what is God's will, what is good, pleasing and perfect" (12:2).

True to his definition of religion, conversion was essentially linked to religion itself. Conversion was not a once-and-for-all act but an ongoing process that must influence both the high points and the low points of life. From this perspective, Solanus' spirituality—which linked conversion and religion—has been expressed quite clearly by Bernard Lonergan. "Fundamental to religious living," he notes, "is conversion." He explains further:

When conversion is viewed as an ongoing process, at once personal, communal, and historical, it coincides with living religion. For religion is conversion in its preparation, in its occurrence, in its development, in its consequents, and also alas in its incompleteness, its failures, its breakdown, its disintegration."[91]

Solanus was aware that he had both his real self and shadow self to contend with. He had to deal with both sides and admit them into his religion and his conversion. He knew the whole process of growth in religion and conversion was life-long, ending only in death. Thus he wrote that, "only in heaven can we be satisfied as being fully and really converted."[92]

What we have done on earth, the "vestibule of heaven," will be the basis for our reward in heaven. Heaven, to Solanus, was "where love of God and our neighbor is the life and the very soul of society and association, where hopeful faith has merged into eternal charity."[93] Since these triune virtues of faith, hope, and charity are the "trace of the Holy Trinity in our immortal souls,"[94] and because the Trinity is the basis for our lives on earth, we should have no fear of passing over to fully experience God at the moment of our death.

Death, for Solanus, was "the happy transition to the heavenly promised abode, where gratitude ripens into perfect love of God and neighbor."[95] Thus he said, "if we prepare for the moment of our passing from time to eternity, it can be like that of a tired child confident in the arms enfolding it."[96]

This attitude should be expected of all people at death's door whose religiosity manifests a provident dependence on God and our neighbor. Yet the actual way Solanus prepared to die shows something more. While he died peacefully, turning his life consciously and rationally over to God, his last days reflected that preoccupation which often accompanies mystics as they prepare to pass over to the Lord. This preoccupation rests in their almost obsessive desire for unity for all people still on earth. Coming closer to that blessed vision of unity

wherein one sees the Trinity face to face, that experience and understanding makes one preoccupied with all the forms of disunity which
still exist on earth, especially among humans.

In describing his last hours Gerald Walker, Solanus' Provincial,
recalls:

> It happened during the last night of his life on earth. I was
> visiting him in the hospital. He seemed to be in utter spir-
> itual darkness, but there was the same love of God and of
> Christ's members. There was the same faith, the same trust,
> the same zeal for souls. At one point he began to writhe in
> pain. I bent over him and asked, "Where does it hurt,
> Father?"
>
> I wish that all the world could have seen the gleam of
> utter joy on his face and heard his words, "My whole body
> hurts. Thanks be to God. Thanks be to God. I am offering
> my suffering that all might be one. Oh, if I could only live
> to see the conversion of the whole world."[97]

He had lived a life of renunciation. Now at the point of death,
Solanus was ready to renounce an immediate entrance into heaven, if
only more people could experience that God to whom he was so united
mystically. Such an approach to spirituality is found in Mahayan Bud-
dhism with its theme of the "Great Renunciation." Although the supreme goal of the spiritual journey is to enter the beatitude of Nirvana,
such a beatitude is considered incomplete if it cannot be shared with
others. This realization gave rise to the Great Renunciation. Only the
greatest, Ru Bodhisahua, was able to make the final act of love—the
vow not to enter into the vision that had been achieved until every
sentient creature had been delivered from the need of their ignorance
and pain.

At the point of being one with God's own being, all humanity is seen
in the process of formation into God throughout the world. At this point
of death the mystic truly knows that God is at the heart of all things and
that all things are in the process of being gathered into one. At that point

of entrance into the Beatific Vision, there is almost a bittersweet feeling; the work is not yet done. As long as a breath is available one's efforts must be oriented to this goal of unity.

Despite this bittersweet feeling, even the feeling itself must be oriented to God's will. To that goal all life must be directed. Thus at the point of entrance into final union with God, Solanus freely dedicated the depth of his being to be at one with his maker: "I give my soul to Jesus Christ."

If the reader of this book will be faithful to the words and deeds of Solanus Casey, his work will continue to manifest concern for two loves: the sick and the poor. With his cause for canonization to sainthood now open, his life can become an inspiration of how our religion also can become "the science of our happy relationship with and provident dependence on God and neighbor."

"As manifested in the lives of the saints," Solanus once wrote, never believing anyone would ever apply his own words to himself, as we have tried to do in this book, "if we strive and use the means God has given us, we too can ascend to great sanctity and to astonishing familiarity with God, even here as pilgrims to the Beatific Vision."[98]

CHAPTER TEN
Epilogue

In 1937, Solanus Casey wrote his sister, Margaret: "I console myself occasionally with the thought that sooner or later the day will come when they will say of poor Fr. Solanus: 'He's gone.' Please God, the struggle for existence will then be over. I just hope that by that time, I'll be able to exclaim with St. Paul: 'I long to be dissolved and to be with Christ.' "

Twenty years later, people did say "He's gone." But, as the decades have evolved since then, he has not been forgotten. Could anybody ever forget Fr. Solanus? Certainly not the thousands who were the recipients of such great charity and concern during his lifetime. And forget him they did not.

Only three years after Solanus Casey's death, those whose lives he had touched founded the Father Solanus Guild. Its stated purpose was: "to keep alive the inspiring memory of Fr. Solanus Casey." These people tried to bring the knowledge of his life to others and to collect information or documentation that might support a cause for beatification and canonization. Finally, by 1966, the Guild had collected enough data to persuade the Capuchin Superiors to take that step. On October 4, Fr. Paschal Siler was appointed Vice-Postulator of the Cause.

The significant steps in the Cause for Beatification and Canonization of Fr. Solanus Casey, O.F.M. Cap. follow:

Nov. 1968   The first biography of Solanus is published. *The Porter of St. Bonaventure's* by James Patrick Derum. It has gone through six printings and sold nearly 30,000 copies.

April 17, 1972 The National Conference of Catholic Bishops gives its *Nihil Obstat* for the Cause.

July 23, 1974 Br. Leo Wollenweber is appointed Vice-Postulator.

June 24, 1976 The Vice-Postulator gives a formal Petition to John Cardinal Dearden, Archbishop of Detroit, to initiate the Cause in the Archdiocese.

Jan. 11, 1977 John Cardinal Dearden issues letter to all the dioceses where Fr. Solanus Lived and worked, requesting his writings.

Dec. 1978   Cardinal Dearden appoints Fr. Charles Dillen, CICM, as Archdiocesan Notary for the Cause.

June 1980   The Collected Writings, transcribed and bound into four Volumes, are taken to Rome and presented to the Capuchin there in charge of Processes of Canonization.

Jan. 15, 1981 All the necessary documents are submitted to the Sacred Congregation for Causes of Saints by the Capuchin Postulator General, Fr. Bernardine Romagnoli, to be examined, studied, and discussed by the Sacred Congregation for possible approval.

June 4, 1982   The Sacred Congregation for Causes of Saints, declares that "This Cause (rests) upon a legitimate and solid foundation" and gives permission for the Archbishop of Detroit "to set up the investigative process on the life, specific virtues and outstanding signs of the Servant of God."

June 19, 1982 Pope John Paul II ratifies and confirms the decision of the Sacred Congregation.

Sept. 21, 1983 Investigative Process opened in the Archdiocese of Detroit. Most Reverend Edmund C. Szoka, Archbishop of Detroit, issues the "Decree Introducing the Cause of the Servant of God, Fr. Solanus Casey, priest of the Order of Friars Minor Capuchin." At the same time he appoints Msgr. Albert C. Allen as Delegate Judge and Msgr. Arthur M. Karey as Promoter of the Faith for the Cause.

Oct. 9, 1984   Investigative Process completed.

Oct. 13, 1984   Acts of the Investigative Process are presented at the Congregation for the Causes of Saints.

Oct. 24, 1983   The Official Testimony beings in Detroit. A total of 53 witnesses—Capuchins, diocesan priests, sisters and lay people—who knew Fr. Solanus over a long period of time, testify on his life and virtues.

Aug. 27, 1984   The last witness completes the official testimony. The final papers and documentation of the Cause are now able to be prepared.

Oct. 8, 1984   The final session of the Informative Process is held with all the officials present. Archbishop Szoka signs the decree to formally close the Process. The boxes containing the Testimony and documentation are sealed by the Archbishop and addressed to the Sacred Congregation for the Causes of Saints in Rome.

Oct. 15, 1984   The completed Process, conveyed to Rome by Vice-Postulator, is handed over to the Sacred Congregation for the Causes of Saints for thorough study and final judgment.

Nov. 7, 1986   Upon examination, the Congregation for the Causes of Saints declares valid the Acts of the Investigative Process. The same day the Congregation appoints Fr. Peter Gumpel, S.J. as Relator for the Cause.

Feb. 7, 1987   Replying to the Petition of Fr. Paolino Rossi, Capuchin Postulator General, the Congregation for the Causes of Saints issues a rescript allowing the exhumation and canonical examination of the remains of Solanus Casey.

July 8, 1987   In the presence of the Archbishop of Detroit, Cardinal

	Edmund Szoka, the exhumation takes place. The body of Fr. Solanus is found to be 95% intact. It is placed in a new metal coffin and reinterred in a side chapel of St. Bonaventure's Church.
June 26, 1987	Responding to Fr. Gumpel's request for an "External Collaborator" from the Province to which Solanus Casey belonged, Fr. Kenneth Reinhart, Capuchin Provincial Minister, nominates Capuchin Michael Crosby as External Collaborator.
July 15, 1987	Fr. Gumpel approves the appointment of Michael Crosby as External Collaborator.
Nov. 1987	The Postulator General directs that the Collected Writings of Solanus Casey be examined by two censors appointed by the Archbishop of Detroit.
March, 1988	The Diocesan Censors complete their work. Both declare the writings of Solanus Casey are free of doctrinal or moral error.
Oct. 10, 1992	The printed and bound three volume *Positio* containing the completed testimonies of 53 witnesses, the biographical and historical section, and the material on the Virtues is delivered to the Congregation for the Causes of Saints.
Oct. 1994	Paulino Rossi, Capuchin Postulator General Informs the Vice-Postulator, Leo Wollenweber, that the *Positio* for the Cause of Solanus Casey would be on the calendar of the Congregation for the Causes of Saints for 1995.
April 7, 1995	The nine theologians who constitute the Designated Committee of Theological Consultants give their unanimous approval attesting to the "heroic virtue" of the Servant of God, Solanus Casey.
June 20, 1995	The cardinals and bishops on the Congregation for the Causes of Saints meet in Ordinary Session to discuss the life and virtues of Fr. Solanus. They give unanimous approval to his life of heroic virtue. They conclude

Solanus Casey's life provides a very inspiring model of virtue for people today.

July 11, 1995 The Congregation for the Causes of Saints meets with Pope John Paul II to offer their opinion on the virtues of Fr. Solanus. The Pope declares that, indeed, Solanus Casey practiced the virtues to a heroic degree. The Holy Father promulgates the Decree of Heroic Virtue and orders its publication. With this promulgation the Servant of God will now be known as Venerable Solanus Casey. He thus becomes the first man born in the United States to be honored by a pope with the title "Venerable."

For further information about Father Solanus Casey, the Father Solanus Guild, or the Capuchin Franciscans, write:

The Vice-Postulator, Cause of Fr. Solanus Casey, 1740 Mt. Elliott Ave., Detroit, Michigan 48207. The telephone number is (313) 579-2100.

Declaration

In obedience to the decree of Pope Urban VII and inconformity with the Apostilic Constitution of Pope Leo XIII, the author declares that he claims no more than a purely human consideration of the events and graces reported herein, and that he submits at all times and unreservedly to the judgment of the Catholic Church.

NOTES

Chapter One

1. Solanus Casey (hereafter noted as SC,) "Letter to Margaret T. LeDoux," April, 1930, *Collected Writings of Father Solanus Casey, O.F.M., Cap,* (hereafter noted as *CW*), I, p. 142. Solanus used abbreviations and many dashes in his writings. I have adapted these for the sake of clarity and fluency.
2. For much of the data referring to the childhood of Solanus Casey, I am indebted to the interviews James P. Derum had with Solanus' brother, Monsignor Edward J. Casey. These were the foundation for Derum's *The Porter of St. Bonaventure's: The Life of Father Solanus Casey, Capuchin* (Detroit: The Fidelity Press, 1968). When a statement is made that seems to need documentation that is not given, such statement can be found in Derum's book from his personal interviews with members of the Casey family.
3. SC, "Letter to Margaret T. Le Doux," Apr. 30, 1930, *CW*, I, p. 143.
4. SC, "Letter to Edward Casey," April 23, 1953, *CW*, I, p. 190.
5. SC, "Letter to Margaret T. LeDoux," *Ibid*, pp. 143–44.
6. *Ibid.*, p. 143.
7. *Ibid.*
8. SC, "Letter to Fr. Maurice E. Joachim Casey," Apr. 2, 1946, *CW*, I, p. 158.
9. SC, "Letter to Margaret T. LeDoux," *Ibid.*, p. 144
10. *Ibid.*
11. *Ibid.*, p. 145.
12. SC, "Fragmentary Note," c. 1949, I, p. 162.
13. SC, "Letter to Miss Margaret Shavey," Oct. 3, 1949, *CW*, II, p. 282.

14. SC, "Letter to Edwin Wilhite," c. Oct. 4, 1950. *CW*. I , p. 128.
15. This paragraph is from Edward Casey's reflections shared with James Derum and noted in his boo, *Ibid.*, p. 26. Unless otherwise notd, those items that seem toc all for a regference are based on Msgr. Edward's recollections noted in Derum's book.
16. Willima Johnston, *The Inner Eye of Live: Mysticism and Religon* (San Francisco: Harper & Row Publishers, Inc., 1978), p. 131.
17. SC, "Letter to James M. Casey," Jan. 29, 1943, *CW*, I, P. 129.
18. SC, "Letter to James M. Casey," July 18, 1938, *CW*, I, P. 111.
19. In an effort to better understand some of the inner dynamics of Solanus Casey, his hadnwriting has been submitted to analysis. Today businesses, among other entities, include handwriting analysis to better determine people's chracteristics. The Library of Congress now includes handwriting under pschology. Selections from various periods of Solanus' life were submitted to two expert graphoanalysts. Sheila Kurtz, MGA, CGA, of New York has been featured in *Forbes* (May 9, 1983) and in United Airlines *Mainliner* magazine (June 1983). Richard Stoller, PhD., of Milwaukee write his doctoral dissertation on graphology. Where the reader may quesiton the basis for statements regarding the inner dynamics of Solanus, such are grounded on the perceptions of others as well as the results of the graphology.
20. Marion Roessler, O.F.M., Cap., June 41 1984, Written Reports Concerning Fr. Solanus Casey, O.F.M., Cap. (hereafter noted as *WR*).
21. Recollection of account by Solanus Casey to Shirley L. Jarosik 1955, *WR*.
22. "Record: Classical Dept., Sept., 1891–June, 1924," Milwaukee: St. Francis Provincial Seminary (archives), pp. 1, 7, 11, 16, 20, 25, 30, 36, 41. Thanks to Rev. Thomas Fait, Archdiocesan Archivist, for providing these records.
23. Students Ledger," St. Francis Seminary, Vol. 1887-001893, p. 171. Materials courtesy of Rev. Thomas Fait.
24. Bonaventure Frey, O.F.M., Cap., Documents File, Vice Postulator's Archives, Detroit, Michigan.
25. SC, "Letter to Maurice E. Joachim Casey," Dec. 15, 1938, *CW*, I, p. 147.
26. SC, *Notebook* 9, c. 1909, p. 27, *CW*, I, p. 18.
27. Cf. Testimonies of Fr. Lawrence Merton and Fr. Marion Roessler, O.F.M., Cap. in *WR*.
28. Years later Solanus would book back at the founders and thank God for the decision that he made that December 8, 1896. As he wrote to his brother Edward in 1943, the connections between the capuchins and the Caseys not only touched history, they had parallels in nature as well:

I spent a few pleasant hours . . . on what I would venture to call the most remarkable hill in our dear old "Badger State," Mount Calvary.

If you picture a modern university—not too large of course—on the plateau-like top of our old Mount Saint Helens (Washington), with a good sized convent of teaching Sisters on the smaller hill to the East over which are seen the farther waters of the Dry Dam (and farther still in the distance, the "Three-Chain-Lakes"), and then with one of the neighboring villages, Burkhardt or Boardman moved in between the two and around them, you have a fair picture of our Mt. Calvary today—the eighty-year-old cradle of the Capuchin-Franciscan Order in this country.

The fertile farms, too, that smile up at that steepled church-crowned mount, or that stretch far to the north and eastward, circling around to the South, are hardly less picturesque than those of the above-mentioned "Garden of Wisconsin," the Udson and Earin Prairies. In fact, I think that just a title would apply most appropriately to this locality as second to none in the whole beautiful state. The smaller hills leading down twelve miles to the foot of the lake at Fond du Lac, as viewed from the "Observation Tower" on the Mount, are similar to those we used to look across fourteen miles to Stillwater, Minnesota.

The well-paved roads as they swing downward over hills and follow ravines—judging from the starry-night trip we made—must be an inviting drive now. What a contrast to the Indian trails of those pioneer days when the two young Pastors—Rev. Gregory Haas, just in his 30s, and John Anthony Frey, only 27 (having waived most promising outlooks in their Swiss native diocese) came to this place to plant the Cross on this Calvary of America and thence proclaimed to sparsely settled whites near and far, and to the savages, the saving truths, the salvation of Jesus Christ.

The former, as Fr. Francis, became outstanding in the Order both here and in Europe. And this not only by his zeal for the Order itself and for religion and justice generally, but one might say, especially by his practical promotion among the Brethren as well as people everywhere, fervent devotion to the Sacred Heart of Jesus. Called to Rome as a Definitor General, he labored untiringly there under climatic difficulties hardly dreamed of in his native highlands or on his Wisconsin Missions. Stricken with real T.B. to which for some time he had been inclined, he returned to America and to his long cherished Mt. Calvary. For professional treatment in his last months of patient struggle for vocational attention he was taken to St. Agnes Hospital, Fond du Lac. There, years before, when in need of a friend, he had been befriended. Next to Calvary, he had made his headquarters there and in days of bitterest opposition, it was where most touchingly he was reconciled with former opponents who sought him out. He peacefully expired on the Feast itself of the Sacred Heart of Jesus.

. . . The younger associate, however, who as Fr. Bonaventure (Frey) became perhaps even more distinguished than his senior partner, was . . . tall, gentle, and handsome but withal prudent and firm. Having built fourteen monasteries, some of them under very trying circumstances, he modestly resigned from active service. Little by little, his hearing gave way and then his sight. But he never lost his keen interest in whatever pertained to the Province and to the Order.

Recollections of Fr. Solanus noted in SC, "Letter to James M. Casey," Jan. 29, 1943, *CW*, I, pp. 232–34.

29. SC, "Letter to James Casey," July 18, 1938, *CW*, I, p. 200.

Chapter Two

1. SC, Notes written on a page of Solanus Casey's copy of the *Rule and Testament of St. Francis*, January 13, 1897. Documents File, Vice Postulator's Archives, Detroit, Michigan.
2. Until the adaptation of the Capuchin-Franciscan way of life after the Second Vatican Council, those studying to be priests were called "Frater." "Frater" was Latin for "brother." The Lay Brothers were called "Brother." With the changes which attempted to return to the spirit of brotherly equality which St. Francis of Assisi envisioned for his followers, all members of the community, especially those in formation, would be called "Brother."
3. SC, Unfinished letter to Rev. Edward Casey, March 14, 1957, *CW*, I, p. 195.
4. SC, "Notebook 9," c. 1897, p. 2, in *CW*, I, p. 2.
5. *Ibid.*, p. 5, in *CW*, I, p. 5.
6. Latin reference to St. Bonaventure, March 20, 1897, *Ibid.*, p. 7.
7. *Ibid.*
8. Solanus Casey had a problem with scrupulosity earlier in his life. He

confided that he was free of the problem as he became more abandoned to God. Confer Mary Therese Bernadine Goodman in *WR*.

9. Jan van Ruysbroeck, *Adornment of the Spiritual Marriage* LXII, tr. C. A. Wynschenn Dom. Ed by Evelyn Underhill (London: John M. Watkins, 1951), pp. 132–34.

10. SC, "Notebook 9," c. 1898, p. 14, in *CW*, I, p. 10.

11. *Ibid.*, p. 7.

12. SC, "Attestation," July 20, 1898. Document in Documents File, Vice Postulator's Archives, Detroit, Michigan.

13. Official vow formulary for the Capuchin Franciscans.

14. While it is true that Frs. Francis and Bonaventure had successive terms by reason of special exception, the exception could have been requested for Father Anthony but was not. This seems to reinforce the general impression that the Chapter delegates had reason(s) for not re-electing Anthony.

15. Fr. Boniface Goldhausen, O.F.M., Cap. 1970, in *WR*.

16. SC, "Notebook 9," c. 1899, p. 19, in *CW* I, p. 12.

17. *Ibid.*, c. Jan. 1900, p. 21, in *CW* I, p. 14.

18. *Ibid.*, April 12, 1898, p. 16, in *CW* I, p. 11.

19. SC, Radio Talk, June 11, 1937, in *CW* I, p. 94.

20. Cardinal Ganganelli, quoted in SC, "Notebook 9," c. 1899, p. 19, in *CW* I, p. 12.

21. SC, "Letter to Mrs. Ella Traynor," Feb. 21, 1904, in *CW* I, p. 71.

22. "Academic Record of Fr. Solanus (Bernard) Casey," Chicago: Province of St. Joseph of the Capuchin Order Archives.

23. SC, Untitled Statement, July 5, 1901. Documents File, Vice Postulator's Archives, Detroit, Michigan.

24. SC, "Notebook 9," June 13, 1902, p. 22, in *CW* I, p. 15.

25. *Ibid.*, c. 1903, p. 21, in *CW* I, p. 15.

26. *Ibid.*, p. 22 in *CW* I, p. 16.

27. *Ibid.*

28. SC, "Letter to Mrs. Ella Traynor," *Ibid.*

29. Fr. Boniface Goldhausen, O.F.M., Cap., Feb. 11, 1963 in *WR*.

30. Bernardus ab Andermatt, "Preacher's Patent," Rome: July 26, 1904. Documents File, Vice Postulator's Archives, Detroit, Michigan.

31. Recent studies have been able to ascertain one's I.Q. within five points of the Stanford-Binet reading from an analysis of handwriting. While this is not definitive, it consistently correlates. The study of Solanus' handwriting was done by Richard J. Stoller, Ph.D., author of *Write Right: Change Your Writing to Change Your Life* (Milwaukee, 1978).

32. SC, "Letter to James M. Casey," Jan. 29, 1943, in *CW* I, p. 228.

Chapter Three

1. SC, "Letter to Fr. Maurice Joachim Casey, O.M., Cap., Aug. 16, 1937, in *CW* I, p. 146.
2. SC, "Letter to Mr. William Spring," March 27, 1935, in *CW* I, p. 88.
3. SC, "Letter to Mrs. Margaret LeDoux," Jan. 3, 1916, in *CW* Ia, p. 5.
4. SC, "Letter to James M. Casey," Jan. 29 1943, in *CW* I p. 234.
5. SC, "Letter to Br. Leo Wollenweber, O.F.M., Cap., Feb, 28, 1943, in *CW* II, p. 119.
6. SC, "Notebook 9," c. 1909, p. 27, in *CW* I, p./18.
7. James Lawless, Jan. 13, 1977, in *WR*.
8. SC, SC, "Notebook 9," c. 1909, p. 27, in *CW* I, p. 18.
9. *Ibid.*, 1909, p. 27, in *CW* I, p. 18.
10. Wa.ter O'Brien, O.F.M. Cap., "Interview with Michael Crosby, O.F.M. Cap., Jan. 11, 1983.
11. Sister Dolora Brogan, CSA, "Interview," with Michael H. Crosby, O.F.M. Cap., Jan 11, 1983.
12. Sister Agrippina Petrosino, CSA, "Interview," with Crosby, *Ibid.*
13. *Ibid.*
14. SC, "Rev. Fr. Stephen Eckart, As I Remember Him," unfinished manuscript, 1948, in *CW* II, p. 251.
15. Ibid.
16. SC, Notes on Vol, III, *The Mystical City of God* in *CW* I, p. 286.
17. SC, "Letter to Mrs. M. LeDoux, Apr. 1, 1915, in *CW* IA, p. 3.
18. Cleus McCarthy, O.F.M. Cap., "Interview with Michael Crosby, O.F.M. Cap., Jan. 11, 1983.
19. Sister Dolora Brogan, CSA, *Ibid.*
20. SC, Sermon on John 2:1ff, "Notebook 2," c. 1915, p. 43, in *CW* I, pp. 35-36.
21. *Ibid.*, p. 36.
22. SC, Sermon on Matthew 13 for the 10:15 AM Mass Nov. 11, 1917, "Notebook 2," p. 47, in *CW* I, p. 50.
23. SC, Sermon on Luke 15:2ff for the 10:15 AM Mass,1917, "Notebook 2," p. 48, in *CW* I, p. 52.
24. *Ibid.*, p. 49, in *CW* I, p. 50.
25. SC, quoting Pope Leo XIII, "Notebook 2," c. 1917, p. 96, in *CW* I, p. 54.
26. SC, "Letter to Rev. Nother Lurana S.A.," Apr. 17, 1912, in *CW* I, p. 72.
27. SC, "Letter to Sister of the ATonement," Dec. 4, 1917, in *CW* I, p. 73.
28. *Ibid.*,
29. SC, "Letter to Br. Lew Wollenweber," Sept, 67, 1945, in *CW* II, p. 125.
30. SC, "Letter to Mrs. Ella Taynor," Feb. 21, 1904, in *CW* I, p. 71.

31. SC, ."Letter to James Casey," July 18, 1938, in *CW* I, p. 199.
32. SC, "Letter to Margaret LeDoux," July 24, 1921, in *CW* IA, p. 9.
33. SC, "Letter to Mrs. Margaret LeDoux," July 16, 1918, in *CW* IA, p. 7.

Chapter Four

1. Fr. Bonaventure Frey O.F.M., Cap., quoted in Celestine Bittle O.F.M., Cap., *A Romance of Lady Poverty: The History of the Province of St. Joseph of the Capuchin Order in the United States* (Milwaukee: The Bruce Publishing Company, 1933), pp. 168–69.
2. SC, "Notebook 9," Aug. 16, 1918, p. 28, in *CW* I, p. 19.
3. *Ibid.*, Dec. 12, 1918, p. 29, in *CW* I, p. 20.
4. *Ibid.*, cir. 1919, p. 35, in *CW* I, p. 20.
5. Sister Rose Cecilia Ascherl OP, "Letter to Michael Crosby," Apr. 12, 1983.
6. SC, "Notebook 3," Aug., 1919, p. 2b, in *CW* I, p. 69.
7. St. Bernard of Clairveaux, in John S. Maddux, "When You Pray," *The Way* XVII, 3 (July, 1977), p. 236.
8. St. Francis of Assisi, *Rule of 1223*, in *Francis and Clare: The Complete Works*, tr. Regis J. Armstrong, O.F.M. Cap and Ignatius C. Brady, O.F.M. (New York: Paulist Press Classics in Western Spirituality Series, 1982), p. 140.
9. John S. Maddux, "When You Pray," *The Way* XVII, 3 (July, 1977), p. 231.
10. *Ibid.*
11. SC, "Letter to Mrs. Margaret LeDoux," July 16, 1937, in *CW* IA, p . 18.
12. SC, "Letter to Mrs. M. C. LeDoux," July 24, 1921, in *CW* IA, p. 9.
13. Book of Minutes of the Friary Discreets at Our Lady of Angels, March 1, 1921 to Nov. 5, 1924, October 25, 1921. New York: Our Lady of the Angels Friary.
14. SC, "Letter to Mrs. Abraham Trabulsy," Dec. 14, 1946, in *CW* I I, p. 195. As the date of the letter notes, Solanus did not write this letter while at Our Lady, Queen of Angels, but while he was at Huntington, Indiana. However, it best reflects his sentiments while he was at New York.
15. SC, "Notebook 1," Nov. 8, 1923, p. 17 in *CW*.
16. SC, "Letter to Mr. Raymond T. Taylor," Feb. 8, 1947, in *CW* II, p. 214. Again, although written later, this letter reflects Solanus' attitude while at Our Lady of the Angels.
17. SC, "Notebook 1," *CW*.
18. Book of Minutes, *Ibid.*, Jan. 14, 1922.
19. SC, "Notebook 1," *Ibid.*, p. 5. Until the new understanding which accom-

panied the Second Vatican Council in the 1960s there was a practice in United States' Catholicism to "adopt pagan (heathen) babies" through donations of various amounts of money. It was a way of supporting foreign missionaries in the form of evangelization that was prevalent at that time, besides the actual "adoption."

20. Fr. Laurence Lisotta, O.F.M., Cap, Sept. 11, 1978, *WR*: His report slightly adapted.
21. Fr. Justin Joos, O.F.M., Cap., Interview with Michael H. Crosby, O.F.M., Cap., Jan. 11, 1983.
22. *Ibid.*
23. SC, "Letter to the Editor," *The Catholic News*, Sept. 27, c. 1922 in *CW* I, p. 74.
24. *Ibid.*
25. *Ibid.*
26. *Ibid.*
27. For an elaboration of how enemies develop an ideology to justify their hostile attitudes consult Ralph K. White, *Nobody Wanted War: Misperception in Vietnam and Other Wars* (Garden City, N.J.: Doubleday Anchor Books, 1970).
28. SC, "Letter to Very Rev. Pater Benno, O.F.M., Cap.," Jan. 25, 1924, in *CW* I, p. 83.
29. SC, "Letter to Mr. James M. Casey," July 18, 1938, in *CW* I, p. 198.

Chapter Five

1. SC, "Notebook 1," p. 14. Solanus made a habit of returning to his original entries that he might make follow-up comments about developments in the various cases. Thus the range of dates. Also, for the sake of easier reading I have tried to make sentences from the phases and code words that Solanus used. Abbreviations have been extended to the full word and corrections have been made to spelling mistakes. The notations from Notebook 1 dealing with those items requested by Fr. Benno will not be footnoted unless for some special reason.
2. Sometimes, as in this case, Solanus noted the "cure" on the day it was announced to him. He then referred back to previous encounters, as in this case.
3. Fr. Marion Roessler O.F.M., Cap., Mar. 11, 1980, in *WR*.
4. SC, "Letter to Mrs. Belle Lyke," May 22, 1946, in *CW* II, p. 175.
5. SC, "Letter to Mrs. Margaret LeDoux," July 16, 1937, in *CW* IA, p. 18.
6. SC, "Letter to Sr. Cecilia Eagen, SC," Nov. 7, 1947, in *CW* II, pp. 240 – 41.

7. *Ibid.*, p. 241.
8. SC, "Letter to Margaret Therese LeDoux," Oct. 19, 1954, in *CW* IA, p. 35.
9. Fr. Herman Buss O.F.M., Cap., July 19, 1977, in *WR*. Br. Andre was Beatified on May 23, 1982 by Pope John Paul II.
10. Fr. Lawrence Merten O.F.M., Cap., Mar. 21, 1980, in *WR*.
11. SC, "Letter to Mr. Merrick O'Laughlin," June 28, 1947, in *CW* II, p. 233.
12. SC, "Letter to Mrs. E. Nettyk," July 18, 1949, in *CW* II, p. 280.
13. William Tremblay, March 15, 1979, in *WR*.
14. *Ibid.*
15. Fr. Blase Gitzen O.F.M., Cap. "Taped Interview" to Michael H. Crosby O.F.M., Cap., Jan. 1983.
16. Bernard Burke O.F.M., Cap., Aug. 9, 1973, in *WR*.
17. Fr. Herman Buss O.F.M., Cap., *Ibid.*
18. Fr. Cosmas Neidhammer O.F.M., Cap., Mar. 16, 1980, in *WR*. The time Fr. Cosmas spent in Detroit with Solanus was from 1938–52. However, almost from the beginning, the routine described by Fr. Cosmas was Solanus' pattern.
19. Maurice Casey, quoted in SC, "Letter to Fr. Maurice E. Joachim Casey," Dec. 15, 1938, in *CW* I, p. 148.
20. SC, "Letter to Mrs. Margaret LeDoux," Apr., 1930, in *CW* I, p. 142.
21. *Chronicle,* St. Bonaventure's, Detroit, Feb. 19, 1928.
22. Fr. Marion Roessler, O.F.M., Cap., *Ibid.*
23. The "Blessing of St. Maurus" can be found in many old prayer books and rituales.
24. Mrs. Bernadette M. Nowak, Mar. 28, 1970, in *WR*.
25. Casimira Scott, Mar. 2, 1977, in *WR*.
26. William Johnston, SJ, "Mysticism for a New Age," *Human Development*, 4,1 (Spring, 1983) p. 28.
27. The description of the Soup Kitchen and Solanus Casey's role in it relies heavily on the written report of his co-worker Fr. Herman Buss, O.F.M., Cap., *Ibid.*
28. Al C. Billard, Apr. 16, 1977, in *WR*.
29. Fr. Herman Buss, O.F.M., Cap., *Ibid.*
30. Mrs. Rita Stanislawski, Jan. 5, 1979, in *WR*.
31. SC, "Notebook 3," 1929, p. 41, in *CW* I, p. 65.
32. SC, "Letter to Mr. James M. Casey," July 18, 1938, in *CW* I, p. 209.
33. William Tremblay, *Ibid.*
34. SC, "Letter to Venerable Br. Leo O.F.M., Cap.," Feb. 28, 1943, *CW* II, p. 120.

35. William Tremblay, *Ibid.*
36. Mrs. Mary Therese McHugh, Dec. 15, 1978, in *WR*.
37. Elizabeth Ann Maher, Apr. 4, 1977, in *WR*.
38. Mrs. Agnes Juergens, Oct. 27, 1978, in *WR*.
39. SC, "Letter to Mr. James Casey," Jan. 29, 1943, in *CW* I, p. 217.
40. SC, "Letter to Margaret LeDoux," Jan. 26, 1937, in *CW* IA, p. 16.
41. SC, "Letter to Mrs. Margaret LeDoux," Jan. 26, 1937, in *CW* IA, p. 16.
42. SC, "Radio Speech on Station CKLW Detroit, June 11, 1937, in *CW* I, pp. 94–95.
43. SC, "Letter to Fr. Maurice Casey," Dec. 15, 1938, in *CW* I, pp. 147–48.
44. Eleanor M. Hagarty, Jan. 25, 1979, in *WR*.
45. Leo Wollenweber O.F.M., Cap., Recollections shared with Michael H. Crosby O.F.M., Cap.
46. Gerald Walker O.F.M., Cap., Apr. 14, 1980, in *WR*.
47. Daniel Brady O.F.M., Cap., "Letter to Michael H. Crosby," Feb. 20, 1983.
48. Casimera Scott, *Ibid.*
49. Mrs. Hazel Maisano, February 12, 1978, in *WR*. Mrs. Maisano does not say what kind of birth control she was practicing, nor what Solanus said about it—just that he could tell she was practicing birth control.
50. Sr. Joyce Pranger, *Rise Early to Meet Your Lord* (adapted) (Denville, N.J.: Dimension Books), 1977, pp. 41–43.
51. *Chronicle*, St. Bonaventure's, Detroit, Sept. 13, 1942.
52. SC, "Letter to Mrs. Margaret LeDoux," Nov. 17, 1942, in *CW* IA, p. 21.
53. *Ibid.*
54. *Chronicle, Ibid.*
55. SC, "Letter to Mr. James Casey," Jan. 29, 1943, in *CW* I, p. 215.
56. SC, "Letter to Mrs. Margaret LeDoux," Nov. 17, 1942, in *CW* IA, p. 21.
57. At this time in the Province of St. Joseph there was a custom that the friars knelt in front of their superior to receive a blessing upon their leaving or returning to the friary.
58. Fr. Michael Cefai, Jan. 10, 1968 in *WR*.
59. SC, "Letter to Father Edward Casey," Dec. 12, 1938, in *CW* I, p. 168.
60. SC, "Letter to Mrs. Margaret LeDoux," Nov. 17, 1942, in *CW* IA, p. 23.
61. SC, "Letter to Mr. Charles K. Chisholm," May 12, 1937, in *CW* I, p. 90.
62. Fr. Marion Roessler O.F.M., Cap., *Ibid.*
63. SC, "Letter to Fr. Marion O.F.M., Cap., July 9, 1945, in *CW* II, p. 144.

Chapter Six

1. *Chronicle*, St. Bonaventure's, Detroit, July 15, 1945.
2. *Ibid.*, July 21, 1945.

3. Fr. Cosmas Neidhammer O.F.M., Cap., Mar. 6, 1980 in *WR*.

4. Western Union Telegram, undated. However this was sent to Fr. Solanus Casey, c/o J. Casey, 124 Warren Avenue, Apartment 109, Seattle, Washington.

5. Most Reverend Clement Neubauer O.F.M., Cap., unsigned, June 14, 1967 in *WR*. The sheet of paper was a formal statement that was to be signed by Fr. Clement; it was dictated but not signed. Clement Neubauer became the first American to be Minister of the entire Capuchin Franciscan Order. He was first appointed by Pope Pius XII at the conclusion of World War II, and then elected in his own right after six years absence from Rome, which he spent as an associate pastor in Appleton, Wisconsin, and then as local superior at St. Felix Friary, Huntington, Indiana.

6. Br. Ignatius Milne, Recollections shared with Michael Crosby, O.F.M., Cap., Sept. 1, 1983.

7. SC, "Letter to Margaret LeDoux," Sept. 9, 1945, in *CW* IA, p. 23.

8. SC, "Letter to Br. Leo," July 30, 1945. In the next paragraph Solanus urged Leo to burn any photographs of himself except for those of his golden jubilee, especially "the one with all the little grandchildren. Some of them are grandparents now themselves." *CW* II, p. 121.

9. SC, "Letter to Muriel Krausmann," Aug. 18, 1945, in *CW* II, p. 91.

10. SC, Retreat Notes, "Notebook 9," Aug. 1945, in *CW* I, p. 253.

11. *Ibid.*

12. *Ibid.*, p. 255.

13. SC, "Postcard to Mrs. Alice Plunkett," 1945, in *CW* II, p. 2.

14. SC, "Letter to Ray Garland," Oct. 22, 1945. This letter was found in Solanus' belongings. Whether a copy was sent to Ray Garland is not known. Solanus would often compose many drafts of letters that dealt with difficult issues; thus it is likely that this was one of the drafts. *CW* II, p. 149.

15. *Ibid.*

16. *Ibid.*

17. *Ibid.*

18. SC, "Letter to Mrs. Mary Kenny," Aug. 28, 1945, in *CW* II, p. 146.

19. Fr. Walter O'Brien, Interview shared with Michael Crosby, O.F.M., Cap., Jan. 11, 1983.

20. SC, "Message to Helena Wilhite," Dec. 14, 1945, in *CW* I, p. 129. A similar poem was sent the Wollenwebers.

21. SC, "Always Christmas Eve—Nay Infinitely More for Daily Communicants," poem in *CW,* II, p. 156.

22. SC, "Letter to Mrs. Edward Wilhite," Feb. 28, 1946. Solanus must have been very inspired by the purported healing of Mrs. Nagle. He repeated the incident and the return visits in an encouraging letter to Sr. Belita in

Atlantic City, N.J. In a letter of September 15, 1945 (in *CW* II, p. 147), he said that he was telling her about Mrs. Nagle's recovery because: "I hope this may give you all a little more courage to pray on and with your friends storm heaven. I often advise a proposition to the poor souls. In other words, if an operation is averted I asked that they donate an enrollment for the Poor Souls, a percentage of the costs of the operation, if it is averted, to go to charity or some good cause, besides prayers and Holy Communions." *CW* I, pp. 130–31.

23. *Ibid.*, pp. 131–32.
24. *Ibid.*, pp. 132–33.
25. Asteria M. Mahoney, Aug. 19, 1977, in *WR*.
26. SC, "Letter to Mrs. E. L. Eichorn." Mar. 14, 1950, in *CW* II, p. 297.
27. *Ibid.*
28. *Ibid.*, p. 298. In the 1940's and early 1950's the term "darky" was not considered a negative term for blacks by whites. However, it was offensive for blacks. Solanus did not know this, as a white.
29. SC, "Letter to Fr. Edward Casey," Mar. 28, 1946, in *CW* I, p. 176.
30. Walter O'Brien, O.F.M. Cap., *Ibid.*
31. Fr. Barnabas Keck O.F.M., Cap., Interview with Michael Crosby O.F.M., Cap., Jan. 11, 1983.
32. Fr. Walter O'Brien.
33. SC, "Letter to Br. Leo Wollenweber," May 23, 1946, in *CW* II, p. 128.

Chapter Seven

1. SC, "Letter to Mrs. Margaret LeDoux," Sept. 22, 1946, in *CW* IA, p. 25.
2. *Ibid.*
3. F. C. Happold, *Religious Faith and Twentieth Century Man* (New York: Crossroads, 1981), p. 123.
4. *Chronicle,* St. Felix Friary, Huntington, Indiana, I (1928–50), May 13, 1946.
5. Fr. Ambrose deGroot, Sept. 25, 1978, in *WR*.
6. SC, "Letter to Miss Muriel Krausmann," Apr. 24, 1947, in *CW* II, p. 99.
7. Dorothy Fletcher, Reflections shared with Michael H. Crosby, O.F.M., Cap., Jan. 7, 1983.
8. *Ibid.*
9. SC, "Letter to Mrs. Abraham Trabulsy," unsigned, Dec. 14, 1946, in *CW* II, pp. 195–96.
10. SC, "Letter to Mrs. Henry Morgan," Dec. 14, 1946, in *CW* II, p. 191.
11. Fr. Ambrose de Groot, "Letter to Michael Crosby, O.F.M., Cap.," June 29, 1984.

12. SC, "Letter to Mrs. Henry Morgan," *Ibid.*

13. SC, "Letter to Mrs. Geraldine Bieke," Sept. 19, 1946, in *CW* II, p. 185.

14. SC, "Letter to Mr. Raymond Taylor," Feb. 8, 1947, in *CW* II, pp. 214–16.

15. *Ibid.,* p. 216.

16. SC, "Letter to Rt. Rev. Edward Casey," May 12, 1947, in *CW* I, p. 182.

17. SC, "Letter to Fr. Simon O.F.M., Cap.," c. 1947, in *CW* II, p. 209.

18. Fr. Blase Gitzen, O.F.M., Cap., Nov. 14, 1969, in *WR*.

19. Fr. Blase Gitzen, O.F.M., Cap., Taped interview to Michael H. Crosby O.F.M., Cap.

20. SC, "Letter to Mrs. Helena Casey Wilhite," June 1, 1948, in *CW* I, p. 138.

21. *Ibid.*

22. SC, "Letter to Mrs. Geraci," c. 1947, in *CW* II, p. 179.

23. *Chronicle, Ibid.,* Jan. 12, 1949.

24. SC, Unfinished "Letter to Miss Mae C. Berling," Feb. 7, 1949, in *CW* II, p. 274.

26. SC, "Think Over," typed notes among Solanus writings, 1948, in *CW* II, p. 253.

27. F. C. Happold, *Ibid.,* pp. 16–17.

28. SC, "Think Over," *Ibid.*

29. SC, "Letter to Very Rev. Fr. Provincial (Edmund Kramer) O.F.M., Cap.," July 18, 1949, in *CW* II, p. 278.

30. SC, "Rev. Fr. Stephen Eckert, As I Remember Him," c. 1948, in *CW* II, p. 251.

31. *Ibid.*

32. SC, "Letter to Br. Leo," Sept. 7, 1945, in *CW* II, p. 126.

33. Fr. Ambrose deGroot, Sept. 25, 1978, in *WR*.

34. SC, "Letter to Edmund Kramer," *Ibid.*

35. Fr. Blase Gitzen, O.F.M., Cap., *Ibid.*

36. SC, "Letter to Fr. Edward Casey," May 30, 1949, in *CW* I, p. 183.

37. SC, "Letter to Gramma Kaufman," Aug. 9, 1949, in *CW* II, p. 281.

38. *Ibid.*

39. Fr. Michael Cefai, Jan. 10, 1968 in *WR*.

40. "The Legend of Perugia," no. 101, tr. by Paul Oligny, in Marion A. Habig, ed., *St. Francis of Assisi: Writings and Early Biographies, English Omnibus of the Sources of the Life of St. Francis* (Chicago, Franciscan Herald Press, 1972,) p. 1077.

41. James Allen Maher, March 7, 1980, in *WR*.

42. *Ibid.*

43. SC, "Letter to Margaret and Frank LeDoux," July 4, 1950, in *CW* IA, p. 32.

44. Fr. Elmer Stoffel O.F.M., Cap., Sept. 1, 1980, in *WR*.
45. *Chronicle, Ibid.* Aug. 13, 1950.
46. Br. Pius Cotter O.F.M., Cap., Reflections Shared with Michael H. Crosby O.F.M., Cap. Oct. 5, 1984.
47. Fr. Blase Gitzen O.F.M., Cap., *Ibid.*
48. *Ibid.*
49. *Ibid.*
50. *Ibid.*
51. SC, "Letter to Br. Leo," Aug. 11, 1951, in *CW* II, p. 132.
52. Br. Booker T. Ashe O.F.M., Cap., Mar. 21, 1980, in *WR*.
53. *Ibid.*
54. *Ibid.*
55. SC, "Mystical City of God—Logical Landmarks," c. 1950, in *CW* I, p. 281.
56. Fr. Francis Heidenreich O.F.M., Cap., Recollections shared with Michael H. Crosby O.F.M., Cap., Jan. 6, 1983.
57. SC, "Letter to Sr. M. Bernice OP," Jan. 15, 1955, in *CW* II, p. 352.
58. Sr. Kathleen Grimes, Feb. 10, 1978, in *WR*.
59. SC, "Letter to Margaret Therese LeDoux," May 5, 1953, in *CW* IA, p. 33.
60. Fr. Benignus of Sant'Ilario M., Min. Gen. O.F.M., Cap., "Letter to Rev. Solanus Casey," Jan. 22, 1953. Documents File, Vice Postulator's Archives, Detroit, Michigan.
61. E. A. Bachelor, Jr.," Detroiters Pay Homage to Priest," *The Detroit Sunday Times,* July 18, 1954.
62. SC, quoted in *Ibid.*
63. *Chronicle, Ibid.,* July 28, 1954.
64. Br. Pius Cotter O.F.M., Cap., *Ibid.*
65. SC, "Letter to Margaret Therese LeDoux," Oct. 19, 1954, in *CW* IA, p. 34.
66. Frank J. Brady, Sept. 23, 1978, in *WR*.
67. *Ibid.*
68. *Ibid.*
69. *Chronicle, Ibid.,* July 21, 1955.

Chapter Eight

1. Fr. Bernard Burke O.F.M., Cap., Aug. 9, 1973 in *WR*.
2. Br. Ignatius Milne O.F.M., Cap., Reflections Shared with Michael H. Crosby O.F.M., Cap., Sept. 1, 1983.
3. Fr. Lawrence Merten O.F.M., Cap., Mar. 21, 1980, in *WR*.

4. Fr. Elmer Stoffel O.F.M., Cap., quoted in Merton, *Ibid*.

5. *Ibid*.

6. Fr. Gerald Walker O.F.M., Cap., Apr. 14, 1980, in *WR*.

7. Fr. Daniel Crosby O.F.M., Cap., June 7, 1984 in *WR*.

8. SC, Unfinished "Letter to Miss Loretta Mary Gibson," Apr. 1, 1956, in *CW* II, p. 313.

9. "Prayer for Peace," typewritten copy (by Solanus) in his notes. Since Solanus indicated in his letter to Miss Gibson (above) that he "heard it first, only after coming to St. Bonaventure's last January" (1956), it would have been typed sometime between then and Apr. 1, 1956. In *CW* II, p. 343.

10. Merten, *Ibid*.

11. *Ibid*.

12. Abraham Heschel, *The Prophets* (New York: Harper & Row, 1962), p. 231.

13. *Chronicle*, St. Bonaventure's, Dec. 2, 1956.

14. Jerry Sullivan, "Life in the Monastery in the Heart of Detroit," *The Detroit Sunday News*, Dec. 2, 1956.

15. *Chronicle, Ibid*.

16. Fr. Daniel Crosby, *Ibid*.

17. SC, Unfinished "Letter to Rev. Edward Casey," Mar. 14, 1957, in *CW* I, p. 195.

18. Rev. Michael Dalton, Nov. 20, 1977, in *WR*.

19. Mrs. Adeline Striewski, July 15, 1977, in *WR*.

20. Mrs. Edward Klemczak, Apr. 5, 1977, in *WR*.

21. The accounts by Sr. Arthur Ann and Sr. M. Margaretta are noted in Derum's book on Solanus.

22. Walker, *Ibid*.

23. Br. Egnatius Milne, O.F.M. Cap., *Ibid*.

24. Walker, *Ibid*.

25. *Ibid*. Fr. Gerald Walker's recollections are based on conversations with Msgr. Edward Casey who talked with the nurse who was with Solanus at time of his death.

26. Fr. Gerald (Walker) of Detroit, O.F.M. Cap., "Father Solanus Casey, O.F.M. Cap., 1870–1957," *The Messenger*, 21 (Feb. 1958). Detroit: Province of St. Joseph, pp. 35–36.

27. Bernadette M. Nowak, Mar. 28, 1977, in *WR*.

28. Burke, *Ibid*.

29. Fr. Gerald Walker O.F.M., Cap., "Funeral Homily," recorded in James Patrick Derum, *The Porter of Saint Bonaventure's: The Life of Father Solanus Casey, Capuchin* (Detroit: Fidelity Press, 1968), p. 274.

Chapter Nine

1. SC, "Letter to Miss Belle Lyke," May 22, 1946, in *CW* II, p. 175.
2. F. C. Happold, *Mysticism* (Baltimore: Penguin Books [rev. ed.], 1970), p. 101.
3. SC, "Letter to Mrs. Helena Casey Wilhite," June 1, 1948, in *CW* I, p. 138.
4. SC, "Letter to Walter McClellen," July 1, 1946, in *CW* II, p. 180.
5. SC, "Letter to Mrs. Helena Casey Wilhite," Apr. 16, 1954, in *CW* I, p. 141.
6. SC, "Letter to Herkenrath Family," c. 1948, in *CW* I, p. 240.
7. SC, "On Atheism," c. 1945, in *CW* II, p. 165.
8. St. Teresa of Avila, "Soliloquies, No 7," in Kieran Kavanaugh OCD and Otilio Rodriguez OCD (trans.), *The Collected Works of St. Teresa of Avila*, I (Washington DC: ICS Publications, 1976), p. 380.
9. Fr. Daniel Crosby, O.F.M., Cap., June 7, 1984, in *WR*.
10. John Macquarrie, "Forward," in F. C. Happold, *Religious Faith and Twentieth Century Man* (New York: Crossroad, 1981), p. 89.
11. SC, "Letter to Mrs. John O'Flaherty," Mar. 23, 1949, in *CW* II, p. 239.
12. SC, "Letter to Br. Leo," Feb. 28, 1943, in *CW* II, p. 120.
13. SC, "Letter to Dr. Koch," Mar. 12, 1946, in *CW* II, p. 168.
14. SC, "Letter to Miss Medora Louisell," Sept. 10, 1947, in *CW* II, p. 235.
15. SC, "Letter to Br. Leo," July 30, 1952, in *CW* II, p. 134.
16. SC, "Letter to Fr. Maurice Joachim Casey," Dec. 15, 1938, in *CW* I, p. 149.
17. Note written on photo of Solanus Casey by himself, c. 1954, in *CW* II, p. 342.
18. SC, "Letter to Charles Bracken, " Jan. 3, 1943, in *CW* II, p. 86.
19. SC, "Letter to Henry S. Morgan," Dec. 14, 1946, in *CW* II, p. 191.
20. SC, "Letter to Peter Doyle," Sept. 13, 1951, in *CW* II, p. 58.
21. SC, "Letter to Miss Mildred Maneal," c. 1945, in *CW* II, p. 162.
22. Karl Rahner, *Encyclopedia of Theology* (London: Burns & Oats, 1974), p. 1010.
23. Benedict J. Groeschel, *Spiritual Passages: The Psychology of Spiritual Development* (New York: Crossroad Publishing Co., 1983), pp. 184–85.
24. SC, Notes written on flyleaf of vol III, *The Mystical City of God*, c. 1939, in *CW* I, p. 270.
25. SC, "Letter to Br. Leo," July 30, 1952, in *CW* II, p. 134.
26. SC, "Letter to Mrs. Alvera McCarroll," Jan. 27, c. 1948, in *CW* II, p. 250.

27. SC, Notes written on Flyleaf of vol II, *The Mystical City of God,* c., 1939, in *CW* I, p. 270.
28. SC, Notes written on flyleaf of vol III, *Ibid.*
29. SC, Notes on Christmas Car, c. 1939, in *CW* II, p. 156.
30. Kathleen Pond, *The Spirit of the Sapnish Mystics: An Anthology of Spanish Religous Prose from the Fifteenth to the Seventeenth Century* (New York: P.J. Kenedy & Sons, 1958). p. 168.
31. A. Poulain, S.J., *The Graces of Interior Prayer: A Treatise of Mystical Theology,* tr. by Leonora L. Yorke Smith, (London: Routledge & Kegan Paul Limited, 1950), p. 337.
32. SC, Note written on flyleaf of vol III. *The Mystical City of God.* c. 1939, in *CW* I, p. 268.
33. SC, "Letter to Mrs. O'Donnell," Aug. 3, 1949, in *CW* II, p. 48.
34. SC, "Letter to Miss Loretta Gibson," Sept. 8, 1951, in *CW* II, p. 312.
35. SC. "Letter to Miss Beatrice Lamb," Sept, 17, 1949, in *CW* II, p. 116.
36. SC, "Letter to Margaret LeDoux," July 16, 1937, in *CW* (no 174), A, p. 18.
37. SC, "Letter to Edwin LeDoux," Sept. 30, 1948, in *CW* IA, p. 29.
38. SC, "Letter to Mrs. Margaret LeDoux," Oct. 19, 1954, in *CW* IA, p. 34.
39. SC, "Letter to Mrs. Margaret Lilly," Jan. 16, 1952, in *CW* IA, p. 46.
40. SC, "Letter to Bridget Ronan," Nov. 24, 1946, in *CW* II, p. 190.
41. SC, "Letter to Mr. and Mrs, Joseph O'Donnell," May 16, 1946, in *CW* II, p. 20.
42. Sc. "Letter to Mrs. Helena Wilhite," Feb, 28, 1946, in *CW* I, p. 131.
43. Msgr. Edward J. Hickey, Dec. 2, 1969, in *WR.*
44. William Tremblay, Mar. 15, 1979, in *WR.*
45. SC, "Letter to Frater Sebastian," Apr. 28, 1945, in *CW* II, p. 140.
46. Willima Johnston, *The Inner Eye of Love: Mysticism and Religion* (San Francisco: harper & Row Publishers, Inc., 1978), pp. 174-75.
47. SC, "Letter to Miss Mae Whelan," Sept., 1942, in *CW* II, p. 179.
48. SC, "Letter to Mrs. Geraci," c. 1947, in *CW* II, p. 179.
49. SC, "Letter to Br. Leo," Feb. 28, 1943, in *CW* II, p.119.
50. SC, "Letter to Sr. Solania," Jan. 3, 1943, in *CW* I, p. 85.
51. SC, "To Recognize the Creator," c. 1948, in *CW* II, p. 263.
52. SC, "Letter to Sr. M. Joseph," May 21, 1945, in *CW* II, p. 141.
53. SC, "Letter to Dorothy Bachor," May 18, 1937, in *CW* I, p. 96.
54. SC, "Letter to Msgr. Edward Casey," Mar. 4, 1957, in *CW* I, p. 195.
55. SC, "Letter to Muriel Krausman," Sept. 21, 1953, in *CW* II, p. 111.
56. SC, "Letter to Mr. and Mrs. Joseph O'Donnell," May 16, 1945, in *CW* II, p. 20.

57. SC, "Maneal," *Ibid.*
58. SC, "Letter to Mrs. Margaret LeDoux," Apr. 1, 1915, in *CW* IA, p. 3.
59. SC, "Letter to John Martin," Aug. 18, 1950, in *CW* II, p. 299.
60. SC, "Letter to Mrs. Geraldine Bieke," Sept. 19, 1946, in *CW* II, p. 185.
61. SC, "Letter to Mr. and Mrs. Peter Doyle," Feb. 11, 1948, in *CW* II, p. 57.
62. SC, "Gibson," *Ibid.*
63. SC, "Letter to Mrs. Helena Wilhite," Feb. 28, 1946, in *CW* I, p. 131.
64. SC, "Letter to Peter Doyle," Sept. 13, 1951, in *CW* II, 58.
65. SC, "Notebook 9," Apr. 12, 1898, in *CW* I, p. 11.
66. SC, "Letter to Bernice Schumacher," Aug. 16, 1946, in *CW* II, p. 183.
67. SC, "Letter to Fr. Maurice Casey," Dec. 15, 1938, in *CW* I, p. 149.
68. SC, "Letter to Miss Winifred Goodwillie," Aug. 5, 1939, in *CW* II, p. 9.
69. SC, "Letter to Margaret LeDoux," May 17, 1950, in *CW* IA, p. 31.
70. *Ibid.*
71. SC, "Letter to Fr. Maurice Casey," Apr. 2, 1946, in *CW* I, p. 159.
72. SC, "Letter to Mrs. Charles D'Amico," Apr. 14, 1948, in *CW* I, p. 248.
73. SC, "Geraci," *Ibid.*
74. SC, "Letter to Mr. Joseph O'Donnell," Mar. 28, 1947, in *CW* II, p. 34.
75. SC, "Geraci," *Ibid.*
76. E. D. Bachelor, Jr. "Detroiters Pay Homage to Priest," *The Detroit Sunday Times,* July 18, 1954.
77. Jan van Ruysbroeck, *Reflections from the Mirror of a Mystic.* tr. by Earle Baille (London: Thomas Baker, 1905), p. 54–55.
78. SC, "Radio Speech on Station CKLW Detroit," June 11, 1937, in *CW* I, p. 94.
79. St. Peter Chrysologus, quoted in SC, "Notebook 9," c. 1899, in *CW* I, p. 13.
80. Andrew Lawrence, ST, in *WR*.
81. SC, "Letter to Mrs. Helena Wilhite," June 1, 1948, in *CW* I, p. 136.
82. SC, "Letter to Mrs. Helena Wilhite," Dec. 25, 1952, in *CW* I, 251.
83. SC, "Letter to Margaret LeDoux," June 1, 1948, in *CW* I, p. 136.
84. SC, "Letter to Margaret LeDoux," Jan. 26, 1937, in *CW* IA, p. 16.
85. SC, "Letter to James Casey," c. 1948, in *CW* I, p. 239.
86. *Ibid.*
87. SC, "Letter to Eileen Casey," Dec. 15, 1952, in *CW* I, p. 252.
88. SC, "Letter to Dr. J. P. Young," Oct. 4, 1947, in *CW* II, p. 205.
89. *Ibid.,* p. 203.
90. SC, "Letter to Br. Leo," May 23, 1946, in *CW* II, p. 128.
91. Bernard Lonergan, S.J., "Theology in Its New Context," in L. K. Shook (ed), *Theology of Renewal,* vol. I (Montreal: Palm Publishers, 1968), pp. 44–45.

92. SC, Note written on picture taken at Monastery Office, c. 1945, in *CW* II, p. 155.
93. SC, "Letter to Charles M. Durrell, MD," Mar. 1, 1947, in *CW* II, p. 226.
94. SC, "Letter to Barbara Bedolfe," Aug. 4, 1949, in *CW* IA, p. 41.
95. SC, Notes written after the death of Fr. Maurice Casey, c. 1949, in *CW* I, p. 162.
96. SC, "Letter to Wallace Bedolfe," Apr. 18, 1953, in *CW* IA, p. 43.
97. Fr. Gerald Walker O.F.M., Cap., in *WR*.
98. SC, "Think Over," 1948 in *CW* II, p. 253.

Index